T0317431

ECOSYSTEM EDGE

ECOSYSTEM EDGE

Sustaining Competitiveness in the Face of Disruption

Arnoud De Meyer and
Peter J. Williamson

Stanford Business Books
An Imprint of Stanford University Press
Stanford, California

Stanford University Press
Stanford, California

©2020 by the Board of Trustees of the Leland Stanford Junior University. All rights reserved.

No part of this book may be reproduced or transmitted in any form or by any means, electronic or mechanical, including photocopying and recording, or in any information storage or retrieval system without the prior written permission of Stanford University Press.

Special discounts for bulk quantities of Stanford Business Books are available to corporations, professional associations, and other organizations. For details and discount information, contact the special sales department of Stanford University Press.
Tel: (650) 725-0820, Fax: (650) 725-3457

Printed in the United States of America on acid-free, archival-quality paper

Library of Congress Cataloging-in-Publication Data is available upon request

ISBN 978-1-5036-1021-7 (cloth)
ISBN 978-1-5036-1186-3 (electronic)

Cover design: Kevin Barrett Kane
Typeset by BookComp, Inc. in 10/14 Minion Pro

Contents

Preface

IT WAS A SUNNY AFTERNOON IN 2008, WHEN THE TWO OF US sat together on the terrace of one of Cambridge's pubs and exchanged some of our latest ideas about research. Peter had finished a second version of the case on ARM, one of Cambridge's hi-tech icons. Arnoud had spent quite some time on understanding how the Cambridge "Silicon Fen," the entrepreneurial network around the University of Cambridge, operated. In our conversation over a glass of Australian Chardonnay we found that the way these companies innovated was different from what we had read in books about innovation in Silicon Valley. Innovation in the Cambridge companies seemed to be less dependent on a single company that would take full leadership and subcontract the development of components to its suppliers. The companies in Cambridge appeared to be much more interdependent and innovated with a network of peers. And the story of ARM was that of a small company mobilizing a large global network to innovate. More than elsewhere these companies seemed to work in a community of interacting organizations, who were also very well attuned to their context, something akin to a biological ecosystem. We were intrigued, and began to talk about innovation through the mobilization of ecosystems in our sessions with executives. And whether it was in Cambridge, Singapore, China, or Germany, these executives responded well and pointed out how their companies were often using ecosystems, though not always in a conscious way. We also started reading the literature and learned that others, in particular J. Moore and R. Adner, had already hinted at the existence of ecosystems and their advantages over traditional supply chains.

Fast forward four years: in 2012 we published a paper in *California Management Review* on "The Ecosystem Advantage: How to Successfully Harness the Power of Partners." Our ideas had sharpened, and through the cases of ARM and Dassault Systèmes, and lots of anecdotal evidence, we were able to pinpoint that ecosystems were more flexible, were better at learning, and were therefore better at innovating in the face of significant uncertainty. We also formulated six keys to unlock the ecosystem advantage: pinpointing the value added to the partners in the ecosystem, structuring different partner roles, stimulating complementary investments by the ecosystem partners, reducing transaction costs, enabling co-learning, and engineering the value-capture mechanisms. This paper helped us tremendously in sharing the role of ecosystems in innovation with a larger group of executives and researchers. The concept of an ecosystem did not meet resistance anymore. The questions in our discussions moved from "How do you understand that you have an ecosystem that can help you?" to "How do you build and grow an ecosystem?"

In the meantime, Arnoud had moved to Singapore. We met up intermittently, in particular at the occasion of programs organized by Singapore's Human Capital Leadership Institute (HCLI). We had the opportunity to discuss our ideas about ecosystems with a wide variety of senior company executives in HCLI's Singapore Business Leaders Programme, and we wrote a few case studies such as one on the ecosystem of Rolls Royce in Singapore. At one of those rare encounters in 2014, the idea of writing a book on the "how to" was born.

We did realize that we needed more in-depth case studies, representing the different continents and industries. Thanks to Eric Baldwin, we developed rich files on ecosystem leaders like Thomson Reuters, athenahealth, Amazon, and *The Guardian*, which harnessed the potential of ecosystems to innovate in different ways. Other cases, like that of Uber and the Ford Motor Company, proved less fruitful.

Notwithstanding the geographical distance and our very busy schedules we were able to develop a common view on how, why, and when ecosystems are a better way to innovate; how to create and build an ecosystem; how to lead it; and how to make money with it. It was not always easy to follow up on our rare conversations, and quite a few times we doubted that the book would ever exist. But we did finally succeed in formulating our common ideas, and that is what you will find in this book.

All of the cases are based on public documents, published case studies vetted by the companies, or conversations with company executives. They told us their story. How we interpreted these to illustrate the concepts of building and managing ecosystems for innovation is entirely our responsibility.

We hope that you will enjoy reading this book and, perhaps more importantly, that you will adjust the way you manage innovation in the face of uncertainty. All companies have the nucleus of a powerful ecosystem around them. But can you mobilize that ecosystem and manage it consciously to become a more effective innovator?

We would like to acknowledge the invaluable contribution of Anand P. Raman in critiquing many of our underdeveloped ideas and helping bring them into sharper focus, his guidance in the development and choice of the case studies, and his tireless work editing and improving the text of our early manuscripts. We also want to thank the teams of HCLI, the Centre for Management Practice and Dr. Havovi Joshi at Singapore Management University, and Cambridge Judge Business School, who all at one time or another gave us assistance, support, and the opportunity to debate our ideas. We also thank INSEAD, Cambridge Judge Business School, and Singapore Management University for giving us the permission to use extensively the case studies on ARM, Alibaba, and Rolls Royce (Singapore).

Arnoud De Meyer and Peter J. Williamson
August 2019

ECOSYSTEM EDGE

1 Addressing the Disruption Imperative

THE SHOCKWAVES IN DETROIT WERE ALMOST DEAFENING. The world had just learned that Tesla Inc. had surpassed the market capitalization of General Motors (GM) to become the most valuable automaker in the United States.

A week earlier, it had overtaken the value of Ford, the company that had pioneered the modern auto industry. GM and Ford had 225 years of experience in the automobile industry between them—while Tesla had all of 15 years. Tesla sold 84,000 vehicles in 2016 compared with GM's worldwide sales of around 10 million vehicles and Ford's 6.6 million. Some questioned the wisdom of these valuations given Tesla's position as a minnow in the industry that had yet to deliver a profit.[1] The sceptics were not wrong; stock market sentiment had changed by the end of 2017, and GM's share price had surged by close to 30 percent while Tesla struggled with the basics of building a car and rolling out its new mass-market Model 3. However, despite these misgivings, it was proof, if proof were needed, that the auto industry had entered a period of disruption.

As far back as 2011, Bill Ford, who headed up one of the most successful automakers of all time, had recognized that selling more cars simply "wasn't going to cut it" either for Ford or for the industry.[2] The emergence of electric vehicles, car sharing and ride sharing, and autonomous driving technology promised to radically transform the automotive industry and undermine car makers' traditional business models.

New players were entering the space, including Uber and technology companies such as Google and Apple. In the words of Bill Ford, "We now have disruption coming from every angle, from the potential ways we fuel our vehicles to the ownership model."[3] Ford's former CEO Mark Fields echoed that sentiment in 2015, noting that the auto industry was at an inflection point, with technology driving rapid innovation and "new, non-traditional partners and competitors now interested in our business."[4]

While incumbent automakers retained their competitive advantage in manufacturing and brand, they were at square one when it came to technologies such as autonomous driving and car sharing/ride sharing applications. The impact of car sharing, as pioneered by Zipcar in 2000, could prove to be significant. Research has found that a single shared vehicle in developed, urban car-sharing markets replaces the purchase of 32 vehicles. The study estimated that car sharing had already displaced 500,000 car purchases and had the potential to cause 1.2 million lost vehicle sales through 2020.[5] More recently, a leading industry analyst had suggested that the emergence of shared driverless cars could lead to a 40 percent drop in US auto sales over the next 25 years.[6] It was clear that the world's established automakers would have to fight to stay relevant.

More and more companies in a wide range of industries are facing similar disruption to their traditional formulas for making money that have served them well for decades. The music business has been up-ended with the rise of new ways to consume music. The top twenty brick-and-mortar retailers in the United States announced that they had shut down three thousand stores in 2017. Macy's, J.C. Penney, Sears, and Kmart were just a few of the chains that had announced sweeping closures.[7] The major restructuring of the French retail giant Carrefour in January 2018 was yet another example of the consequences that e-commerce had on the traditional retailers. In 2017, the *Financial Times* identified four more industries ripe for disruption by technology, the sharing economy, start-ups, and new business models: Travel agents; manufacturers and distributors of small components, in part because of 3-D printing; financial advisers, with the rise of robo-advisers; and auto repairers due to low-maintenance electric vehicles and fewer accidents with driverless cars.[8] The banking industry too is poised for disruption by blockchain-based financial services and other forms of "fintech." Other sectors such as fast-moving consumer goods (FMCG) are being disrupted by the greater consumer choice and price transparency that comes with online marketplaces. Their media strategies are being challenged by social media, and calls to guarantee the sustainability of their products and traceability in their supply chains, along with the prospect of new technologies that allow consumers to personalize the products they buy, are further disrupting their extant business models. New technologies also mean that instead of selling jet engines, companies such as Rolls Royce, Pratt and Whitney, and General Electric sell "aircraft power by the hour."[9] Companies like Michelin sell road kilometers instead of tires. In effect, new technologies such as digitalization, the application of big data analysis and machine learning, and artificial intelligence (AI) are disrupting business models in industry after industry.

How should you deal with the wave of disruption that will eventually hit your industry? How do you become one of the disruptors? The specifics of successful strategies will obviously vary with the situation. However, we believe they all share one characteristic: A successful strategy, in the future, will depend on how well you proactively lead your *ecosystem*, by engaging with different partners who bring fresh competencies and capabilities that will fuel innovation and transform your organization. You need to catalyze a deep and vibrant ecosystem of partners around your company. This goes far beyond working more closely with your supply chain, open innovation, or co-innovation with your customers.

The nature of innovation is changing: Instead of just product and process innovations, customers are now demanding innovative, integrated solutions to complex needs and problems. To deliver these integrated solutions you will need to access the capabilities of partners, drawing on know-how and capacity in a wide variety of related industries.

The potential to reap economies of scale has also changed. In the past, scale economies were driven by your company's size. Today and tomorrow, the benefits of scale will increasingly depend on the total sales of your ecosystem, including both you and all of your partners.

The concept of competing on speed also needs to be rethought. Companies used to think about speed as being "first to market." Today, however, launching your product or service ahead of competitors is a poor predictor of who will come dominate the market. Instead, the winners are increasingly those companies that are first to scale up an innovative idea. Speed to scale, capitalizing on the magnitude of the opportunity rather than simply opening it up, is key. Harnessing the network effects that your ecosystem can provide, where every additional user increases the value of the product or service to all the other partners and customers in the ecosystem, is frequently decisive in winning the race to scale. The Facebook ecosystem, for example, reached five hundred million users in 2010, just six years after the company was founded.[10] That same year, MySpace users declined to seventy million, having plateaued at just over one hundred million users.[11] This was despite being launched one year earlier and the backing of its huge new owners, News Corporation. Speed to scale had won out. While Myspace went into decline, two years later Facebook had surpassed one billion users. It now has over two billion active monthly users.

To benefit from these fundamental shifts in the competitive landscape requires a radical transformation of your business model. It involves learning to proactively catalyze, shape, and lead an ecosystem in ways that will harness its potential to radically transform your business model to cope with disruption, uncertainty, and rapid technological change. It means learning to thrive in a world where competition that pits one ecosystem against another replaces rivalry between individual companies.

Catalyzing the development of a powerful ecosystem around your company will also transform your prospects by giving you what we call the "ecosystem edge." It will help you leverage powerful network economies; focus your company on what it is really good at; enable you to harness the power of partners in the areas where they excel; and help you innovate faster, become more agile, and grow in a world where digitalization is now infusing every industry. These benefits are now more than "nice to have"; companies must transform themselves by creating ecosystems today in order to survive and prosper tomorrow.

To understand the practical steps you and your team can take to achieve the ecosystem edge, we focus on eight core examples in this book: Alibaba Group, Amazon.com, ARM, athenahealth, Dassault Systèmes S.E., The Guardian, Rolls-Royce, and Thomson Reuters. We selected these firms from a variety of different industries to demonstrate that it is not only platform players or e-commerce companies that can harness the potential of ecosystem advantage. There is also huge potential for companies in traditional industries, such as manufacturing, mining and energy, pharmaceuticals and life sciences, and fast-moving consumer goods (FMCG), to enhance their success and respond to industry disruption by embracing ecosystem thinking. We also selected these case studies from different continents: an ecosystem is not unique to a particular location. We found ecosystems delivering innovation, greater scale economies, and increased profits both in industrialized and emerging economies.

In order to explain what this entails, let's begin by taking a look at Alibaba, China's giant e-commerce company, which has transformed retail in China and beyond through its many innovations.

Alibaba: The Power of Ecosystem Advantage

Alibaba Group is one of the best examples of an organization that has successfully leveraged the power of its ecosystem to gain competitive advantage. At its initial public offering (IPO) on the New York Stock Exchange in September 2014, this Chinese conglomerate was valued at over $225 billion.[12] Its market capitalization has since soared to reach almost $530 billion in January 2018. The group and its affiliate companies span twenty-five business units that include the world's largest business-to-business marketplace (Alibaba.com), business-to-consumer e-commerce (Taobao and Tmall.com), online payment (Alipay.com), and cloud computing (Aliyun.com). More recently, it has expanded into new areas, including digital media and entertainment, credit scoring, travel services, and virtual mobile telecommunications. Its affiliate, Ant Financial Services Group, includes the world's largest money market fund, Yu'e Bao, which had 325 million customers and assets exceeding $170 billion by early 2018.

For the year ending December 31, 2017, Alibaba Group's revenues exceeded $39 billion. Yet it had achieved this massive scale and spread of operations with little more than sixty-six thousand employees (with just seven thousand more in Ant Financial, itself estimated to be worth more than $150 billion in 2018). The Group's e-commerce businesses were more than twice the size of Amazon.com, a company with over five hundred fifty thousand staff. So how did Alibaba achieve such results, recording annual sales revenues of over $590 thousand per employee?

The first clue as to how Alibaba has created so much new value can be found in the opening paragraph of the Group's website: "We operate an ecosystem where all participants—consumers, merchants, third-party service providers and others—have an opportunity to prosper."[13] Alibaba had come to believe that the route to success lay in understanding how to enhance its own competitive advantage by promoting and leading the development of its ecosystem developed with time and experience. Key to this was a focusing on the creation of attractive opportunities for an increasingly diverse range of partners.

But Alibaba's journey also shows some of the hurdles that must be overcome to gain an ecosystem edge. Learning how to harness the power of its ecosystem was not always easy for the Group. Alibaba had started out as a classic intermediary between buyers and sellers. Learning to become an ecosystem enabler required it to make difficult choices that included abandoning some of its existing profit streams. In the face of huge uncertainty, and accepting that a large network of partners would never be fully controllable, Alibaba's founder, Jack Ma, had a strong belief in the power of the ecosystem model.[14] To date, this belief has proven right.

Alibaba's experience with its Taobao and Tmall.com units illustrates some of the key characteristics of ecosystem strategies and the requirements for its success. In 1998, Ma was asked by a company sponsored by the Ministry of Foreign Trade and Economic Cooperation (MOFTEC) to assist Chinese companies to become involved in "electronic commerce," based on private networks, to facilitate electronic data interchange. Ma believed the real potential lay in open networks enabled by the Internet, and so he gathered eighteen people in his apartment and outlined his vision in a discourse lasting two hours. The group was so inspired that they clubbed together $60,000 to launch "Alibaba"—a name they felt embodied the idea of "open sesame to the treasures of the world." Alibaba's origins thus trace back to 1999, when it first launched the website Alibaba.com, a business-to-business (B2B) portal to connect Chinese manufacturers with overseas buyers.

Alibaba did not have a clear vision of what their future ecosystem would look like at the time. The idea was simply to make the internet accessible, trustworthy, and beneficial for all. Those noble aspirations, however, were not enough to ensure that the new venture was financially sound. Alibaba.com had a rocky time in its early years. Although it earned a margin by selling products through its site, the costs involved in handling new products (such as uploading and maintaining product details on the site) was high. By 2001 it was burning through the $25 million funding it had raised from investors, such as Japan's Softbank, Goldman Sachs, and Fidelity, at the rate of $2 million per month, and was left with less than $10 million in the bank.

The first phase (of three broad stages) in Alibaba's transition to becoming an ecosystem enabler came in response to this cash drain. Alibaba moved from a pure platform intermediary to become a service provider, charging membership fees to users. It had already recognized that reaping economies of scale was critical to spread fixed costs and drive down unit costs. But it now understood that it would never achieve the scale it was aspiring to if it continued to act as a principal buyer or seller in its own right. For that massive scale, Alibaba would need to start thinking only about growing the size of its own operations to harness the power of a huge number of partners who could take the business beyond its own limited capabilities at the time. That, in turn, meant making it easy for partners to develop their own businesses, limiting its own activities, and focusing on selling Alibaba's support to potential buyers and sellers.

The launch of Taobao heralded the second stage in developing an ecosystem: Taobao was conceived as a marketplace that encouraged others to serve customers. Alibaba role was to concentrate on providing the "platform" through which e-commerce could flow, and take a commission for connecting buyers and sellers. It was evident that the platform would need to be standardized as much as possible to gain scale economies. Additionally, partners needed to be able to differentiate themselves on that standardized infrastructure platform. To achieve this mix of standardization and differentiation, limiting the boundaries of the platform would be key.

"Our objective was to develop a platform of infrastructure that can attract a wide range of partners and boost growth and scale," recalled Wang Jian, then chief technology officer of Alibaba Group. He went on to explain that Taobao had spawned a myriad of partner businesses: from companies that designed sophisticated shop-fronts for vendors and creators of advertising right through to companies that recruited models for photo shoots. Wang Jian also drew attention to Alibaba's policy of nurturing small partners, and commented, "Small customers can become big customers, so the technology for both should be the same. Alibaba wants to make sure small customers have a future." But during phase 2, Taobao was still acting as a kind of intermediary or "middleman" between buyers and sellers. That had to change. As Ming Zeng, the then group strategy officer put it, "We realised our ability was so limited compared to the potential of the market as well as the task facing us." As Taobao developed, "it learned a lot of painful lessons by trying to over-control and becoming the bottleneck," he added.[15] The need to step back and move from intermediary to ecosystem orchestrater, was one of those key lessons. And because it meant surrendering significant control to partners, it was a difficult truth to swallow.

This led to a third stage in the emergence of ecosystem thinking at Alibaba: that it needed to become an "ecosystem enabler" and focus on becoming a provider of e-commerce, infrastructure, and services for all e-commerce market participants. Doing so would allow Taobao to gain the network advantages associated with large numbers of buyers and sellers. If Alibaba could position Taobao as "the place to go" for consumer e-commerce, it would trigger a positive spiral whereby the larger it grew, the more attractive it would become for buyers and sellers. By 2008, this thinking had led to the adoption of the "Big Taobao" strategy that aimed to encourage a large number of diverse potential participants to join and exploit new opportunities while addressing their challenge of reaching out to the vast but underdeveloped Chinese consumer market. The idea of becoming the leader of a thriving ecosystem with its own momentum, driven by partners joining and exiting, expanding in new directions, had taken root.

In order to successfully transition from an intermediary to ecosystem enabler, Taobao needed to reduce its role as the controller of activities around the platform. It now encouraged shop owners to take the initiative of working with other participants in the ecosystem, such as other sellers, providers of complementary services and the online shoppers themselves. It thus began to encourage shop owners to organize more joint marketing activities, and to work more directly with providers of other services that could improve their offerings.

This shift of focus to becoming an enabler for the development of a broader and deeper ecosystem around Taobao and Tmall.com also required Alibaba to change its revenue model. In 2009, advertising made up 85 percent of the revenues of Taobao and Tmall.com, and came from various sources including paid items appearing prominently in search results and additional fees for prime advertising positions on the sites. But reliance on these advertising and transactions fees would have to be reduced in order to enable the growth of the ecosystem and improve service to customers. Growth in Alibaba's revenues and profits would have to come from Taobao and Tmall.com opening new revenue streams and sources of value from which Alibaba could capture a share. As Ming Zeng explained to us, "Because you are no longer taking a cut as a middleman, an ecosystem enabler has to be continually finding innovative ways to create new and unique value added from which it can take a profit. Revenue growth will come from taking a small cut on an ever-expanding volume of interactions of many types."

To become an ecosystem enabler, Alibaba had to learn, therefore, to stop doing things; in some cases, even things that had become sizeable activities, such as running special promotions for some product categories. Some of these decisions were relatively easy, while others were more difficult. Observed Wang Jian,

> It was very clear that Alibaba should not sell products—but the boundaries of the ecosystem are not easy to determine. Take software services. In principle, Alibaba knows it should leave them to partners, but in the short-term partners may not be willing or equipped, and so it would be easier for Alibaba to provide this service. But that would lead to unsustainable complexity and fragmentation. The solution hitherto has been for Alibaba to provide the basic building blocks, such as the exchange platform and a very rudimentary CRM system for every shop owner on Taobao. Alibaba is clear that it will not provide anything that is useful only to a single seller or even a small group of sellers—it must be offerings that are used by large numbers of participants.[16]

To maintain the health of the ecosystem, Alibaba also found that it was critical to resist the temptation to encroach on its partners' businesses. Brian Li, then vice president of strategy, explained, "Someone in Alibaba will, perfectly reasonably, say: 'we see a new application is becoming popular, why don't we build one to do this?' But a good ecosystem leader needs to say 'no'; we should instead encourage partners to build this type of app, so that we draw on their capabilities and drive improvement and learning. By [Alibaba] taking this approach, users now have a choice of multiple apps within our ecosystem."

Fundamental to Alibaba's thinking was the belief that if it could create value for the end customer, it would find a way to earn money for itself. This meant focusing first on creating customer value, and then thinking how to capture and share a portion of that value. The Wangwang instant messaging feature on Taobao is a good case in point. It is of great value to buyers and sellers; it helps to build trust. Alibaba also learned that many Chinese buyers wanted to see the physical address of the seller on the website before they would trust them; so Taobao provided addresses even though suppliers argued that it was unnecessary in a world of electronic commerce. Likewise, Alipay ensured that the net proceeds of each sale were transferred to sellers once the delivery had been acknowledged by a buyer—in contrast to competitors such as 360buy which kept the money for a month after the sale to enhance their cash flows.

Ming Zeng explained how this fit into Alibaba's ecosystem thinking, "Alibaba is a hub, so everything needs to go through it. Conceptually that enables you to charge a toll for passing through, which is our revenue. The higher the flow through, the more our revenues."[17] It was through this change in mind-set that Alibaba was able to create new business models to deliver growing profits.

An example of the new business model is the creation of "Taobao Ke," a traffic aggregation system developed by Alibaba's employees that won a CEO Innovation Award from Ma. Taobao Ke aggregates and analyses user data from more than five hundred thousand websites, receiving data on billions of page views per day. It starts by Alibaba agreeing with a website to carry a link that would direct potential customers to a Taobao store. The owner of the shop on Taobao agrees to pay a commission of around 10 percent of the gross sales when a lead comes through that website. The website owner receives 90 percent of that commission and Taobao retains 10 percent (or 1 percent of the gross sales value achieved). This kind of arrangement was common across the internet. But Taobao Ke developed new ways of adding value from analyzing and using data to improve the match between a Taobao store and the websites to which it was linked to achieve that required technology-heavy capacity that could analyze in an automated way the contents of a website, and also work out which of the one million-plus Taobao stores were most likely to be of interest to its users. Alibaba then proposes the optimal links to both Taobao storeowners and websites. This improves the value and efficiency of the arrangement for both parties. Alibaba adds even more value by making the system dynamic, using the mass of data accessed through Taobao Ke to continually learn and improve the matching between Taobao stores and other websites.

Taobao Ke is, therefore, an example of the kind of co-learning opportunities that ecosystem thinking creates. Storeowners learn more about what kind of websites are useful "shop windows," as it were, to attract businesses. This could even vary by time of day or location. A wide variety of websites (including noncommercial information and community sites) would understand how to create a new revenue stream from click-throughs. Utilizing this new knowledge generated a growing profit pool. The partners improved their yield from each visitor. Alibaba itself generated a substantial stream, taking a small toll from each of the between five hundred million and one billion users that moved through Taobao Ke every day.

While Alibaba could not completely control its ecosystem, it could play a leadership role by acting as an enabler and catalyst for the development of the ecosystem. As a pivotal player in the ecosystem, it could influence and shape its future evolution. On the other hand, there was also a downside of being the hub in the ecosystem because, as Ming Zeng says, "every problem comes at you." Despite this burden, he also pointed out a corresponding upside, "You are sitting at the hub of a system that generates lots of new knowledge so you can continuously learn from experience, problem solving, learning by doing, and contact with the front line."[18] Hence, being at the center of all flows of information gave Alibaba the opportunity to steer the whole network in ways that generated new value and profit streams, without actually controlling it.

Alibaba also discovered another insight that all ecosystem leaders need to take on board: a recognition that knowledge creation in the ecosystem is much greater than your own learnings—even as the "ecosystem leader." Considerable learning also occurred between partners within the ecosystem, which could improve performance and strengthen the ecosystem even when it did not involve Alibaba directly. Sometimes, Alibaba needed to tap into the cross-communication and learning taking place between partners to help the process of discovering new value and profit opportunities along. At other times, that intervention was unnecessary.

The social networking sites around Taobao were a good example of why Alibaba had to reassess continually what role it should play. Alibaba had originally set up a social network site called Tao Jianghu within Taobao, with the aim of connecting younger users and creating a buzz in this group around the site. Over time, many similar social networks emerged around Taobao. None reached a scale sufficient to support the Taobao ecosystem as a whole; and instead, the proliferation of small social networking platforms created internal competition within the Taobao ecosystem. As a result, Alibaba had to take the initiative, and catalyze the growth of a single, vibrant social network that would match the Taobao identity and support its business model.

The success of Alibaba illustrates many of the advantages of ecosystems that we advanced above: ecosystems can generate new sources of customer value; enable new business models; access diverse partner capabilities and knowledge; and reap huge network economies. Alibaba also demonstrates how an ecosystem can ignite a positive spiral where successive improvements in the offering combined with easy access and greater choice attracts yet more customers. This growing customer base, in turn, attracts new partners who bring new capabilities and ideas that further improve the quality and convenience it offers to customers.

Alibaba's experience also provides our first inkling into some of the things an ecosystem leader needs to do to catalyze, foster, and leverage their ecosystem: provide a compelling vision of the opportunity; step back and make room for partners; foster joint learning among partners; capture the data and knowledge the ecosystem generates to open up new revenue streams; and focus on the increased profits that come from enabling the ecosystem to grow rather than squeezing it dry for short-term returns.

The Case for Ecosystem Strategies

The kind of radical transformation Alibaba has achieved in e-commerce and many other consumer services in China is not limited to new emerging economies. New business models from personalized autonomous transport through to digital music or mobile e-commerce are now creating a wave of change across most industries all around the world. Ecosystem strategies enable you to retake the initiative in the face of these disruptive forces by allowing your company to flexibly harness the new and broader range of partner capabilities necessary to underpin these new business models. To succeed in an industry ripe for disruption requires access to capabilities and experience outside the orbit of existing players, such as knowledge of other industries, different distribution channels, alternative marketing approaches, new ways of interacting with customers, and novel technologies. Ecosystem strategies are ideally suited to unlock access to this new knowledge. And properly executed, they enable you to leverage this new knowledge to reap massive network economies that far exceed the traditional economies of scale available to any company acting alone.

They can also help you successfully tackle some of the pressing challenges many business leaders face today: the dilemma of meeting rising customer demands while keeping your company focused on what it does best; the challenge of delivering more innovation, faster; and the need to make your organization more agile.[19]

Additionally, ecosystem strategies allow you to meet the rising demands of customers for more functionality, more customization and personalization, and solutions rather than simply products—while staying focused—by leveraging the capabilities of partners to provide many of the pieces of a broader offering. Unlike classic outsourcing, which often acts as a straightjacket on the contributions of partners, engaging them in your ecosystem allows you to harness their capacity for innovation, learning, and flexibility, as well as their specialized capabilities. These benefits flow from the fact that in an ecosystem partners coordinate their investments, jointly innovate, and continually evolve out of self-interest, not because of inflexible contractual obligations. And as more partners and customers are attracted to the ecosystem, you are likely to benefit from the network economies we mentioned above. The larger and more diverse set of partners and customers the ecosystem engages with, the greater will be the benefit to each individual participant, including your own company. Being part of this positive spiral will enable you to reap economies of scale from across the entire ecosystem, far beyond your own size.

Proactively developing your ecosystem helps promote innovation that can benefit your business. Business ecosystems can deliver more innovation because they access a wider range of ideas, experiences, and capabilities through a multitude of partners than is available to any company alone, or even to a tightly prescribed alliance. As partners form new relationships and interact in new ways, they generate learning that enables innovation in what is offered to customers and the ways it is produced and delivered. And as new partners join the ecosystem, they continually enrich this diversity, helping fuel creativity and speeding up the pace of innovation.

Ecosystem strategies can also help your organization become more agile. Some of that increased agility comes because leveraging an ecosystem enables you to harness the power of a large, dynamic, and partly self-organizing network of partners to help you serve your customers. Like a living organism, the ecosystem continually evolves and adjusts to meet their changing needs. As the leader of the ecosystem, your own organization needs to adjust the way it gets things done so that it can effectively leverage an ever-changing partner network. These new roles, processes, and leadership styles that you will put in place will further help transform your existing structure into a more agile organization.

Making It Happen

This book explains how your business can become more successful in a world of disruption, uncertainty, and rapid technological change by gaining this ecosystem edge that comes from proactively catalyzing, shaping, and leading a business ecosystem in ways that will harness its potential. We cast you, the reader and your company, in the role of the "ecosystem leader" in an ecosystem. Indeed, many observers of ecosystems have stressed the key role of a hub or keystone company, or ecosystem leader as we term it, to provide the stability for the development of the ecosystem and its final success in stimulating innovation.[20]

As the ecosystem leader, you cannot completely control that ecosystem or prescribe its precise structure. Nor can you play the role of an omniscient dictator, moving around all the chess pieces and interceding between them. Instead, you play an active role in stimulating and shaping the business ecosystem around your company by using smart power, rather than by imposing strategies as the largest or most resource-rich participant.[21] We will show how, by promoting and guiding the development of your business ecosystem as an ecosystem leader, you can enhance your company's competitive advantage and its ability to generate sustainable profits.

We will also show how leading the development of a vibrant ecosystem will allow you to benefit from the opportunities and deal with the uncertainties associated with the new wave of creative destruction, rather than falling victim to it. As we have already seen, industry disruption challenges companies to find ways to bring together new combinations of technologies, know-how, experience, assets, and capabilities that no single company has at its disposal. That means creating strategies and organizational structures that bring the potential power of partnerships to the fore as core to your business model and future success. It also means leveraging the power of a diverse and changing set of partners, many of whom you can influence but not control, to accelerate learning, experimentation, and innovation in your organization.

In short, it is time to get serious about harnessing the full power of your business ecosystem. This ecosystem is the network of organizations and individuals around your company that can co-evolve their capabilities and roles, and align their investments to create additional value and/or improve efficiency,[22] and this to the benefit of all partners in the ecosystem.

The good news is that your company already has the kernel of a business ecosystem. No company is an island; it depends not only on its immediate customers and suppliers, but also on its customers' customers, end users, providers of complementary products and services, governments, those who contribute to training its workforce, and many others. A few are formal "partners," but many beyond these formal partners impact the success or failure of your business by their actions, investments, and learning. Some of the broader participants in your company's ecosystem are identifiable. Others, such as specifiers that set the directions in your industry, opinion formers, or those developing tools that help users deploy your product or service, may have an important impact on your business without you even being aware of them.

Your first reaction might be "So what? I cannot control my ecosystem. I might even not be aware of it." Look at it this way. Few executives doubt that positioning their companies in their markets is a key element of strategy, even if the market dynamics are outside their control. But back in the 1950s, when most companies felt themselves to be at the mercy of market forces over which they had little influence, the idea seemed radical. Similarly, a strategy that depends on shaping your ecosystem might seem similarly radical today. Smart companies are leading (although not fully determining) the development and behavior of their ecosystems in ways that help make them more successful, and their businesses more innovative and more sustainable.

Another reaction may be: "Yes this sounds good, but it can only be done by a large company like Alibaba. I am a smaller player; how can I do it and what is in it for me?"

Ecosystems Strategies Are Not Only for Large Companies

To see how ecosystem strategy can provide the key to rapid growth for start-ups and medium-sized companies as well as large, established players, we can look to ARM, an information technology hardware company from the UK. Despite limited resources this small company, a world away from the crucible of Silicon Valley, became a leader in an industry that normally requires huge capital investments. They did so by building a very successful ecosystem for the design of its chips.

ARM started with twelve engineers in a fourteenth-century barn near Cambridge in the UK in 1990. At the end of July 2016, Japan's Softbank paid $32 billion, 43 percent above ARM's closing price, for a firm with sales of just $1.5 billion, and profits before taxes of $500 million. This looks like a high price for a relatively small company, even if its profitability was impressive. Why was ARM so valuable?

ARM is not a household name even though almost all of us are indirectly its customers. One reason is that ARM is a pure IP (intellectual property) company that designs, but does not manufacture, a specific type of microprocessor known as reduced instruction set computing (RISC) chips. These chips use fewer instructions. Thus, the devices that use them consume less energy than conventional designs. That makes it possible for you to use your smartphones longer without running out of power. The processors based on ARM's designs are used in over 95 percent of all the world's mobile phones, as well as other mobile devices and more recently in intelligent devices that can talk to each other over the internet. Most of your smartphones and tablets, your smart watch, and the GPS in your car all likely use ARM's processors.

One of ARM's attractions to Softbank is that it benefits from participating in a fast-growing market. We hear the buzz about smart cities, the Internet of Things (IoT), wearable technology, driverless cars—all of which require processors of the type that ARM helps to design. But paying $32 billion for a company with fewer than four thousand employees with no manufacturing capabilities and only producing IP—wasn't that a bit over the top?

The price was paid, we believe, not just for ARM's tangible assets, but also for its unique innovation ecosystem. It is another example of how ecosystem strategies can generate massive value for shareholders as well as customers and partners. ARM had created an extensive network of partners that co-innovate and codevelop with it. These partners are chip designers, manufacturers, and distributors (e.g., Samsung, the producers of equipment for design and testing of chips), the original equipment manufacturers (e.g., Apple for its iPhones or Huawei), and of course also the app developers and content providers. Some partners design processor chips based on ARM's IP; others have fabrication plants that produce the chips. ARM is a master at orchestrating this network—without controlling all the participants. How can it do so? After all, it is a relatively small company and it has to lead an ecosystem with giants. Given the capital requirements for building chip fabrication plants, it could never have succeeded in doing so in-house. But it was successful with its intellectual property (IP) development because it had established itself at the center of knowledge exchange between diverse partners. The key was to create an ecosystem where, by working with ARM, partners could together achieve lower costs, better use of expensive wafer-fabrication capacity, and a faster rate of technological advancement than acting alone. We will describe in more detail this knowledge network and how ARM catalyzed its emergence in chapter 3.

An important lesson here is that small innovators can be as successful as their larger counterparts by using their soft power to lead an ecosystem of innovators. ARM is good at mobilizing and guiding an international network of knowledge partners that stretches from Munich to Melbourne, San Francisco to Seoul, and Guangdong to Geneva. And although some of the participants in its ecosystem are huge companies such as Apple, Huawei, and Samsung, ARM has been able to take on the mantle of ecosystem leader in the network.

ARM's success in creating enormous value by in-building and leveraging its ecosystem is all the more remarkable because it has achieved this in an industry where the conventional paradigm is one of vertical integration. Trying to replicate the kind of integrated operations Intel has built up would have required an investment of billions of dollars. ARM was launched with an investment of less than $3 million. But by clever leadership of the ecosystem, it was able to not only break in, but also to become a pivotal player. One important lesson here is that the ecosystem leader needs to control the temptation to become too greedy. Like Alibaba, it knew when it had to leave a juicy chunk of value for its partners to keep them motivated and engaged. ARM was highly profitable, but it was also willing to share a fair slice of the value created in the ecosystem with its partners. As one ARM executive told us: "We get rich if our partners get rich." Thus, ARM's partners were motivated to scale the ecosystem quickly. As the ecosystem grew, so did ARM, enabling it to grow without the capital necessary to build its own distribution machine.

ARM's experience also demonstrates that it has been astute in the way it used this ecosystem to innovate as a small company in the high-technology sector. Therefore, it has virtually no competitors. When Softbank bought ARM, it was actually tapping into a collaborative innovation engine that involved a vast network of companies.

To Lead the Ecosystem or Simply Participate?

Whether you are running a large company or a smaller one, we have adopted the perspective of ecosystem leader to explain how you can harness the power of partners to make your business more successful. But there are also many lessons in this book for companies who choose, instead, to become active participants in an ecosystem led by someone else. These include how best to participate in the process of discovering new value; speeding up your pace of learning and innovation; interacting with other partners in the ecosystem; and, importantly, monetizing your role in the ecosystem.

As we embark on the journey to understand how to leverage an ecosystem to thrive in a world of industry disruption, the question of when it makes sense to take a leadership role versus participating more or less fully must be considered. A useful way to structure this decision is to think about two dimensions of your relationship with your potential ecosystem partners.

1. How pivotal is your potential role in the ecosystem? Or to put it another way, how much will your partners need to depend on you?
2. How critical will any specific partner be to successfully executing your future business model? In other words, how much will you need to depend on a specific partner?

The answers to these two questions interact to determine the four possible routes you might follow as depicted in exhibit 1.1. If you have the potential to play a critical role in enabling the ecosystem system to deliver its value proposition, then it makes sense for you to try to adopt the leadership role and catalyze and shape the development of the ecosystem in ways that benefit your business. As we saw in the case of ARM, even a relatively small company can become the ecosystem leader if its potential to contribution is essential to the ecosystem delivering value to customers and other partners. But you will probably be able to assume this role only if you are not heavily dependent on a specific partner who is also vying to lead the ecosystem. Again, ARM's experience is instructive here. ARM is heavily dependent on its partners to deliver its ecosystem's value proposition in RISC chips. But it need not be dependent on any specific partner for its ecosystem to succeed. The more original equipment manufacturers (OEMs) and chip fabricators, for example, that join the ecosystem, the better. But if one specific potential partner refuses to join the party, even a large and powerful one, the ecosystem can still thrive. In ARM's ecosystem this was in fact the case: for many years Intel refused to join and instead sought to promote its own, competing proprietary technology. When the ecosystem became the de facto global standard, Intel eventually joined as a partner.

The converse scenario is where you can provide a significant, but not critical, contribution to the ecosystem and are also highly dependent on a specific partner to complete the value proposition. Here it makes sense to participate as a follower in the ecosystem and seek to maximize the benefits you draw from it under the leadership of someone else. This is the case for the myriad of partners in Alibaba's ecosystem. Even those that are huge and powerful companies in their own right are dwarfed by the massively greater scale of the ecosystem as a whole and need to accept Alibaba's leadership as the pivotal player.

The two other scenarios demand compromise strategies. If you can potentially play a key role enabling the ecosystem to deliver potential value, but to do so you must also depend on another specific partner, then a struggle for leadership is likely to ensue. Here you find yourself in the realm of "co-opetition" seeking to lead the ecosystem when you can, but cooperating with initiatives that the other powerful partner takes. This is likely to be an uncomfortable position. As we will see, ecosystems tend to be most successful where one company acts as clear ecosystem leader, nurturing and strengthening the ecosystem as well as pursuing its own interests. Co-opetiton may, however, be a necessary

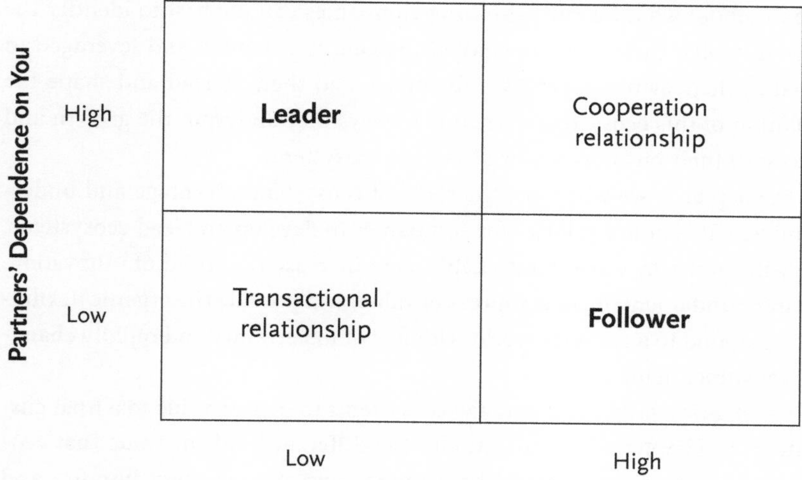

EXHIBIT 1.1. Deciding Whether to Lead or Participate in an Ecosystem. Source: authors' research.

fallback if you are unable to adjust the business model to reduce your dependence on a specific partner and assert your own leadership of the ecosystem.

Finally, if you are in a situation where your potential contribution and significance to the ecosystem is low and your engagement is not heavily dependent on a specific partner, then purely transactional engagement with the ecosystem, taking advantage of opportunities as and when they arise, is probably the right approach. In this case, the ecosystem is unlikely to contribute much to your success. Given the huge potential of ecosystem strategies to transform your business, this would be a lost opportunity. We would encourage going back to first principles and rethinking how by taking leadership of a new and different ecosystem you could harness the power of potential partners to gain the ecosystem edge.

The Way Ahead

A key theme of what follows in the book is how ecosystem leaders can best harness the potential power of ecosystems to deliver levels of innovation, new value creation, and flexibility that far exceed what traditional supply networks, focused alliances, or trading platforms can ever hope to achieve. This book is about what forward-thinking companies can do: first to identify the ways in which their existing ecosystems can be extended and leveraged to enhance their own competitive advantage, and then, to lead and shape the evolution of this ecosystem over time in ways that underpin the growth and success of their businesses as well as their ecosystems.

In chapter 2, we will trace the roots of ecosystem advantage and understand why it is now a priority for companies to develop and lead ecosystems. We will show why ecosystems enable us to increase the speed of innovation, tap into fundamentally new sources of value, and provide the organic flexibility to respond to a complex world with lots of uncertainty and rapidly changing consumer demands.

Companies design and manage ecosystems to deliver value to a final customer.[23] In chapter 3, we will explore the different kinds of value that ecosystem strategies can create. These range from new product bundles and customer solutions to more efficient business models and completely new industries. The opportunity to create new sources of value is the starting point for any successful ecosystem strategy. Because partners will need to contribute to create this new value, it is clear that additional value will have to be shared. By promoting co-learning and innovation, ecosystems can create massive new pools of value, providing more than enough to be shared around.

Ecosystems derive much of their vitality and success from network economies. Once an ecosystem is well established or becomes the dominant player in its market, new partners will flock to join, contributing to a spiral of success. But when a new ecosystem is in its infancy, partners will be leery of engaging and investing. In chapter 4, we focus on how an ecosystem leader can kick-start a new ecosystem and get the flywheel of success turning.

Once an ecosystem is up and running, the challenge is to grow it to the scale necessary to deliver profits. This is the topic discussed in chapter 5. Growth is about attracting new customers and new partners, but it also requires the ecosystem leader to help attract the right partners: those with the capabilities and knowledge the ecosystem needs to thrive. To attract the right partners, the ecosystem leader needs to establish an architecture for the ecosystem going forward where partners can find their niche. Wherever possible, it needs to resist the temptation to undermine its partners by encroaching on their territory. And it needs to find ways to encourage partners to invest in the growth of the ecosystem. By doing so, it can leverage others' investments as well as its own, opening the way to generating increasing returns as the ecosystem scales up.

Even ecosystems that achieve scale can falter in the face of competition with better ideas and value propositions. The ranks of almost-forgotten firms who led ecosystems that atrophied, from Netscape through to Myspace and Symbian, is testimony to this risk. For an ecosystem to be sustainable in the long term, it needs to go on pulling in new knowledge, learning, and innovating. Chapter 6 shows what lead companies can do to create the conditions for continuous learning and innovation in the ecosystem.

The kind of ecosystems many of tomorrow's companies need to build to cope with disruption may never be as efficient as classic supply chains, focused alliances or trading platforms for delivering highly specified products, services, and tasks. The co-learning, innovation, and flexibility that ecosystems offer usually come at a cost in terms of lower efficiency and higher transaction costs. Ecosystem leaders therefore need to think carefully about what they can do to reduce this relative disadvantage, by making the interactions within their ecosystem as efficient as possible and enhancing the system's overall productivity. This is the topic of chapter 7.

Ecosystems, of course, also need to make money for the ecosystem leader (as well as its partners). Value needs to be created, and captured. Chapter 8 focuses on the different ways that a vibrant ecosystem can be monetized while ensuring that the process remains fair to those who jointly create its success.

We then turn to the question of how your personal leadership style and the structure of your own organization will need to change in order to successfully lead an ecosystem. It is clear that one of the key advantages of ecosystems, compared with vertically integrated firms or joint ventures, is their flexibility. Ecosystems are dynamic organisms that can continually change with changing market conditions. Partners come and go and the configuration of the ecosystem can continually adapt. Self-organization often plays a big role, but the ecosystem leader can also help create the conditions for the ecosystem to adapt when it needs to. As was illustrated by the influence of Jack Ma at Alibaba, this requires a different type of personal leadership: one that looks beyond your own organization to the broader network on which your success depends. Among other factors, the senior management team of a company that wants to lead an ecosystem requires better collaborative skills and a higher tolerance for ambiguity and uncertainty than those running a more integrated firm or a well-honed supply chain. It also necessitates a restructuring of your company's internal organization. New roles will need to be created, new performance measures implemented, and employees will need to be equipped to operate comfortably in a world of "co-opetition". The characteristics of successful ecosystem leaders and the necessary changes to your internal organization are discussed in chapter 9.

Chapter 10, the concluding chapter, looks at the future of ecosystem strategies and their role in addressing an ever more volatile and uncertain world. At some point in time, your ecosystem may require restructuring, or may have outlived its usefulness. As partners' roles become more stable and the market matures, there may be less need for flexibility and adaptation. The higher costs of coordination and potential for redundancies inherent in a dynamic ecosystem may then be less justified. Ultimately, therefore, it may make sense to transform the ecosystem into something closer to a traditional supply chain, create a joint venture with key ecosystem partners, or acquire key partners to reap the cost efficiencies offered by closer vertical integration.

You may then need to spawn a new ecosystem in adjacent markets or underpin a new business model. For example, as its e-commerce ecosystem matured, Amazon led the growth of a new Amazon Web Services (AWS) ecosystem alongside, which provided on-demand cloud computing platforms to individuals, companies, and governments on a paid subscription basis. It is now investing managerial effort and money in catalyzing a new mobility ecosystem with self-driving vehicles at its core. Similarly, ARM is striving to replicate the success of its ecosystems for mobile phones and servers in the rapidly emerging arena of the Internet of Things.

We will use a diverse set of cases to illustrate our concepts. All of what we write is based on published materials or insights from our interviews. The risk with case studies is of course that they capture a snapshot of a particular moment or a phase in a company's evolution. But the competitive environment is dynamic and by the time you read this book, there will no doubt already be changes in what these companies do. For example, when the original case on ARM was written, it was an independent company. By the time we wrote this text, Softbank had acquired the company, and their ecosystem continues to evolve. Thomson Reuters spun off the division that we describe as Refinitiv in 2018. It was acquired by the London Stock Exchange in August 2019 for US$27 billion. Keep this in mind when interpreting the cases, looking for lessons that can help shape your own strategy, rather than silver bullets.

2 The Roots of Ecosystem Advantage

THE UNDERLYING RATIONALE THAT EXPLAINS WHY YOU CAN gain a competitive edge by proactively leading your business ecosystem is simple: any company's success depends, at least in part, on how effectively it co-opts the complementary capabilities, resources, and knowledge of the network of firms, institutions, and individuals that are around it. That *business ecosystem*, a term coined by business strategist James Moore in 1993, is a network of organizations and individuals that co-evolve their capabilities and roles and align their investments to create additional value and/or improve efficiency.[1] Within that ecosystem, an "ecosystem leader" catalyzes its emergence and guides its development.

This is by no means an entirely new idea. The management of the Commons in mediaeval Britain was based on a network of such partnerships. Similarly, the management of water on the rice terraces in Java required collaboration in an ecosystem of peers. Such partnerships preserve individual incentives and a degree of autonomy. The system maintains flexibility while enabling parties with different, but complementary, capabilities to work together for their joint benefit.[2] Studies of the woolen textile cluster in fourteenth-century Prato, Italy, estimated to involve in its time some twenty-four thousand people, show how specific artisans and traders contributed to and leveraged the mutual strength of a network. Many centuries later, leveraging a similar network propelled clothing companies such as Italy's Benetton and Spain's Zara into the global market.

In the United States, business ecosystems have existed for over a century. One example is Maine's "lobster gangs," which emerged in the 1820s. A study by anthropologist James Acheson dispelled the notion that the lobster fisherman was the eastern version of the cowboy, struggling alone for survival against the elements. Instead, Acheson found him to be part of a thick and complex web of mutually beneficial relationships.[3] The ecosystem of the lobster gangs was based on bringing together individuals with different skills and family ties in ways that not only ensured a continued livelihood for its members, but also conserved the limited resources from overexploitation. In any port, there was an informal, often unspoken, agreement about where each member of the fishing community could lay his traps. They would also lay the strings of their traps in one direction, such as north to south, so that they did not tangle their lines in someone else's gear. Youngsters who wanted to enter the fishery started with a few traps or worked as a stern man, baiting traps and carting gear, for one of the established lobster fishermen. Eventually, they would be allowed to take over their own territory after an apprenticeship.[4]

These ecosystems often proved more effective than other forms of organization. In a research project by the Environmental and Cultural Conservation in Inner Asia (ECCIA) from 1992 to 1995, satellite images were used to compare the amount of land degradation due to livestock grazing in the regions of Mongolia, Russia, and China. In Mongolia, where shepherds were permitted to move collectively between seasonal grazing pastures, degradation remained relatively low at approximately 9 percent.[5] However, degradation in Russia and China, which implemented state-owned pastures involving immobile settlements, and in some cases privatization by households, was much higher at around 75 percent and 33 percent respectively.[6] The collaborative effort on the part of the Mongolians proved much more efficient in preserving grazing land.

Successful geographic clusters are another type of organization with a long history that embodies many of the principles that we see reflected in modern business ecosystems. Alfred Marshall already mentioned them in his seminal *Principles of Economics*, published in 1890, where he characterized clusters as a "concentration of specialized industries in particular localities" that he termed "industrial districts." He argued that concentrating industries in specific regions created four types of advantages: knowledge spillovers, a skilled labor pool, development of supporting industries, and sharing of resource inputs.[7]

Urban economists have described similar benefits that firms obtain by locating near each other so that interaction is facilitated and encouraged. They call it agglomeration. In 1991, Nobel laureate Paul Krugman argued that as more firms in related fields of business cluster together, their costs of production may decline significantly: firms have competing multiple suppliers, and as a result greater specialization and division of labor.[8] Even when firms compete in the same industry cluster, there may be advantages. The cluster attracts more complementary suppliers and customers than would an isolated company. In simple terms, the basic concept of agglomeration economies is that production is facilitated when there is a clustering of economic activity.

In industrial economics, the terms *agglomeration* and *clustering* have evolved and now imply the ways in which economic efficient specialization arises through clustering in a particular industry-zoned urban area. Since the 1980s, and in particular since the publication of Michael Porter's *Competitive Advantage of Nations*,[9] the term has been associated with an important element of dynamic industrial development in Central and North-Eastern Italy. There, after the Second World War, clusters of small and medium-size enterprises (SME) experienced strong growth. One of the reasons that these industrial districts thrived in Italy was because they brought together in one place different firms engaged in producing a very specialized product. Thus, the Prato district produced woolen fabric, while Sassuolo was known for its ceramic tiles or Brenta for women's footwear. Proximity combined with focus on a common goal encouraged the players to interact and exchange knowledge, resources, and capabilities that benefited everyone within the network.

There is a long history, therefore, of different mechanisms companies and individuals have used to enable them to come together and leverage the complementary capabilities and knowledge of potential partners, to cooperate in ways that promote joint learning, and to coordinate their investments to the benefit of both the individual and the group. Some of these mechanisms, such as the mediaeval commons, were governed by a set of well-defined rules. Others relied on mutual recognition and self-organization. Sometimes partners interacted directly, but in others, such as in clusters, coordination and knowledge exchange were often indirect. The "partners" may not have even been aware of each other, but proximity allowed them to gain the benefits of being part of a network.

But if mechanisms and structures that enabled companies to gain the benefits of reaping network economies were so effective and widespread, why then did managers come to neglect them?

The Decline of Ecosystem Thinking

From the late nineteenth century, the quest to reap economies of scale at the level of corporations became the driving force for business in industry after industry. This led to three key developments that meant that the commons and clusters, and the thinking behind them, lost importance, fading into obscurity by the early twentieth century.

First, the quest for economies of scale favored the standardization of products and processes so that they could be easily controlled and repeated. The result was the vertically integrated corporation, managed by a corporate hierarchy, and its cousin the government bureaucracy. The belief took hold that coordination through formal transactions and contracts was necessary to eliminate "free-riding" because common interests could not ensure collective action and contribution to the common good.[10] Thinkers such as Weber and Michels argued that it was natural that as organizations grew in size and complexity, they would tend to create bureaucratic forms and oligarchies in order to ensure reliable coordination between individuals.[11]

The second reason was that the pursuit of growth and scale had led to the internationalization of business. As business activities spread across the globe, it became more difficult to rely on coordination through proximity, mutual adjustment, and face-to-face interactions. As a result, tighter control and formal reporting replaced the loose understandings that underpinned the informal networks of the past. Formal organization gained importance over ecosystems.

Thirdly, in the quest for standardization and economies of scale, the architecture of many products became more modular. This allowed the emergence of complex international supply chains where tightly defined interfaces between the participants enabled efficient coordination and uncertainty reduction. Given the available technology, the only viable approach to govern the interactions among participants in the chain was to use market mechanisms. These markets comprised large numbers of participants independently, and often myopically, responding to price and volume signals. Such arrangements may have been efficient for short-term optimization, but they lacked the mechanisms to promote partnerships that would enable coordination and co-evolution between participants with specialist capabilities and knowledge. In the drive for efficiency and scale economies, the downsides of decreased joint learning and innovation and reduced flexibility tended to be ignored.

At the same time, working with ecosystems, based on shared ownership and co-ordination between self-interested parties, began to get a bad name among economists. In 1968, ecologist Garrett Hardin published an influential article in the journal *Science* entitled, "The Tragedy of the Commons." One of his arguments was that if all the members of a group used the common resources for their own gain and with no regard for others, then all of the common resources would eventually be depleted.[12]

Rediscovering Ecosystem Advantage

The argument advanced in "The Tragedy of the Commons" became widely accepted until Nobel Prize–winning economist Elinor Ostrom and her collaborators revisited it in 1999.[13] They found that the tragedy of the commons was neither prevalent nor difficult to solve; and locals often came up with solutions to the problem themselves. In fact, other researchers have shown that in many circumstances, even self-interested individuals will find ways to cooperate, because collective restraint serves both the collective and individual interests.[14]

The tide thus began to turn in favor of looking for ways to cooperate that went beyond the limitations of corporate hierarchies, bureaucracies, or impersonal markets. But it was also acknowledged that pure self-organization could not always be relied upon. The simple governance structures observed by Ostrom may well work for local, tangible resources such as grazing or fisheries—but it was not clear how it would translate to the management of resources that transcended well-defined boundaries. These included resources such as the earth's atmosphere and its implications for climate change, air pollution, or those with potential international spillovers, such as oil resources.

The management of knowledge, the essential driver of corporate innovation in the modern world, shares similar problems. Many types of knowledge are not easily contained within well-defined geographic or corporate boundaries. When new technologies or know-how are jointly created through the interaction of multiple partners, proprietary rights are unclear. Likewise, when companies or other organizations invest in so called "market making"—investments designed to stimulate the uptake of new types of products, services, or technologies—from which everyone can benefit, it is difficult to link individual contributions to returns. So, while the idea of promoting the business cooperation and resource sharing that characterized the commons and industrial districts of the past is back in vogue, it is unlikely that those benefits will be achieved if we wait for them to self-organize. Instead, the kind of ecosystems that were illustrated by Alibaba and ARM involve an ecosystem leader establishing an overall architecture and structuring the key interfaces and incentives, and co-opting a small number of strategic partners. Only then do they rely on self-organization within the network. Once a virtuous cycle is established, partners join, depart and interact between themselves without constant intervention by the ecosystem leader. In fact, in some cases, the ecosystem leader may not know the identity or even the existence of some of the partners who are co-evolving their capabilities and aligning their investments while also helping bolster the ecosystem's competitive advantage as they pursue their own self-interest.

Therefore, what we see in the quest to rediscover the advantages of the old commons and industrial districts and clusters is the emergence of a hybrid organizational form that sits between the extremes of a corporate hierarchy and a free market.[15] Traditional corporate hierarchies have the advantages of lower transaction costs; the ability to maximize alignment between different specialist activities and players and optimize the interfaces; and the ability to reduce risk, uncertainty, and variability. But they are not suited to innovating customer-driven solutions that require complex combinations of knowledge that need to be drawn from different companies and organizations scattered around the world. Nor are they suited to quickly and flexibly reconfigure in the face of a volatile environment; witness the struggles large companies face when they try to implement programs of organizational change.

At the other extreme, free and open markets excel at flexibility. Today, some markets adjust prices every millisecond. And they are highly efficient in facilitating exchange, so long as the commodity being traded is easy to price. This is the reason commodities exchanges for products like wheat or pork bellies use standardized contracts. Standardization enables these markets to sidestep the problem of pricing underlying commodities where the quality or location varies. But when it comes to exchanging messy commodities, such as knowledge or new technologies that are difficult to value and price, markets typically fail. This is because efficient markets rely on participants acting independently (and myopically) in response to price signals; they are, however, ill-suited to the challenges of coordinating diverse players and encouraging them to co-invest and share learning for the common good.

These hybrid organizational forms, such as ecosystems, can, of course, exist without a leader. But then they probably would underperform in creating innovative value for the ultimate customer. We argue that with the right leadership, ecosystems promise to deliver several of the advantages of both corporate hierarchies and efficient markets. The ecosystem leader provides some of the better alignment, coordination, simplified interfaces, and greater certainty that a corporate organization can achieve. At the same time, because the leader is unable to fully dictate who participates or impose tight control on partners, ecosystem structures are able to bring together diverse partners with some of the flexibility and incentives for entrepreneurship and innovation that are characteristic of open markets.

The Competitive Advantages of Ecosystems Are Becoming More Important

At the very time that the world is rediscovering the advantages of ecosystems as a way of organizing business activities, the global environment has been changing in ways that put a premium on the advantages that ecosystems can deliver.[16] In the twenty-first century, the demands of consumers, as well as the technologies available to satisfy them, have changed dramatically. Customers increasingly demand customized solutions, rather than standardized products and services delivered in homogeneous volume. While the solutions themselves may appear to be simple, delivering such solutions often requires numerous innovations and complex coordination of different elements. Yesterday's simple mobile phones have been replaced with smartphones that demand a range of technologies ranging from audio electronics and global positioning to photographic imaging, as well as interfaces with myriad services. In dense urban environments, cars have been replaced by services that offer transport by the hour. This requires the collaboration of rental car companies with urban authorities who provide the space where these cars can be parked, new designs for cars, new security systems, different types of insurance, new billing systems, and so on. Food now needs to be traceable in the same way as for pharmaceuticals, requiring coordination, tracking, and validation of the activities of a large number of partners operating at different stages along the value chain.

At the same time, the knowledge and capabilities necessary to satisfy ever more demanding customers no longer reside in just a few, large-scale specialist units. Instead, in more and more industries, the required knowledge and capabilities are abundant and widely dispersed. This makes it difficult to bring them together under the umbrella of a single, vertically integrated firm. Those with some of the key technologies or know-how, for example, may be unwilling to surrender their independence and become employees, they may balk at demands to relocate, and promising companies may resist being acquired. Think, for example, of all the ingredients that have to come together to create autonomous vehicles. It requires a deep understanding of pattern recognition and artificial intelligence, improved sensors, thorough knowledge of automotive design and manufacturing, changed regulations and innovations in insurance, to name just a few. None of these capabilities are currently neatly bundled inside one company or industry. In the face of these trends, the fact that ecosystem structures help diverse sources of capabilities and knowledge to come together, interact and share learning while maintaining some of their independence, makes this way of organizing increasingly attractive.

Additionally, the dramatic fall in the costs of information and communications technologies (ICT) also favors ecosystem structures. Modern ICT means that widely dispersed capabilities and knowledge can be effectively and economically coordinated without geographic co-location. The same benefits historically delivered by clusters and industrial districts can now be replicated by ecosystems that connect partners virtually across the world, rather than being restricted by proximity to a single location, such as a common, a region, or a fishery. In some cases, this coordination can be governed using open-market mechanisms. But many of today's products and services depend on the exchange and sharing of complex, messy, and often tacit knowledge, which can't be easily codified, and coordination, which, as we have seen, the market is ill-equipped to facilitate. Ecosystem structures provide a way of overcoming these limitations to help companies respond to customer demands for solutions and to take advantage of advanced ICT.

This presents company executives with an unparalleled opportunity: the chance to benefit from network economies by harnessing the potential of partners with different knowledge and capabilities, by allowing these assets to be focused on a common goal, and by dynamically coordinating them to drive innovation and improvement. Increasingly, therefore, innovative companies have begun to look for a more strategic approach to enhancing their own competitive advantage by leading the formation of extensive and vibrant networks of partners who can directly, and indirectly, help make their business more successful.

Ecosystem Strategies Can Contribute to Your Success in Three Main Ways

Three characteristics of ecosystem strategies make them particularly well suited to helping companies thrive in the current environment of high uncertainty, disruption, increasingly demanding consumers, new opportunities to leverage ICT and rapid change.

One, ecosystem strategies are highly effective at promoting *joint learning*.[17] Both Alibaba and ARM succeeded by stimulating their ecosystems to generate more learning across the network of partners at a much faster speed than any single participant could achieve alone. A successful ecosystem thus brings together many partners with diverse capabilities and know-how, and helps them interact with each other. In the pursuit of their own self-interest, this interaction generates considerable learning and creates new knowledge. Some of this learning and knowledge will be captured as proprietary knowledge by companies who can use it to enhance their own businesses and open up new profit streams.

Alibaba, for example, captures the huge amounts of data that enable them to understand better the behavior of the partners in their ecosystem in China. They then use this treasure trove of data for everything from offering customized offers to potential buyers to developing improved credit scores it can sell or use to make better lending decisions.[18] But much of the knowledge the ecosystem generates will become a semi-public good that can be shared between numerous partners within the network, each of whom will use it in their own way. In the process, both individual businesses and the ecosystem as a whole will become more successful. In the case of Alibaba's Taobao, for example, interactions in the ecosystem set in train a cycle of continuous, joint learning between the parties. Sellers, website owners, and Alibaba, all benefit from it in different ways.

Two, ecosystem strategies allow a company to take *leadership* of a complex network of partners, making the ecosystem more efficient in innovating, delivering, and supporting products or solutions than a pure self-organizing system. A case in point would be a cluster such as Silicon Valley.[19] Clusters bring together companies and other actors with diverse capabilities and know-how in the same city or region. Proximity enables them to interact easily, providing opportunities to share their knowledge, to spark innovations, to form alliances, and to construct new value chains. In the process, industrial clusters enable joint learning, much of which becomes a public good, a process that the nineteenth-century economist Alfred Marshall described thus: "The mysteries of the trade become no mysteries; but are as it were in the air, and children learn many of them unconsciously."[20] But the ability of traditional clusters to access diverse capabilities that are today scattered around the world is necessarily constrained by geographic boundaries.

The virtual cluster that results from a business ecosystem, often enabled by ICT, can generate even more learning and create still greater value more efficiently if it is catalyzed, shaped, and engendered by an ecosystem leader, rather than relying on traditional self-organization alone. The ecosystem leader acts to make sure that the investments diverse partners make are aligned so that individual investments build on each other.[21] Alibaba's state-of-the-art ICT systems, for example, ensure that when sellers invest in improved customer interfaces, its distribution partners align these with investments in improved warehousing and delivery facilities so that new capabilities for tracking, reliability, and speed can be leveraged for everyone's benefit.

As partners invest, and the ecosystem grows, a positive spiral of network effects kicks in. Each new partner or customer that joins increases the value of the ecosystem to the individual participants. Economies of scale and scope are no longer limited by the size of the individual businesses but can be reaped across the scale of the ecosystem as a whole.

As we also saw in the case of Alibaba and ARM, the ecosystem leader can promote the emergence of a favorable environment for co-learning: an architecture that allows for specialized partner roles to complement each other; a technological roadmap and rules of the road that help partners coordinate their investments; and a common language, communication mechanisms, and governance structure that reduce the transaction costs associated with partner interactions. Taking advantage of opportunities to lead what could otherwise be a chaotic and wasteful evolution of the ecosystem can benefit all the partners as well as the end customer. Smart ecosystem leaders can also capture a portion of that additional value for their own bottom lines.

Three, ecosystem strategies allow a high degree of *flexibility*, enabling partners to constantly adjust their activities to changing circumstances. Unlike an impersonal market, however, these adjustments can be made in concert with the changes other partners are making with an eye to improving the attractiveness of the product or solution the ecosystem delivers while protecting self-interest. A vibrant ecosystem can, therefore, enable activities, assets, and capabilities to be constantly reconfigured in response to unexpected shifts in the environment. Ecosystems allow companies to break free of the inherent rigidities associated with traditional joint ventures or classic, "hub and spoke" alliance structures where the partners and their roles tend to be predetermined and set in stone.

Hence, even as ARM's ecosystem developed, it was constantly reconfigured through the actions taken by both the ecosystem leader and other partners. New partners entered, roles changed as scale and specialization increased, and new connections were forged while old ones disappeared. In this process of flexible evolution, fresh sources of customer value were created and new revenue streams were created and captured. By fostering self-organization and adjustment within a framework promoted by the ecosystem leader, ecosystem strategies offer a way to mix the flexibility of an open market with the discipline of an internal organizational hierarchy. In that process of constant reconfiguration, you probably also improve your own internal organization and processes. You learn what you are good at, what others are good at, how you can grow in a world where digitization is impacting every industry, and how your own organization structure needs to adapt. As a result, your own value creation processes become more effective, and you can learn what it takes to be a leader in tomorrow's world.

Successful ecosystem strategies can therefore unlock:

1. *Rapid innovation:* by drawing on the ecosystem's capacity to generate faster and more diverse types of learning and knowledge than any company can achieve alone;
2. *Fundamentally new sources of value:* by enabling novel, but uncertain, opportunities that can be realized by bringing together a much more diverse range of capabilities and experience than exists in any single company, delivering network economies, and reaping scale economies across the ecosystem as a whole;
3. *Organic flexibility:* because the ecosystem can constantly evolve and restructure in response to a changing market by combining the capacity for self-organization with focus and coordination enabled by an ecosystem leader.

As we will see in chapter 3, the combination of these three characteristics make ecosystem strategies especially well-suited for twenty-first-century market conditions and the threat of disruption that more and more businesses face today.

Ecosystem Strategies Are Not for Everyone

Despite the powerful advantages of ecosystem strategies in today's business environment, we recognize that there are other types of organizational networks that might be effective in helping companies achieve their goals. These include joint ventures, hub-and-spoke alliances, platforms, supply chain networks, agreements with complementary partners, and immersion in localized industrial clusters. But ecosystem strategies have something more to offer. As will become clear in subsequent chapters, there are distinctive *advantages of ecosystem strategies that come from the fact that co-learning and innovation lie at their very core*. They provide the flexibility and greater scope for experimentation needed for innovation and constant improvement combined with the focus and discipline provided by a lead player that is necessary to quickly scale-up and efficiently deliver new products and customer solutions.

Unlike traditional geographically co-located clusters, ecosystems are able to work over long geographical distances. Niklas Zennstroem, one of the co-founders of Skype, argued that co-location has lost much of its value in innovation, and that it may become a liability for companies that can benefit from operating globally. He believes that the battle between technology hubs such as Silicon Valley is a thing of the past:

> While this geographic battle for supremacy is compelling, its effect is actually to make location less, not more, important. For instance, thanks largely to the Internet itself, almost everyone has access to the same information; for most people, the days of having to be close to a data centre are long gone; and investors such as us are looking globally for promising companies we can help. While every location has its opportunities and disadvantages—it is easier to find top computer scientists in San Francisco, for instance, but easier to hold on to them in Helsinki—where you start out is no longer a helpful predictor of your chances of success. Today, the truth is that great companies can come from anywhere. In a way, we have the wrong obsession with geography. In technology, as in life, it is not where you come from–it is where you are going that counts.[22]

Ecosystem strategies also enable a company to more effectively internalize some of the same externalities that are generated in a cluster. Rather than knowledge simply being "in the [local] air," as Alfred Marshall postulated, the links between partners with an ecosystem make it possible for some of this knowledge to be "privatized" or shared between a limited number of parties.

This provides more opportunities to capture the value for the different partners in the ecosystem, not least the ecosystem leader. In a recent study of how pharmaceutical companies internalized biotechnology in the 1990s, the ecosystem approach proved to be superior compared to in-house development. A distinctive feature of biotechnology during the 1990s was the small number of scientists and entrepreneurs who really understood its potential. For traditional pharmaceutical firms, the challenge was to get access to this limited supply of skilled people, most of whom enjoyed working in universities and start-ups in a small number of locations (e.g., San Francisco, San Diego, Boston, and Cambridge). Moving into these clusters of activity early on was therefore a good way of building capability.[23]

Traditional supply chain networks, like those in automotive companies such as Toyota or apparel manufacturers such as Zara, are effective for efficient production and supply of goods with well-defined specifications. However, they generally do not create much learning between partners. With the tasks of each participant in the chain tightly defined and performance focused on narrow measures such as cost, predefined quality standards and on-time delivery, there is little scope or incentive for joint innovation. The value chain leader may accumulate knowledge as it orchestrates its tightly defined supply chain and interacts with end customers and transfers this back to its suppliers. Yet, even this learning and flexibility will be constrained by straightjacket specifications, supplier contracts and narrow performance targets. These features deliver efficiency benefits when the requirements of product or service are buttoned down, but they hinder the development of new customer solutions, sources of value, or new business models and businesses where experimentation and learning are key. They are therefore less effective in coping with disruption.

Focused alliances and joint ventures may well be about sharing knowledge or even co-developing new products, but again they often live within a very structured contractual framework between a small number of partners. As a result, they are not well suited to deliver the kind of new customer solutions and business models created by Alibaba and ARM, where the roles of different partners, and even which types of partners need to be involved, is uncertain and evolving. In this case, it is almost impossible to design a focused alliance to do the job.

One could, of course, set up multiple, bi-lateral alliances with what has been termed "complementors."[24] But this kind of hub-and-spoke arrangement places a significant burden on the ecosystem leader, not only because of the investment required to set up the network but also the ongoing resources required to manage it. The management of such an arrangement includes the need to act as conduit for communications, be a go-between to achieve complementarities, and act as an arbiter of disputes between every partner in the web. Recall the warning from Alibaba's strategy director, Ming Zeng, quoted in Chapter 1: "We learned a lot of painful lessons by trying to over-control and becoming the bottleneck."

Trading platforms for the gig economy like Airbnb, Grab, or Deliveroo enable many independent suppliers and users to come together. Partners using the platform can come and go, but the information exchanged between participants through the trading platform is limited and tends to be highly standardized. The platform leader may accumulate a massive trove of Big Data that opens up new opportunities. However, because the exchanges between other parties are very structured, opportunities for joint learning and innovation, as well as the flexibility to jointly reconfigure and evolve value propositions, tend to be shut down. As mentioned earlier, while most of Alibaba's businesses have trading platforms at their core, it was only by adopting a broader ecosystems mind-set and working jointly with partners in creative ways around these platforms that the company could kick-start the formidable innovation engine that has been the real source of its success.

We therefore are convinced that ecosystems, a hybrid that sits between markets and hierarchies, are ideally suited to cope with disruption, be it technological or otherwise. We know they are not a panacea, and ecosystems are not the solution to cope with all forms of uncertainty. But when one needs to innovate in the face of significant uncertainty and disruption, well-led ecosystems have clearly an advantage over other organization forms.

When thinking through how to capture these potential advantages of leading an ecosystem, it is worth keeping front of mind what an ecosystem is not. This clarity is becoming ever more important as the growing popularity of the term *ecosystem* has led to its frequent misuse. Clearly an ecosystem is not just a complex supply chain, nor is it simply a digital platform or marketplace. Nor is it a static structure that a leader can completely manage or control. As recent research has pointed out, these kinds of misconceptions are more than semantics. They can result in many of the most important benefits of ecosystems being overlooked. At worst, they can lead to exactly the wrong kinds of decisions.[25] Always keep in mind that the ecosystem is a network that brings together partners with different capabilities and knowledge to flexibly innovate, coordinate and co-evolve in ways that create new value. And the role of the ecosystem leader is to catalyze and guide its development.

Having presented our core thesis on why and when ecosystems can be to your advantage, we will now examine how they can help you to create new sources of value.

3 Discovering New Value

DEVELOPING YOUR ECOSYSTEM OPENS THE WAY TO CREATING more value for the customer than would be possible by any company acting alone outside an ecosystem. This ability of the ecosystem to generate additional value is critical to its success. As we mentioned in chapter 2, business ecosystems are less efficient than hierarchical organizations, but they make up for this efficiency gap by providing greater scope for joint learning, rapid innovation, and flexibility. This additional value is precisely what will pay for the additional cost that the ecosystem leader and partners will incur.

Potential Ecosystem Value Creation

What kind of additional value can an ecosystem create? We have observed four ways ecosystem strategies can unlock new value.

New Product Bundles

The bundles enable a product to deliver richer functionality to the customer. Apple's iTunes Store and App Store, for instance, have given hardware products, such as an iPhone or an iPad, an almost infinite set of new functionalities by engaging millions of partners who create and offer music, video, and many different kinds of apps.

New Customer Solutions

The ecosystem leader brings together and decides how to better combine a diverse range of capabilities from partners, kicking off an iterative learning cycle with lead customers, to more effectively satisfy customer needs. The case of Dassault Systèmes S.E. (DS) is an interesting example of how an ecosystem leader can bring together hundreds of knowledge partners to create ecosystems in automotive, life sciences, or aircraft design to support innovation. DS is an international software company headquartered in France with a turnover of $3.975 billion in 2017, and a market capitalization of more than $43 billion in early 2019.[1] It started in the early eighties as a spin-off from the Dassault Aviation Company, a manufacturer of military aircraft and business jets such as the Falcon. It developed powerful computer-aided design (CAD) software for the aerospace industry. In its early days, it was among the pioneers in 3D modelling, and worked closely with its sister company Dassault Aviation. This gave it a good understanding of what was needed to design an aircraft. But its real breakthrough in that industry came in the nineties when it collaborated closely with Boeing to design the 777 aircraft, the first to be designed without producing a physical prototype. Opting for a purely virtual model to do all the testing before producing the first product required considerable know-how to flow from Boeing to DS. Even then, DS did not have all the technical expertise to model, for example, the aerodynamics of the plane. As often is the case, such specialized know-how rests with boutique companies that are masters of very specialized skills. DS went on to integrate these capabilities into what it dubbed the "CATIA 3DEXPERIENCE platform," and developed a "virtual twin" of the product: a complete and detailed computer image of the physical product.

In developing solutions for other industries, DS always works very closely with a partner who has a deep understanding of that specific industry. In doing so, they develop new concepts that then can be applied to service the needs of other customers. For example, in the early 2000s, they worked with Toyota to understand how to integrate the virtual design of the product, the manufacturing process, the supply chain, and the after-sales service. This, in turn, led to the creation of the DS Product Lifecycle Management (PLM) system that enabled the integration of the design, development, manufacturing design, and administrative processes, such as documentation needed for certification in many other industries. This approach continues to serve DS well even today. In June 2018, for example, it announced a twenty-year partnership with EDF, the major French integrated electricity company, and Capgemini, a global consulting company, to digitize and modernize processes and engineering methods for the nuclear engineering industry.

In a similar way, DS works with industry leaders and hundreds of specialized expert companies in fields including mining, pharmaceuticals, marine engineering, fashion design, consumer products, energy, and cities. The concept of a virtual twin world has proven effective for many different applications. For instance, to produce a first virtual twin of a city, it worked closely with the National Research Foundation of Singapore, and many other government-linked organizations in Singapore to integrate urban planning, government services, energy supply, security, social integration, economic development, sustainability, access to health services, and so on. With images and data collected from these public agencies, including geometric, geospatial, and topological, as well as legacy and real-time data such as demographics, movement or climate, users of "Virtual Singapore," a dynamic 3D city model and collaborative data platform, are able to create rich visual models and realistic large-scale simulations of Singapore. Users can then digitally explore the impact of urbanization on the city-state and develop solutions that optimize logistics, governance, and operations relating to environmental and disaster management, infrastructure, homeland security, or community services.

The choice to work with Singapore was not an accident. Bernard Charlès, president and CEO of Dassault Systèmes recalled:

> Singapore is the most advanced city in the world in terms of leveraging technology to plan and manage its transformation over the next decades, and its government's forward-thinking vision towards a Smart Nation parallels our own mission to harmonize product, nature and life through 3D universes. Cities are some of the most complex "products" created by humanity. Through more efficient and accurate predictions of future experiences within these cities using state-of-the-art tools and applications, we can better anticipate national resource planning or provision of services, and contribute towards a more sustainable quality of life. We hope to see other cities echo Singapore's exciting initiative.[2]

The capability to create a virtual twin of a city has now enabled DS to work with several booming cities such as Jaipur in India to develop detailed 3D models for their urban development.

Using this approach, DS has catalyzed the development of a number of ecosystems with more than eight hundred partners, bringing together lead customers in industries ranging from automotive to life sciences, as well as dozens of services, software, and technology partners and educational institutions. Their ecosystems deliver a bundle of software solutions covering every aspect of PLM, from the first sketch of an idea to the documentation used in maintenance, optimized for each different industry's needs. DS's PLM ecosystems have enabled increased faster innovation, a wider set of solutions, and a lot more customization for the needs of its users, than DS could have managed alone. As Charlès put it, "As we are shifting towards an experience-centric world, the ecosystem and the combinative nature of creation are becoming more valuable than each individual piece of IP. While innovation is inseparable from the transmission of knowledge within an ecosystem, we have to find new models . . . with the right balance between individual contribution, investment and total value creation for the consumer and society."[3]

New Platform Economies

Customers gain the benefits of innovative offerings, better value for money, more choice and less risk when a company establishes a platform and nurtures an ecosystem around it that opens up possibilities for partners and customers to share products, services, and knowledge. The most prominent examples of ecosystems built around platforms are two-sided markets, such as Uber, Lyft, Didi Chuxing, Grab, and Airbnb, which not only allow potential buyers and sellers to transact efficiently, but also enable efficient flows of information about needs and capacities between the parties and, of course, the ecosystem leader.

Ecosystem leaders can do more than simply set up an exchange to make the ecosystem successful. They need to find ways of attracting and nurturing potential partners and customers, monitoring the evolution and learning in the network, and catalyzing its development. But the possibilities for new value creation by harnessing platform economies is not restricted to establishing two-sided markets. As we have seen in the case of ARM, the firm has created value by establishing a platform in the form of its RISC-chip architecture, reducing the costs of designing and manufacturing these chips while speeding up innovation.

New Industries

The potential to create value sometimes entails creating a completely new industry, where companies that have never interacted before come together for the first time. Of course, a new market that brings them together can sometimes do the job. But, as we saw in chapter 2, a market is unlikely to be effective in promoting the kinds of knowledge exchange and co-learning required to build a new industry, especially when its future is shrouded in uncertainty. Creating the new mobility industry, for instance, will not just involve automotive companies. In fact, automakers may be one of the less important contributors. A new mobility industry will need infrastructure providers, designers and manufacturers of new types of sensors (both on-board and embedded in the environment), software and artificial intelligence (AI) companies, entertainment to occupy the passenger in an autonomous vehicle, and regulators and municipal governments, to name just a few of the likely participants. Hence, a new ecosystem that promotes experimentation and learning between the partners, and helps to coordinate their investments, is essential to unlock the enormous potential from tomorrow's mobility solutions. For example, when Didi Chuxing Technology Co, the Chinese ride-sharing, AI, and autonomous technology conglomerate, announced in August 2018 that it would invest $1 billion in its auto-services business and break it off into a separate unit, it stated, "In the future, Didi will continue a win-win collaborative network with partners throughout the automotive industry chain to build a new transportation ecosystem designed for a future of shared mobility."[4]

The Value-Creation Imperative

Creating the new value that ecosystem strategies can deliver by enabling new product bundles, new customer solutions, and new platform economies, and thus spawning new industries sounds attractive. But why is it becoming an imperative for more and more companies?

The answer lies in the fact that the global competitive environment is changing in ways that demand a much broader range of capabilities, and it offers new opportunities to engage with others. Three developments in the global environment are particularly significant in favoring ecosystem strategies: the fact that customers are increasingly demanding solutions and experiences rather than products, the rising knowledge content of many products and business activities, and new opportunities being created by advances in information and communications technologies.

Customers Are Demanding Solutions and Experiences

As we mentioned in chapter 2, customers are increasingly demanding solutions and experiences, rather than simple products or services. The value they are looking for comes from experiencing the use of a product or a service that is tailored to their specific needs and preferences. This is also a trend in business-to-business markets, where customers have begun to demand services (such as "power by the hour" or "miles of road use" rather than jet engines or tires). Delivering such experiences often requires complex and integrated systems.

Delivering even seemingly simple experiences like an impromptu meal out with friends is becoming more complex. Apps with location-based services on your smartphone help you to choose the restaurant with the food you like with the shortest waiting time. Other apps show you how to get there using the fastest route with a choice of travel modes. Social media links enable you to share the experience or rate the food and service. Complex supply chains spanning the world have probably brought exotic ingredients to the restaurant so that you can savor your preferred dishes. Companies can no longer satisfy the demands for these kinds of solutions and experiences acting alone. Innovative solutions and experience are becoming almost impossible to deliver by relying exclusively on the knowledge and capabilities of a few large specialist units within your own organization or linking with a few subcontractors. In more and more industries, the relevant knowledge and capabilities necessary to innovate are scattered among players and across the globe. Not only is the challenge of satisfying today's customers demanding a wider range of competencies—in today's world of volatility, uncertainty, and ambiguity, the activities and interactions between businesses underpinning your offering need to be reconfigured quickly and flexibly.

At the same time, many companies increasingly face pressure to focus on fewer core activities to reduce investments and avoid the increased costs of complexity. This focus enables them to target their capital expenditure on deploying the latest technology for their core processes and to concentrate on deepening their core competencies.[5] "Focus and win" has become a popular catch phrase. But shrinking a business to a focused core of activities is at odds with customers who demand experiences and solutions that require more integration and complexity and that bring together multiple products and services, often in customized bundles.

There are many other examples of this trend. Simple mobile phones have been replaced by smartphones that can offer a myriad of services. In dense urban environments, cars have been replaced by services that offer transport by the hour. Complex financial products involving everything from insurance to equity release are replacing simple mortgage loans. In each of these cases, value is created by a combination of products and services that are delivered by an extensive group of partners. For instance, the concept of car rental by the hour anywhere, anytime, as it was developed by Zipcar (now a subsidiary of Avis) in Britain, the United States, Canada, Spain, France, Germany, Turkey, Belgium, and Taiwan; Paris's now defunct Autolib or Car2go; and DriveNow in Berlin, required collaboration between a huge range of partners, including property owners and local authorities (who provided parking spaces) through to credit card companies, breakdown and cleaning services, and insurance companies.

One answer to the demands to "shrink your core, but expand your offering" problem is to outsource more to partners.[6] But it is difficult to reliably deliver a complex solution bundle involving multiple technologies, capabilities, and services using vertical integration or the kind of subcontracting relationships common in traditional supply chains, where relationships and incentives are often antagonistic.[7] Rather than outsourcing a few well-defined activities, delivering complex customer solutions requires the management of complicated interactions and exchange of knowledge between many mutually dependent partners, as well as trial-and-error learning—tasks to which ecosystem strategies are much better attuned.[8]

Knowledge Content Is Rising

A second important trend is that the knowledge content of many products and business activities is rising. The increase in the number of knowledge workers dealing with tacit and uncodified knowledge means that simple, standardized or physical interfaces no longer meet the needs for interaction and exchange required in many industries. Instead, knowledge that is more complex must flow between partners; boundaries of responsibility are blurred and need to be managed, as do the claims to intellectual property that are often jointly developed.

Ecosystems allow new value to be created by combining knowledge from a diverse group of partners. DS, the market leader in PLM systems, does this by creating application-specific user groups that collaborate on specially designed social network platforms.[9] As we saw earlier, the basic principles of modeling and design of products and processes may be common across many industries, but effective software solutions need to incorporate in-depth—and very often tacit—knowledge of the industry in which it will be used. Designing cars or aircraft requires very different skills than designing fashion or applications for geological analysis. To digitalize the operations of mining companies, DS had to work with a mining group like Australia's BHP Billiton, equipment suppliers like Atlas Copco, and university labs like the French engineering school UniLasalle, to just name a few. To access diverse industry-specific knowledge, DS collaborated, and continues to do so, with hundreds of partners, including system integrators, customers, and suppliers. For each of its solutions, it has created user communities on an internally developed enterprise platform for social networking called 3DSwYm, which was designed to dynamically share and leverage knowledge. This enables DS to uncover and harness individual talents and ideas inside and outside the company, including partners, suppliers, consumers or any other stakeholder. Connecting via communities helps this diverse group coalesce around key objectives and focus on how the ecosystem can create value. These communities also foster powerful synergies by creating an open and participative approach.

Sophie Planté, CEO of 3DSwYm, Dassault Systèmes stated that "3DSwYm empowers everyone, regardless of domain, to innovate and add value, share their experience and put forward ideas, fostering a strong sense of belonging and engaging everyone in the enterprise's challenges and vision. . . . The result is a unified 360-degree view of activities and interactions shared across the [ecosystem]. 3DSwYm becomes a real-time social dynamic referential environment, offering effective decision and action support, leveraging social innovation to help transform the organization." Monica Menghini, then executive vice president of Industry and Marketing at Dassault Systèmes added, "We are offering customers a value creation platform. Many disciplines within a company create value. All industries, from banking and insurance to retail, fashion, construction, energy, life sciences, transportation or aerospace, need to break down barriers and ensure value is created by all. 3DSwYm lies at the heart of our Social Industry Experience strategy."[10]

This sharing across the ecosystems has enabled DS to become, and stay, relevant, innovative and successful across the eleven different industrial sectors for which it has now delivered software applications.

As knowledge management becomes increasingly central to competitive advantage, the model of an extensive ecosystem that allows knowledge and innovation to be generated rapidly through joint learning across a wide range of different partners, each stimulated by different contexts, histories, and cultures, is becoming more critical to success.

Developing an ecosystem with many partners enhances innovativeness, because it offers the opportunity for a thousand flowers to bloom. This makes ecosystem strategies—which have the ability to side-step many of the issues faced when trying to move and transplant knowledge, much of it embedded in the people, systems, and cultures of external organizations—increasingly appealing to boost innovation and discover new value.

Disruption and Uncertainty Are Becoming Endemic

Because of these three developments, companies now operate in an environment with increasing uncertainty, challenged by disruptive competitors who want to rewrite the rules of the game. Rapid technological evolution, the interconnectedness of the world of trade and business, and geopolitical instability are no doubt some of the reasons for this rising uncertainty. Witness the US financial crisis of 2008 and the ensuing years, when the interconnectedness of the banks and financial institutions brought down some of the most revered financial institutions. Or consider the fate of telecom operators, who made tons of money from SMS traffic, but now face stiff competition from internet-based social networking companies such as WeChat, WhatsApp, Line, Telegram and Viber.

Ecosystems, where partners can collaborate through loosely coordinated development and experimentation, can absorb uncertainty more effectively than traditional hierarchies or even subcontracting relationships, where deliverables have to be precisely specified in advance and structures are more difficult to reconfigure.[11] As we shall see in chapter 5, this advantage is reinforced by the ability of ecosystems to enable ecosystem leaders to reap economies of scale and network advantages with lower capital investment. This is particularly important in winner-takes-all industries, where increasing returns to scale are decisive.[12] Disruption, meanwhile, can be countered by the ability of ecosystem strategies to unlock new platform economies or create new industries.

Information and Communications Technologies Offer New Opportunities

While ecosystem strategies provide opportunities to create value in ways that address these challenges, some business leaders may have refrained from implementing them because of a fear of the complexity involved. But advances in ICT are making new business models such as ecosystems increasingly achievable and also more cost-effective. These technologies enable business ecosystems to marshal economically diverse resources and knowledge scattered across the globe, and create a "digital commons." In the past century, networking between diverse and dispersed partners was often thwarted by the prohibitive costs of ICT. Although remote communication may not be a perfect substitute for face-to-face interaction in the near future, technological advances and falling unit costs are enabling more complex and dispersed ecosystems to become economically viable.

The way DS brings together its engineers and those working at its partners through ICT showcases how coordination of the development work across dozens of locations can be achieved. DS's software platform enables engineers within its own labs or with partners, in places as far-flung as France, the United States, Japan, China, and India, to work together on a 3D design in real time with only an internet connection. This capability is a significant advantage for any company with a global engineering and manufacturing strategy. ICT can therefore enhance the breadth and depth of collaboration. Everyone, regardless of location or whether employed by the company or a partner, or working as a freelancer, can collaborate across business processes, from the lowest level of detail to the full product definition, bringing together the requirements and the functional, logical, and physical definitions of the product. Additionally, difficulties due to differences in language have been reduced significantly by DS creating a set of standard technical instructions for the actions that designers can take, which are language independent.

One of DS's users is Renault, the French automotive company and part of the Renault-Nissan Alliance. It has deployed DS's solution since 2009 across all its geographies and brands. The online access to the digital mock-up of its models and virtual twins has led to a simplification of collaboration between engineering sites. This use of a unique, collaborative interface for all developers worldwide supports simultaneous product/process engineering to get the design "right the first time"[13]

Renault's original engineering processes, divided into three different silos with three different solutions, was transformed by adopting the unified collaborative DS platform using a single, standardized data model, and solutions that are deployable "out of the box" for all engineering divisions. At the heart of Renault's strategy to transform its product development was DS platform's virtualization of the entire product lifecycle within a flexible, precise, and truly collaborative environment. And it also reinforced collaboration with Renault's partners and suppliers to ensure performance and data consistency between globally dispersed teams.

Renault wanted an integrated and collaborative PLM environment enabling greater operational transparency and the possibility to validate scenarios through virtual simulation and online management of the digital mock-up. This significantly eased decision-making throughout the stakeholder community and across the entire product lifecycle of Renault automobiles, from conception through to design, compliance, simulation, and manufacturing.

Discovering New Value: The Ecosystem Leader's Role

Each of the four ways in which the development of an ecosystem can unlock new value—through new product bundles, new customer solutions, new platform economies, and spawning new industries—shares a common characteristic: they require a process by which new customer value is discovered. The new value is not just assembled or delivered from existing elements by following a predetermined blueprint; it has to be identified. Business ecosystems come into their own by facilitating the process of discovery.

Discovering new sources of value requires the three key capabilities that ecosystems excel at: a huge potential for rapid, joint learning and innovation; the ability to harness the capabilities of diverse players and channel them toward a common goal through the leadership of an enlightened company; and the flexibility for continuous reconfiguration in the face of an uncertain, fast-changing environment.

Given these demands, what can you do as an ecosystem leader to catalyze and promote the discovery of new value through your ecosystem strategy?

Focus Externally

The first thing you can do is to cast your eyes on what is going on outside your company, starting with potential customers. Few ecosystem leaders have succeeded by coming up with a new value proposition internally, designing their ideal ecosystem, and then determinedly trying to build it. Most started with a broad idea of where the potential for new value might lie, and then start talking to possible customers or piloting a product, service, or putative platform to engage them. In many cases, the value and the shape of the ecosystem that subsequently emerged was not exactly where or how they had expected it at the outset.

In fact, the value potential of some ecosystem strategies has emerged from early failures; in trying to understand and overcome the reasons why the initial customers rebuffed their first offerings, future ecosystem leaders have discovered where the value potential actually lies. The story of how ARM developed its first successful product shows how arduous, but also ultimately rewarding, the value discovery process can be. It might have been consigned to the role of just another specialist supplier had it not been for the negative reaction of the then leader in mobile phones, Nokia, to the first proposal that chip supplier Texas Instruments (TI) had pitched, which incorporated ARM's designs. Among a long list of problems, Nokia pointed out that the ARM processor needed too much memory because the software code was too heavy. This made the product too expensive. But Nokia also recognized that there was not an offering on the market that provided the required performance and that the solutions to these problems were not obvious. In order to break new ground, they suggested the formation of a consortium consisting of TI, ARM, and Nokia to develop a new solution.

As a result, ARM found itself working closely with a partner who, as an original equipment manufacturer, was ARM's "customer's customer" (two steps removed in the value chain), as well as its direct customer, TI. The benefits of these kinds of close interactions with diverse partners, which went beyond ARM's immediate customers, became obvious very quickly. ARM gained a detailed understanding of Nokia's priorities and needs. Besides, it received detailed knowledge from TI about how to interface with its digital signal processing technology and what made a chip efficient to manufacture. This was the germ of what was to become ARM's global ecosystem. Working with a network of partners and genuinely listening to their needs can help discover new value.

This ARM story also demonstrates something about the nature of the new value that can underpin a sustainable ecosystem. There has to be additional value for end customers. In this case, it was better functionality with longer battery life. But there was also additional value for the partners involved. For Nokia, that was the ability to deliver performance at low cost and hence a more competitively priced product. For TI, it was the opportunity to sell more chips. ARM itself directly benefited from increased revenues received on its designs from license fees and royalties. The indirect value for ARM, however, was even more important. By interacting with its partners, ARM gained valuable knowledge about next-generation product requirements from Nokia and new chip-fabrication technologies from TI. That knowledge enabled ARM to come up with a whole new generation of designs. The putative ecosystem not only delivered short-term revenues, but also began to prime an innovation engine with knowledge that ARM's competitors lacked.

Such an innovation engine can create a virtuous cycle of value discovery. As ARM's ecosystem grew, it discovered other types of new and additional value. Handset makers such as Apple or Samsung worked with ARM because they could share the costs of developing a flexible platform on which they could build their devices. That allowed them to concentrate their resources on developing their own proprietary technologies atop ARM's base. Being part of the ecosystem for RISC chips also allowed the handset makers to choose from a wide range of semiconductor manufacturers, rather than being locked into proprietary technology. And it improved their chances of finding supplies whenever an upswing in the cycle led to shortages. For semiconductor fabricators such as TI and TSMC, the ability to sell to a wide range of OEMs helped them gain scale economies and manage capacity utilization. End customers benefited from improved reliability, lower costs, and faster access to technological advances that underpinned greater functionality and longer battery life. Ecosystems can deliver different types of value to many different partners.

Our next case study, athenahealth Inc., illustrates exceptionally well the process of discovering additional value through a relentless external focus. What has become today an extensive health care ecosystem, started out in the United States as Athena Women's Health, a clinic founded when partners and former consultants Jonathan Bush and Todd Park acquired an obstetrics practice in San Diego, California, in 1997. Neither was a physician, but the former health care consultants thought they could efficiently and profitably manage a medical practice. Positive clinical outcomes, combined with lower prices, led to its growing popularity and revenues, and the practice soon expanded to more than a dozen clinics spread across California.

Despite their success, Athena faced a problem common to medical practices: being paid. The process of verifying and processing insurance claims, and thereafter being reimbursed, proved time consuming, costly, and difficult. Insurers, both Medicaid and private insurers, took weeks or months to reimburse claims. As a result, and despite growing revenues, Athena faced recurring cash-flow problems. To address this issue, Bush and Park recruited Park's younger brother, Eddie, to develop a web-based billing system to track patients, handle medical billing, and carry out insurance eligibility checks.

Bush and Park soon recognized the potential value of their software solution, dubbed AthenaNet, for other health care practices. One important, and unexpected, signal came when Bush approached potential investors about funding the growth of the business. The latter expressed more interest in backing the software than the company's medical practice. Realizing that Athena would be more valuable as a health care IT solution provider than as a medical practice, Bush and Park relaunched Athena Women's Health in 1999 as athenahealth, a health care IT company. They began selling their cloud-based solution to medical practices across the country, focusing primarily on small- and medium-size physician practices providing outpatient care.

The new company's first, and flagship, product was AthenaCollector, a cloud-based billing and practice-management software. It was followed by an integrated electronic health record service, a patient portal and automated messaging service, and an order transmission service that facilitated referrals, ordering labs, prescriptions, and inpatient admissions. Over the next decade, athenahealth's software added more functions, such as options for maintaining patient records, communicating with patients electronically, processing insurance claims, as well as handling billing and reimbursements. By 2010, the company was earning annual revenues of almost $250 million.

Still, when the founders looked at the potential to create more value in the health care market, they realized they were only scratching the surface. It also dawned upon them that the limited capabilities within their own company presented a bottleneck to unlocking that potential. Drawing analogies from the success of Salesforce.com and Apple, the leadership recognized, as athenahealth's VP of business development, Kyle Armbrester, recalled, that "it was not features and functions that drove their success. Rather, they've created huge value by supporting developers and start-ups that want to plug into their businesses."[14]

If the transition from a women's health clinic to a software solution provider was somewhat of an accident, the transition from a product-based strategy to an ecosystem strategy was quite deliberate. athenahealth's leadership began to take steps to catalyze the development of an ecosystem of health care software solutions around their cloud-based IT product. The aim was to create what they called "the health care Internet."

To start the process of discovering new value, the company launched a program called "More Disruption Please" (MDP) in 2010. This emerged after it had asked: "How can athenahealth become more valuable to its customers by leveraging the efforts of outside players?"[15] At the heart of MDP was the conviction that "the rapid pace of change in health care made it impossible for any one entity to deliver every practice's needs. By integrating with our MDP partners, we can bring each one's focused expertise to our clients, offering specific functionalities that address caregiver needs."[16] Explained Armbrester, "It's simply impossible for us to be the best in the world at developing everything our clients could possibly need, and we need to offer more services than we could ever possibly build ourselves. Instead, we can take pride in being the person who introduces our clients to those who are best at a certain service. Not building and owning everything actually allows us to go to market with richer products. By offering connectivity to the AthenaNet core, we open our platform to an array of innovative solutions for our client base."[17]

Another key aspect of athenahealth's external focus for discovering new value through an ecosystem strategy is: do not look only at what you have the capability to deliver; focus on the customer value that can be created if you also harness the capabilities of others. The strategy has certainly worked for athenahealth until now: From $250 million of revenues when MDP was launched in 2010, it surpassed $1.22 billion in 2017, making it one of the leading cloud-based health care IT companies in the United States. Seeing potential to grow it yet further, private-equity firms Veritas Capital and Elliott Management Corp. agreed to purchase the company for $5.7 billion in November 2018.

Concentrate on the Overall Value an Ecosystem Might Create

When trying to discover new value that an ecosystem strategy might unlock, narrowing the focus too early is usually a mistake. Yet, many companies do just that: they quickly narrow their field of vision, looking for products or services that may generate revenues or lucrative "profit" pools within the value chain required to deliver them.

Such myopia is natural; in the classic supply chains that companies are used to, there is a more or less fixed amount of value determined by the price the customer will pay for a product or service. Revenues and profits are, therefore, largely the result of who gets what share of the value generated; that is, how the proverbial pie is carved up. If one party gets more, the other gets less. Only recently have companies at the head of these supply chains come to realize that if they work with suppliers to improve efficiency and better align their capacity, they can eliminate sunk costs.[18] That is the kind of thinking ecosystem leaders need to adopt on a broader canvas. At the outset, much of the new value an ecosystem can deliver, can be only hazily perceived. So, the focus needs to be on discovering more value potential: what will increase the size of the pie?

That is exactly what ARM did. When it was thinking about the value that could be gained by catalyzing an ecosystem to change the way OEMs satisfied their need for RISC-chip designs and speed up innovation, that was not the time to worry about whether the new process might prove a gold mine for its chip fabrication partners such as TI, Intel, or Taiwan Semiconductor Manufacturing Company (TSMC). In fact, if catalyzing the development of an ecosystem helps partners make more money, that is probably a good thing for everyone. If its partners were to make more money, that would not mean necessarily that ARM would make less. Discovering more value creation would mean both could capture more value. If the partners were more successful, the resulting ecosystem would be robust and sustainable. The key question was simple: Could developing an ecosystem benefit ARM? At this stage they needed to forget notions of trying to maximize their share of the pie because, as the old adage goes: "a high share of nothing, still amounts to nothing."

Focusing on increasing the size of the pie rather than trying to maximize its share is a bet that Amazon.com Inc. (Amazon) made when it launched Amazon Marketplace in 2002.[19] That platform enabled third-party sellers—ranging from individuals to start-up and medium-sized businesses—to offer their products on Amazon's website. Amazon took that bold step, despite the fact that opening up its website to third-party sellers meant allowing competitors to sell on an equal footing with Amazon's retail offerings. In the short term, Amazon could have captured more of the value that the ecosystem was then creating by locking out competitors to protect their own offerings and maximize their share of the pie. But CEO Jeff Bezos had a bigger opportunity in mind. Recalling the decision, he said, "The basic thought was: Look, we have this website where we sell things and we want to have a vast selection. One of the ways to get vast selection is to invite other sellers, third parties onto our website to participate alongside us, and make it into a win-win situation."[20]

By opening the ecosystem to third-party sellers, customers were offered a larger and more varied selection at a range of prices, even as Amazon avoided stocking risky inventory. More and more customers were attracted, and the ecosystem grew dramatically. In 2006, Amazon extended its support to third-party sellers further by creating "Fulfilment by Amazon," a service that provides storage, shipping, payments, and customer handling to small and medium-sized businesses using the website. By offloading selling, payment processing, and storage and distribution services to Amazon, which could benefit from economies of scale, smaller businesses could focus on simply developing and manufacturing their products, dispensing with the need to create a sales and distribution infrastructure, thereby cutting their costs and reducing time to market.

As a result, the Amazon ecosystem was able to offer more competitive prices and a more responsive service. More partners made investments that expanded and strengthened the ecosystem even further, opening up new profit opportunities for Amazon. Amazon took a cut of the expanded flow of transactions, deals that would otherwise have been lost to competitors such as eBay. It also earned revenues from providing fulfilment services while reducing its own costs through increased scale. In hindsight, Amazon's decision to open up to third parties looks like a stroke of genius, but it has its roots in a simple idea: focusing on maximizing the size of the ecosystem opportunity rather than on your share of the pie.

Of course, as we will see in chapter 8, a balance must be maintained. Extracting an attractive stream of profits without harming the vitality of the ecosystem is critical for the ecosystem leader.

Making New Connections

Discovering any of the new sources of value requires new connections. These links may be between different products and services, capabilities, or knowledge assets that have not interacted earlier because they were isolated by boundaries between companies, by geographical distance, by technological incompatibility, or simply by the perception that nothing would be gained by bringing them together. To discover new value, every ecosystem leader needs to stimulate new connections.

Apple's iTunes and App Stores are good illustrations of how this can happen. Both of these innovations facilitated connections between hardware, musicians, software developers, providers of services (everything from your airline to your restaurant or online grocery service), and payment providers in ways that had never been done before. ARM's ecosystem brought together, directly and indirectly, semiconductor fabricators and tool developers, including knowledge from competitors in different sectors that had never before been combined. DS created new mechanisms for the knowledge of PLM and software engineers to come together with that of system integrators and suppliers, and interact with the industry-specific know-how of everyone from designers and modelers to maintenance staff across industries. Looking for ways to make new connections for innovating is a key role that ecosystem leaders can play in discovering new value.

Looking for Value Potential from Network Economies

In working out which new connections might be most useful to promote to discover new value, it is vital to consider the complementarity between potential partners in the ecosystem. The people to be connected may well be quite far apart from each other. ARM gradually discovered, for example, that the most fertile complementarities in its ecosystem were to be found in the knowledge that existed with the heads of the product and technology development staff in the OEMs and its engineers, even though these were two stages removed from each other in the classic value chain.

Another consideration is whether connections have the potential to generate positive network economies. As we know, the more people with telephones, the higher will be the potential value of a phone to any individual; the higher the chance, then, that the person to be contacted has one. In an ecosystem, positive network economies depend on more than the number of customers and partners in the ecosystem. The amount of value the ecosystem generates can also be influenced by the intensity of the interactions between participants, the types of interactions, the diversity of the partners' capabilities, and the quality of those interactions, particularly the amount of new knowledge they create.

The fact that the new value an ecosystem generates depends on the nature of the interactions between the participants in an ecosystem—not just the number—opens up several possibilities to create mechanisms by which the ecosystem leader can help the ecosystem discover more value. Certainly, one thing an ecosystem leader can do is to attract more participants into its ecosystem. As we mentioned in chapter 1, Alibaba for example, launched its Big Taobao strategy in 2008 with the aim of encouraging a large number of potential new participants to join the ecosystem. It did that by allowing partners to join for free, and by making it easy for them to engage with it through a standardized portal and offerings tools, such as preconfigured shopfront templates.

ARM's annual partner meeting shows us a different mechanism to help the ecosystem discover new value through new connections. The annual partner meeting is a three-day event unique to the industry, as it brings together a wide cross-section of ARM partners to a single venue, typically one of the colleges at Cambridge University. Although the criteria for inviting partners has varied over the years, the invitees usually include the OEMs and providers of complementary products and software as well as ARM's direct customers. The role of this event is to provide an opportunity for ARM to present and discuss information, such as its current roadmap, with partners. Equally important are the large number of one-on-one meetings that take place between partners, sometimes involving ARM and sometimes independently, during the event. Facilitating this multitude of face-to-face contacts is an important way to help the ecosystem discover new, and often unexpected, sources of value.

Another mechanism to stimulate connections used by ARM is to promote virtual interactions between the broader community in its ecosystem, tens of thousands of developers and other participants, through its ARM Connected Community website. Managed by dedicated ARM executives, this online community provides free access to extensive resources for developers, a forum for developers and engineers to exchange ideas with support from the ARM ecosystem, and company and product listings classified by product category, market application, and ARM technology—all linked to partner sites.

Attracting a More Diverse Set of Partners

Another way an ecosystem leader can promote value discovery is to help attract a more diverse set of partners into the network. That was athenahealth's primary objective for launching its start-up accelerator in 2014. The accelerator is designed to attract start-ups with well-developed products that need additional resources in order to achieve scale. In addition to workspace and seed funding ranging from $250,000 to $2 million, athenahealth offers expertise drawn from its employees and network of clients and partners, as well as access to its client base. It is focused on start-ups that are interested in joining athenahealth's marketplace, but are not yet ready to do so. The aim was, as program director Mandira Singh pointed out, "to lower the barrier of entry for the best solutions."[21] This, in turn, brings more diversity into the ecosystem. Encouraging new entrants to collaborate with existing partners forges new types of connections. By bringing together previously isolated capabilities and pools of knowledge in this way, athenahealth is able to help its ecosystem discover new value.

Promoting Value Creation by Enhancing the Quality of the Interactions

The ecosystem leader can promote value discovery by initiatives that improve the quality of interactions between its partners. Alibaba made a conscious effort to improve the quality of the interactions in its ecosystem. Many of the websites in Alibaba's ecosystem, such as those run by clubs or local information portals, carry links to other sites. But the quality of those links is usually poor, providing little relevant information to the viewers. By proposing optimal links to both Taobao storeowners and websites, Alibaba enabled its ecosystem to discover more potential value. As we mentioned in chapter 1, it then made the system dynamic so that Taobao Ke, the traffic aggregation system, could continually learn more about the behavior of buyers. That helped it to improve the matches between the linked websites and Taobao stores in real time. As a result, the links could vary by the time of day or the user's location, helping the ecosystem identify the potential to generate more value.

Sometimes discovering new value requires the ecosystem leader to launch a specific off-line initiative. That was the case when Thomson Reuters, the global provider of news, data, and business intelligence, launched its "Legal Tech Innovation Challenge" in 2016. This became part of a new division carved out to become an independent venture in 2018 under the name of Refinitiv. The London Stock Exchange Group acquired it in August 2019. We will discuss this fifth case in more depth in the next chapter, but it is worth noting here that working with Stanford University's Center for Legal Informatics (CodeX), Thomson Reuters invited partners in its ecosystem, as well as legal professionals, programmers, entrepreneurs, data scientists and any other interested parties, to develop new applications that improved the efficiency of the legal system by providing high-value analytics.[22] Participants in the challenge were given access to federal court docket data, company information, and other data from Thomson Reuters and its partners. The outcome was a new model that could predict the likelihood of the success of motions to dismiss before specific judges in federal courts based on key details about the case. The director of innovation for the Thomson Reuters legal business observed: "Our customers are increasingly looking to the next generation of technology solutions to build and advance a better functioning legal system." By creating a mechanism for learning with partners in its ecosystem and beyond, Thomson Reuters was able "to combine (our) proprietary content and domain expertise with a broad range of leading technologists to further fuel innovation and advance the practice of law."[23]

From Discovery to Realization

When thinking about how to discover the new value that an ecosystem can deliver for you, it is worth remembering that your company may already have the roots or the kernel of an ecosystem today. It can include customers, vendors and suppliers, providers of technical expertise (such as universities and research institutions), and other players, including influencers and regulators. To build on this seed, it is worth asking yourself the following questions:

1. How can I transform the kernel of an existing ecosystem into a full-blown ecosystem?
2. What can I use it for? Creating new products or customer solutions? New platform economies? Or would I be able to develop a new industry?
3. What is it that I need to develop the ecosystem for? Is it to compensate for the focus that my company needs to pursue to stay efficient? Or is it to capture knowledge that I cannot develop myself? Or both?
4. What kind of ICT capabilities do I need to develop to manage the coordination and communication in an international ecosystem?
5. How do I create a vision of the value that the ecosystem can deliver, as opposed to the value that my focused company would be able to create alone? And how do I ensure an outside focus to capture the detail and the dynamics in the value required?
6. Is there any network effect in the ecosystem that could create otherwise non-existing value?
7. How do I develop the correct portfolio of partners in the ecosystem, encourage new connections between them, and promote and capture learning?

Seeing the potential to create new value for customers is the first step in catalyzing the development of a successful ecosystem. How you can realize that value is the subject of the chapters that follow.

4 Kick-Starting a Virtuous Spiral

YOU HAVE STARTED TO IDENTIFY THE NEW VALUE THAT CAN be created by leading the development of your ecosystem. But how do you get partners to join you? Partners will readily flock to an ecosystem that is successful; the benefits of joining it will be obvious. But when an ecosystem is in its infancy, its success in creating and capturing value is still unproven. The benefits of joining are uncertain, and so your grand vision is likely to be spurned.

Additionally, large, established companies often face yet an additional problem in kick-starting the growth of an ecosystem, particularly when the aim is to create a new business model in response to disruption of their existing industry. Partners hear fine words about the leader's intent to create an inclusive, innovative and flexible ecosystem. But they frequently question whether an established company is really committed to creating something more than a quasi-supply chain or a tight network of collaborators where it calls all the shots.

As we mentioned in chapter 1, when Ford launched its "blueprint for mobility," it may have intended to develop an ecosystem involving a large number of diverse partners to re-create the auto industry.[1] It quickly entered a partnership with Zipcar to become its largest supplier of vehicles, followed by research partnerships with universities, including MIT and Stanford. It has since partnered the ride-hailing company Lyft to develop an autonomous vehicle, and with Domino's to pilot autonomous pizza delivery. But in parallel, Ford also began pursuing acquisitions. It invested $75 million in Velodyne, maker of

LiDAR, a key autonomous driving technology; acquired machine learning and computer vision company SAIP; and made investments in Nirenberg Neuroscience, a machine vision company; as well as a Silicon Valley–based 3D mapping company. Then, in January 2018, Ford announced that it would work together with Silicon Valley–based Autonomic to build a new open platform called the 'Transportation Mobility Cloud' to help cities develop infrastructure communications, including connected traffic lights and parking spots.[2] But later that month, it revealed that it was acquiring its partner, Autonomic, as well as another transportation software company, TransLoc. It also explained that it would be reorganizing its internal mobility subsidiary in a bid to accelerate the delivery of new products, like micro-transit services and self-driving cars. This hesitation between building an ecosystem, and then integrating the partners within Ford illustrates how challenging it may be for a large organization to remain disciplined about building an ecosystem.

In chapter 10, we will look at when and how such acquisitions and internal investments made by ecosystem leaders can help them realize their vision. But a word of caution is in order: when kick-starting the development of an ecosystem in its infancy, convincing potential partners that you are serious about developing a broad and deep partnership network with real collaboration between the players is key. Flip-flopping between different partner platforms and signaling what seems like a preference for acquisition over partnering can muddy the waters. Partners will ask themselves whether you are really serious about building an ecosystem characterized by collaborative innovation, joint learning, and the flexibility to adapt to a fast-changing, uncertain environment. They might well suspect that while you talk about catalyzing a new ecosystem, force of habit will lead you to try and develop a tried-and-tested supply network, where you predetermine specific partner roles and deliverables and control communications, IP creation, and profit in a system that is open only in name. Faced with those risks, and the attraction for most companies to opt for structures that offer greater control and predictability, how do you credibly kick-start the development of an ecosystem? We propose six steps, outlined below

Demonstrate That You Really Believe in the Ecosystem

The case of Thomson Reuters, which we briefly mentioned in chapter 3, provides a good illustration of how an incumbent can successfully demonstrate that it is committed to kick-starting an ecosystem to innovate in the emerging fintech industry. Its experience is particularly instructive because its natural inclination wasn't to build an ecosystem. It was only after initial failure that it was able to convince potential partners that they were serious about catalyzing the growth of an ecosystem by adopting a new approach.

The merger of the Thomson Group and Reuters in 2008 created the world's largest news and financial information company. Its revenues touched $12 billion that year and continued to grow, fueled largely by acquisitions. Revenues peaked in 2012 at $13.1 billion, and then began to gradually decline, falling to $12.2 billion in 2015.[3] In July 2016, Thomson Reuters sold its Science and Intellectual Property business, so that it could focus on its core areas of information services for Finance and Risk, Tax and Accounting, Legal, and Reuters.[4] Its main competitors in that business were other newsgathering organizations and providers of business information and intelligence, such as Bloomberg and Dow Jones.

In 2011, in an initiative to compete with Bloomberg's terminals, which had become ubiquitous worldwide, Thomson Reuters launched Eikon, replacing its existing desktop offering. Like Bloomberg's terminals, Eikon provided investment professionals with market data, financial information, analysis and messaging tools. But despite Thomson Reuters's marketing efforts, Bloomberg remained, by far, the market leader. By late 2013, Bloomberg had three hundred fifteen thousand subscribers or 57 percent of the market compared to one hundred ninety thousand for Thomson's Eikon, or 34 percent of the market.[5] Even that disappointing growth had partly relied on acquisitions.

Thomson Reuters's leadership identified lack of innovation as its key challenge to winning market share. To address this issue, the company took several steps, such as shifting funding from acquisitions to innovation, establishing new performance metrics, and creating ways for "intrapreneurs" (internal entrepreneurs) to share ideas. But Bloomberg steadily surged ahead, generating $8.8 billion in revenues in 2015 from its terminals and data feeds, outpacing Thomson's $6.5 billion.[6] It was clear that Thomson was not on track to achieve its ambition of becoming the market leader. Their traditional approach to innovation was just too slow and would never enable them to beat the competition.

This painful experience prompted Thomson Reuters to look out, and take note of global trends—one of which was the rise of fintech. Fintech heralded the creation of fundamentally new business models, if not a new industry, that would require capabilities and knowledge way beyond what Thomson Reuters had access to internally. Therefore, it came to believe that partnerships with external partners would be central to its efforts to promote innovation, particularly at the intersection of regulation, business, and technology.

The core desktop segment, served by its Eikon product, was one area where Thomson Reuters sought to capitalize on third-party partnerships to create new value for customers. As far back as 2012, Bloomberg had created an open applications portal to enable complementary, third-party applications to be accessed through its terminals.

In an effort to catch up and kick-start its own applications ecosystem, Thomson Reuters launched the Eikon applications studio (App Studio) in late 2015. The logic was clear: it needed innovation; and as Albert Lojko, global head of the company's desktop platform explained, "When you think about financial technology, overall, it's been very closed and proprietary, and that, at some level, stifles innovation."[7] But as a latecomer who had first tried to go it alone, it had to convince potential partners that it was now serious about catalyzing the development of its ecosystem. That was not an easy task. How could it be credible to its partners that it really wanted to build an ecosystem? And how could it lower the hurdle for partners to join?

Thomson Reuters took a four-pronged approach to this challenge. One, its communications emphasized that App Studio would enable partners to benefit by integrating their software deeply into its Eikon product. Its message was that: "App Studio, Eikon's third party development suite, enables clients and vendors to embed their applications, content and work flows into Thomson Reuters' Eikon, creating an integrated end-to-end solution. This open approach allows users to benefit from access to financial apps created by third party developers globally, built directly into Thomson Reuters' Eikon."[8]

Two, it opened up its development system, providing a software development kit and application programming interfaces (APIs) to make it easy for partners to join its ecosystem and link directly into the Eikon user experience.

Three, to further enhance its credibility, Thomson Reuters committed to the Open Data Initiative (ODI), a London-based nonprofit organization, it had joined in 2014. ODI, as the name implies, promotes efforts to make more data open, so anyone can access, use, and share it. Together, Thomson Reuters and ODI published a series of white papers in 2015 and 2016 that defined best practices and processes on data identifiers and ways to manage data so that it could "break out of the many silos that exist within and between organizations." Thomson Reuters and the ODI argued that data should be "shareable by default"—that is, data should be structured, and managed, in ways that facilitate accessibility and interoperability to maximize the value that could be extracted from it. Data, they argued, is more valuable if it is open and shared, and the challenges to making data shareable are culture rather than technological. The full benefits would only be unlocked if "everyone takes a position of collaboration and reuse."[9] Even data that never used to be communicated outside an organization delivers benefits, when shared, by opening up an organization's (or an individual's) ability to combine it with other sources and forms of data to see it in a broader context.[10]

Four, Thomson Reuters emphasized to potential partners that it already had a track record in developing open ecosystems, citing its successful partnership with Stanford's Center for Legal Informatics, federal court recorders, third-party data providers, and law firms (described in chapter 3).[11]

Thomson Reuters had first tried to make a go of the Eikon on its own, but failed. Only when it opened up its development system, provided tools to help its partners connect easily, and joined networks such as ODI, did potential partners start believing that it was serious about building an ecosystem, enabling it to gain traction.

The lesson from Thomson Reuters's experience for any company that wants to kick-start the development of its ecosystem is clear: It is not sufficient simply to announce your intention to build an ecosystem. As an ecosystem leader, you must make a credible commitment to not only working with partners, but also letting the ecosystem evolve in ways that you may not be able to control. And the claim that you want to build an ecosystem must be backed by tangible commitments to share some of your knowledge and capabilities and to build the tools that partners will need in order to achieve common, even if uncertain, goals.

As we have already observed, partners often impose a higher burden of proof on large companies before being convinced that they are serious about developing a vibrant and flexible ecosystem. This is because large, established players usually have a history of tightly controlling their supply chains. They often inadvertently reinforce this perception of a bias in favor of command and control through attempts to get their ecosystem up and running by offering contracts to potential partners or opting to acquire partners rather than collaborating with them. Smaller companies generally have an easier time establishing credibility around the plans for an ecosystem. When ARM and

Alibaba were relatively new start-ups in the early 2000s, for example, their lack of resources made it easier to convince partners that they wanted to embrace the concept of an ecosystem even if it would not be fully under their control. But the risk for start-ups is that when they grow, their leaders may feel more powerful, even become arrogant, and begin to believe that partners are superfluous to their future plans.

Co-opt Foundation Customers

For an ecosystem to take off and create new value, it needs foundation customers. Finding those initial customers, before the ecosystem becomes well established, is one of the most difficult challenges that an ecosystem leader faces.

We argue that there are two ways to overcome it. One is to proactively go out and seek a foundation customer, one who will co-invest in getting the ecosystem up and running. The other option is to create a "honey pot" that will attract a critical mass of customers to the ecosystem.

Finding a Foundation Customer

ARM's experience in developing an ecosystem to extend the use of its designs to mass-storage devices, such as disk drives, offers an example of the first approach. By the late 1990s, ARM had established a large and vibrant ecosystem around its designs of RISC processors for mobile phones. It needed to duplicate this success in other areas, which was a step into the unknown. As Liam Goudge, one of ARM's product managers at the time, said, "We wrote down every single market we could think of, and mass storage stuck out a mile at the time. We knew nothing about it. We did not even know who the main players were, but we cobbled together all the information we could find. We grouped together a basket of qualities that we decided were important. Building volume was very important to ARM at the time."[12]

Given the nine-month product cycle for disk drives, ARM optimistically thought it would take around eighteen months to co-opt a foundation customer, work with it, and get the new ecosystem up and running. Coincidentally, Goudge learned just then that a field applications engineer in ARM's US office had received a query from the California-based Quantum, the second-largest independent maker of disk drives. On the back of that contact, Goudge and a colleague introduced ARM's technologies and plans to Quantum. Although it appeared to be interested and short-listed ARM,

Quantum eventually chose a Japanese competitor. Undeterred, Goudge moved to the United States and started making phone calls "to any of our existing partners that had anything to do with mass storage." After six months of relationship building—or, as Goudge said, "Showing them our mettle and working our way in"—Cirrus Logic evinced interest in the idea. But Cirrus Logic was a chip supplier, while the knowledge ARM needed to get the ecosystem off the ground was buried in the makers of disk drives: companies such as Western Digital, Seagate, and Lucent, who were ARM's customers' customers.

Fortunately, Cirrus had strong connections with Western Digital. Goudge was able to visit them frequently over a two-month period, often accompanied by John Rayfield, who later became ARM's Director of Research. They thought they had made a breakthrough when Western Digital agreed to evaluate ARM's offering, the ARM7, for one of its new disk drives. However, their hopes were dashed when Western Digital came back with the scores on its evaluation matrix. It recognized that ARM's design had advantages, but also pointed out that the ARM7 had key deficiencies that would slow the speed of the disk drive, and complicate Western Digital's product-development process.

Goudge and Rayfield were not ready to give up their quest to build a new ecosystem for mass-storage devices. With the aid of a Western Digital employee who had become a friend, Goudge arranged a meeting between Western Digital's top management and Robin Saxby, ARM's then CEO. At the meeting, Saxby declared, "I want your business; what do I got to do?" On hearing of the problems with the ARM7, Saxby said, "Alright, we'll fix it." ARM eventually lost the account to another semiconductor company but, as Goudge recalled, it had made two key advances. ARM had heard from the customer exactly what it needed, and ARM had shown Cirrus the extent of its commitment to building the new ecosystem. Added Goudge, "We showed Cirrus that we would step up to the plate, and that we would be in the lab at midnight on Sunday, solving their problems with them."

Rayfield decided to start working on the two key technical problems identified by ARM's potential foundation customers. Back in Cambridge, he started assembling the knowledge that ARM had accumulated. With the goal of creating a new ecosystem, he also tried to figure out how to widen the performance beyond Cirrus to meet the requirements of a range of broader applications and other potential partners and customers. He gathered ideas from sources as diverse as a small technology company in Israel and research taking place in New Zealand. Finally, ARM was ready to go back to Cirrus, and one of its OEM customers, Lucent, with a proposal.

This time around, Cirrus and Lucent agreed to join ARM's initiative to kick-start a new ecosystem. The troika issued a press release announcing their collaboration with the aim of creating a new design, the ARM9E. Rayfield recalls what happened next, "When this hit the newswires, it generated a lot of interest. Lucent put its full marketing organization behind it. It made ARM's (technical) people in Cambridge flip! Once they had calmed down, they agreed to work on it. We called it product development by press release!" When Saxby received a call from Lucent, congratulating him on the ARM9E initiative, he emailed Rayfield telling him that he had replied to Lucent, "Good, glad you like it." But Saxby's email message to Rayfield continued, "But, John, can you tell me what is the 9E?"[13]

Some eighteen months had passed since the first brainstorming session with Western Digital, and no one knew what the design would look like—yet. It would emerge over time as the partners pooled their knowledge and worked together. However, the foundation customer for the new ecosystem was in place, which was critical to getting a positive-spiral of growth underway.

Attracting a Critical Mass of Customers

A second way of recruiting anchor customers is to put in place a "honey-pot." That approach is likely to be more viable when a critical mass of customers is required to get the ecosystem going. Alibaba's experience when it set out to develop a new ecosystem in financial services through its affiliate Ant Financial provides a good example of how you can attract very rapidly a large group of customers. Alibaba created a powerful magnet to attract the Chinese consumers in the form of the Ant Fortune app. This was a one-stop portal designed to attract China's vast population of consumers, who had limited options for money management and investment. The app offered an easy way of accessing more than nine hundred financial products provided by over eighty banks, asset management firms, and Chinese mutual fund companies through Ant Financial's collaboration with Fund123.cn. Alibaba ensured that the funds were initially sold on a no-load basis, so users did not need to pay sales commissions on their investments. The Ant Fortune app also attracted customers by providing free stock-market information for the bourses in Shenzhen, Shanghai, Hong Kong, and the US NASDAQ exchange.

The Ideal Foundation Customer

Four qualities stand out as ideal in a foundation customer (see exhibit 4.1):

1. Foundation customers must have a need that existing solutions can't satisfy. If customers can buy suitable solutions at reasonable prices, why should they join your ecosystem? As we saw, Cirrus and Lucent needed chip designs that would help their devices run faster and would be easy for developers to work with. They couldn't find the right solution on the market, so once they were convinced of ARM's commitment and capabilities, they were willing to join its ecosystem.
2. Real foundation customers must be willing to invest time and resources to codevelop innovative solutions. All the foundation customers in our examples were willing to share their knowledge and capabilities to help get an ecosystem that would satisfy their needs off the ground. They also had the resources and bandwidth to invest time, energy, and, sometimes, cash, to make that happen.
3. It is also an advantage if foundation customers can make a significant volume of purchases from the ecosystem. In the case of the ARM9E, Cirrus and Lucent were global companies with the potential to buy large quantities of chips. At Ant Financial, the potential for rapid expansion of the ecosystem came from the fact that the foundation customers who found the proposition attractive were in the millions.
4. Finally, an important quality to look for in a foundation customer is the recognition that the ecosystem will not service them exclusively. If they believe in exclusivity, the growth and development of the ecosystem will be constrained; the foundation customers will seek to keep the resulting innovations and benefits to themselves. In the business-to-business sector, this means that foundation customers need to accept that the benefits will be shared as the ecosystem expands, but that they can compete by staying ahead of the game, maintaining their role as innovators in the ecosystem. In consumer businesses, it is important for the ecosystem to create what economists call public goods. Those are benefits that all customers can enjoy without detracting from the utility other participants derive. In the best case, consumers will benefit from greater choice and faster innovation as the ecosystem expands.

1. **A foundation customer should have a need or opportunity that existing solutions in the market can't satisfy.**
2. **They should be willing to invest time and resources in codeveloping innovative solutions.**
3. **They should offer the promise of significant sales volume once the innovation is launched.**
4. **They should recognize that if they have initial exclusivity, this will only be temporary before others catch up and they need to move on to the next innovation.**

EXHIBIT 4.1. Criteria for a Good Foundation Customer. Source: authors' research.

Develop and Share an Initial Road Map for the Ecosystem

With a vision of the value to be created by the new ecosystem and the foundation partners in place, the next step is to provide them and potential new partners with the information they need to see how they can fit into, contribute to, and benefit from the emerging ecosystem. This requires you to lay out an initial road map for how you think the ecosystem will develop going forward; and because the ecosystem will change as it develops, the initial road map cannot be too prescriptive. It will have to adapt to changing demands, opportunities that open up, and failures along the way. But if the road map is too unpredictable, partners will not have the signposts they need to decide how and where to invest. Ecosystem leaders therefore need to find a balance between avoiding too many twists and turns that will destabilize partners' plans, while communicating what has been learned and when it is necessary to change direction in order for the ecosystem to succeed.

We will introduce an additional case, Rolls Royce in Singapore, to explain the role of such a road map. The experience of Rolls-Royce in creating a flow of skilled workers when it established its first aircraft-engine manufacturing plant outside the UK at Seletar in Singapore is a good example of how to achieve the appropriate detail in the road map.[14] When it came to Singapore, Rolls-Royce was a pioneer in establishing aircraft-engine manufacturing facilities in Asia. Therefore, there was no ready pool of suitably skilled labor in Singapore or in the region. The company's management decided that the best solution was to catalyze the emergence of an ecosystem for talent development. As a senior Rolls-Royce manager told us,

> When we set out to build this facility, it was touted as the facility of the future. You can operate a facility like this anywhere, but what's the difference between one place versus another? It's the people. We needed to build 250 engines a year on time, meeting customer expectations and unit cost targets while creating customer value. This necessitated a real focus on building highly skilled human talent. In the UK, you can hire a trained technician very quickly because there are so many similar established industries. Rolls-Royce in the UK has a very mature and seasoned workforce, where you can find people on the shop floor with thirty, forty, even fifty years of experience building engines. But we can't afford to take those people and bring them here to Singapore. So how do you train and transfer knowledge?[15]

Despite its size and experience, Rolls-Royce knew it would never be able to train the large number of people it needed on its own; securing the help of local partners would be critical. Rolls-Royce could have contracted local institutions to do the job, but that would, at best, have rectified the problem in the short term. What Rolls-Royce needed was a sustainable flow of qualified people across a wide range of aero-engineering disciplines. That would only be possible if it was able to catalyze the development of an ecosystem that would harness the potential of local institutions, partners, and the Singapore government, and encourage them to invest in new programs and more training capacity. In order to do so, Rolls-Royce needed to provide a road map for how that ecosystem could develop in Singapore.

Rolls-Royce's potential partners included the Singapore Workforce Development Agency (WDA), the National Trade Union Congress's e2i (Employment and Employability Institute), Singapore Airlines Engineering Company, the Institute of Technical Education (ITE), and various polytechnics. The company began by laying out a plan for making the training challenge more tractable by minimizing the number of tasks each technician would be expected to do, while ensuring that there would be complete equivalence with the company's quality and standards. Tin Ho, Seletar's operations director explained, "We didn't change how we build, we just sliced it into smaller chunks. We use the term *depth not breadth*. This way, we can get a technician trained quicker; they get more repetitions, so skills are developed faster. Then, once they're capable, we can broaden those skills."[16]

Rolls-Royce laid out a road map that involved training and recruiting new employees from Singapore's Institute of Technical Education (ITE) and the polytechnics. Within three years, Rolls-Royce and its joint venture partners would need to employ more than twenty-two hundred trained staff, of which over 85 percent were expected to be locals. New curriculum materials would need to be developed. A joint program of internships would need to be set up for students to move between educational partners and Rolls-Royce to gain practical experience during their courses. An aerospace industry-related scholarship fund would have to be established. Rolls-Royce set out how it could contribute to these initiatives, including the provision of industry-specific education materials, help with curriculum development, internships, and funding. The initial road map also suggested how partners might be involved and the benefits they could gain.

Sharing this initial road map proved important in starting the ecosystem and secured Rolls-Royce's leadership: it became the only company in the aerospace industry with a high level of involvement with the ITEs and polytechnic institutes in Singapore. Chamlark Ang, the head of Rolls-Royce's HR Service Delivery (Asia Pacific), noted that by 2015, "70 percent of the ITE modules and curriculum were influenced by Rolls-Royce. What we wanted is for the new recruits to already have the theoretical knowledge that they needed to work at Seletar."[17] In collaboration with Rolls-Royce, Nanyang Polytechnic (NYP) even established an engineering degree program in Aeronautical and Aerospace Technology. The company ended up recruiting as much as two-thirds of each graduating cohort from all its partner schools.

Returning to the case of Alibaba, it developed and communicated, as we saw in chapter 1, a similar road map for potential partners when it set out to create the Taobao ecosystem. It established that, rather than acting as a principal, it would provide the platform on which e-commerce could flow and would take a commission for connecting buyers and sellers. To gain scale, the platform would be standardized as much as possible. Partners would then need to work out how to differentiate themselves.

The road map will of course evolve as the ecosystem develops; it is, by the very nature of learning and innovation in an ecosystem, dynamic. This evolution will not depend on the actions of the ecosystem leader alone, nor will it be entirely under the leader's control. Instead, the way the ecosystem develops will depend on the actions of partners, on what they learn, and how they interact among themselves, often independent of the ecosystem leader. As Alibaba discovered, for example, when it pulled back from certain activities, ecosystems are most successful when a degree of partner independence triggers creativity, innovation, and flexibility. But the initial road map provides a framework and the necessary signposts for partners to invest in ways that will stimulate learning, innovation, and the ecosystem's future development.

Communicating a road map may not always be easy. It is important, therefore, to have several communication platforms that can reach both the foundation partners and potential new partners, some of whom the ecosystem leader might not even be aware could contribute. Social media, networking platforms, and conferences, therefore, all have a role in helping share the road map as widely as possible.

Communicate the Value of Joining

In order to attract partners to the road map that has been laid out, the ecosystem leader needs to be able to communicate a strong value proposition to potential partners. An ecosystem will prosper only if it is attractive to all the partners that need to be involved, who also must succeed once they join.

In our experience, ecosystem leaders often start with the wrong question when identifying potential partners. The temptation is to formulate a list of partners based on their size, reputation, or importance in the industry. Taking that approach amounts to putting the proverbial cart before the horse.

The first question an ecosystem leader needs to ask is what set of capabilities will be necessary to get a positive spiral of learning, innovation, and growth underway in the ecosystem. Will the ecosystem need to attract partners with capabilities in certain technologies, or those who can deliver capacity, or maybe those who supply complementary services? Does the ecosystem need partners that can provide access to new customers, based on their reputation or existing relationships? Will it also need partners with strong market-making skills to unlock latent demand and overcome the conservatism of potential buyers? Asking these questions will enable the lead corporation to understand the key capabilities that the ecosystem needs to get started.

The capabilities list is unlikely to be complete, or 100 percent correct, at the outset, and unanticipated needs for capabilities will emerge as the ecosystem develops. But to start the ecosystem, the ecosystem leader needs a working hypothesis about the key capabilities that will be required. Listening to foundation customers is a good way to develop that hypothesis.

Armed with a shopping list of the critical capabilities required to get the ecosystem going, the search for the right partners can begin. They can be assessed against the capability gaps they will fill. Again, there is a basic choice about how best to recruit the first partners: by proactive targeting or attracting them with a honey pot. Both approaches need to be underpinned with a clear value proposition that will encourage partners to engage with the ecosystem. And then once the ecosystem is up and running, new partners who bring novel skills will be attracted to it.

Alibaba gives us an example on how to create a honey pot. When it launched the Ant Financial ecosystem, it used the fact that it already had three hundred fifty million customers using its Alipay online payment and escrow service as a honey pot to attract partners. Alibaba itself lacked capabilities in financial services, but with an average of eighty million transactions flowing through Alipay each day, the potential benefits of working with Alibaba to build a new ecosystem around financially active customers was obvious.[18] Thomson Reuters may have had to work harder to demonstrate the value to its potential partners of joining its putative fintech ecosystem. The value proposition for its foundation partners was that membership would speed up their ability to innovate, helped by access to some of Thomson's intellectual property. It also tried to convince partners to join by offering distribution power and brand recognition. Lojko pointed out that "giving app developers' access to Eikon would enable innovation, which would otherwise be hindered by lack of a distribution channel for start-up developers and the inability to achieve scale. There is huge distribution reach you get by being part of Eikon."[19]

Dassault Systèmes (DS) took the approach of proactively targeting lead customers in each new application industry when it wished to expand. In automotive, for example, it was Toyota; Gucci for consumer goods and retail; Novartis for pharmaceuticals. In seeking to engage early with these partners, DS was looking for some of the ideal characteristics we have described: leading-edge companies that need solutions not available on the market, a willingness to invest time and resources in co-innovation, and recognition that the benefits would be available to others as the ecosystem expanded, but they would enjoy first-mover advantage.

Rolls-Royce opted to use both approaches in concert to get its Singapore aero-engine ecosystem off the ground. It used its brand, leading-edge technology, and reputation for skills development as a honey pot to engage key government agencies such as Singapore's Economic Development Board (EDB). As Trevor Orman, director Quality, BPI & IT at Rolls-Royce, expressed it, "The government saw the banner of Rolls-Royce as an important asset for Singapore. And it was not just the brand, but also the product. We would be producing our most advanced large aero-engines and components, our flagship products, in Singapore. It was not just a warehouse, or some nuts and bolts manufacturing, but the Trent 900 and hollow titanium wide chord fan blades, which would get you on the cover of *Flight Magazine* for being built in Singapore. And the EDB knew that."[20] Thus, the value proposition for Singapore was clear: a large investment, the creation of new high-value jobs, an upgraded stock of human capital, and an enhanced reputation as a site for hi-tech manufacturing.

With national backing in place, Rolls-Royce proactively targeted partners who could bring specific capabilities and knowledge. These including Singapore Airlines (SIA) and SIA Engineering Company (SIAEC), and academic institutions including ITE and Singapore's polytechnics. Each partner was presented with a tailored value proposition. SIA, for instance, benefited from having an engine manufacturing facility on its doorstep, giving it greater share of voice in product development, more responsive service, and exchange of knowledge that could help improve its operating and maintenance processes. SIAEC provided capacity for training in general aviation workshop principles while earning revenues from the excess capacity in its training center. Joining the Rolls-Royce ecosystem gave the ITEs and polytechnic institutes in Singapore opportunities to develop new courses, expand student numbers, opportunities for their students to experience the industry firsthand through internships, and assured employment opportunities for graduates.

Shrink the Entry Barriers

Partners may well understand the value that an ecosystem brings, and be prepared to join it. But the costs of doing so may turn out to be a significant barrier. Finding ways to lower the entry costs and make it easy to join the ecosystem is, therefore, a must.

There are several initiatives an ecosystem leader can take to help reduce the costs that partners incur when they join the ecosystem. The obvious first step is to waive any joining fee. But successful ecosystem leaders have gone much further. They have developed standardized interfaces, not only between themselves and their partners, but also to facilitate connections between partners in their putative ecosystem. Alibaba has been very successful in attracting partners by consciously making it very easy to join their ecosystem. When starting each of its ecosystems, including Taobao and Ant Financial,

Alibaba, for example, made it easy for partners to join established standard data-exchange interfaces. That way, when an order was placed on Taobao, data was immediately shared with the seller and the logistics provider. Alibaba also aimed to make it as easy as possible for new sellers to open a Taobao store by providing software tools to get their shop-front up and running for free.

Another example of how entry barriers can be lowered is to enhance compatibility of technical standards. ARM, as we have seen, worked with OEMs and semiconductor fabrication partners to adapt its RISC-chip designs to make it easy for partner engineers to build them into their products and fabrication processes, smoothing their way to joining its emerging ecosystem. And going to your potential partners can also help. Thomson Reuters opened laboratories around the world—in Boston; Zurich; London; Cape Town; and Waterloo, Ontario—to make it easy for customers and partners to engage with its innovation ecosystem. By establishing centers around the world, Thomson Reuters Labs made it easy to "collaborate with customers and partners to solve big problems and rapidly prototype and validate solutions using data science and lean techniques."[21] By reducing the barriers to partner engagement, Thomson Reuters has also been able to fuel innovation by connecting, as Mona Vernon, vice president of Thomson Reuters Labs, put it, "world class data sets and deep industry expertise with innovation communities around the globe, including world-renowned universities and academic research centres."[22]

Look for Partners That Can Bring Their Own Ecosystems

One of the key benefits of ecosystem strategies is that they offer the opportunity to harness a diverse range of knowledge and capabilities from different companies and focus them to achieve the common vision set out by the ecosystem leader. But it is obviously a tall order for an ecosystem leader working alone to attract many partners at the outset. One way to side-step this problem is to look for foundation partners who can bring their own sub-ecosystems of partners to the undertaking.

Consider, for instance, Rolls-Royce's decision to engage with the Economic Development Board (EDB) of Singapore as a foundation partner. EDB did not bring specific technological know-how, training capabilities, or production capacity. And it probably did not need to play a major role in the ecosystem once it was established. But its cross-organizational role in Singapore's economic development meant that it was a key player in starting the ecosystem. EDB opened the gates to Rolls-Royce's engagement with a myriad of other partners that were part of EDB's ecosystem. That included everyone from SIA to the institutes, polytechnics, and other suppliers that were key to getting Rolls-Royce's new aero-engine ecosystem off the ground. In ARM's case, its engagement with Cirrus brought access to a sub-ecosystem that included key players such as Western Digital and Lucent.

Similarly, Ant Financial's foundation partnership with Fund123.cn brought a large sub-ecosystem that included a number of fund managers, allowing Ant to kick-start the ecosystem with an immediate array of money market and equity funds in which potential customers could invest. And Alibaba's Taobao attracted logistics partners by offering to invest in a system that would provide real-time tracking data so their efficiency and service levels improved. Each of these foundation partners, in turn, brought their own networks of small, last-mile delivery companies, allowing Taobao to offer a door-to-door service.

Attracting foundation partners that bring with them sub-ecosystems provides a multiplier effect that can help get a new ecosystem off the ground and running quickly.

Ready to Kick-Start the Development of Your Ecosystem?

As we discussed in chapter 1, most potential ecosystem leaders already have in place some of the key components to start an ecosystem. Every company has relationships not only with its immediate customers and suppliers, but also with a broader group that includes providers of complementary products and services, governments, those who contribute to training its workforce, and many others. Having explored the capabilities required to move the ecosystem forward, putative leaders can ask which of the existing relationships can be developed or repurposed to help. Ecosystem leaders then need to make sure they have answered the following questions:

- How do you ensure that your ambition to establish an ecosystem is seen to be credible? How do you avoid it looking like a disguised attempt to start up a traditional supply chain?

- Foundation partners are key to the successful start of an ecosystem. Do not go for the easy solution of looking for the biggest or the most established partners. Instead ask yourself: Which capabilities do I need? What are the characteristics of ideal foundation partners?
- Potential partners need an initial road map of how the ecosystem will develop to encourage them to engage and invest. They know this will evolve over time as the ecosystem learns and innovates. But ask yourself how you can establish some signposts that can guide your partners to the roles they can play and where they need to consider investing to enable the ecosystem to create and capture value.
- Potential partners will want to know what is in it for them when they join the ecosystem. Have you articulated a set of value propositions for partners that will entice them to join? Have you communicated those value propositions broadly to reach potential partners, some of whom you may not have identified as potential contributors?
- Have you made investments and developed interfaces that reduce the costs and barriers that might impede partners joining your ecosystem?
- Have you identified ways to attract partners that can bring their own sub-ecosystems and so help speed up the growth of your ecosystem?

5 Ecosystem Growth and Scale-Up

ONCE AN ECOSYSTEM IS UP AND RUNNING, THE ECOSYSTEM leader needs to focus on how it can be scaled up rapidly. This includes attracting more partners, encouraging them to invest in the ecosystem, facilitating learning and innovation, and balancing growth with the need to maintain the quality of what the ecosystem delivers to customers. So, the ecosystem leader will need to be part cheerleader, part orchestrator, part coach, and part "regulator" in the ecosystem.

By successfully playing these different roles, the leader will help the ecosystem grow, innovate, and create more value. But crafting the right set of initiatives to do this requires a careful balancing act. The ecosystem leader needs to provide an architecture that accommodates different partner roles. At the same time, this architecture needs to be flexible enough to avoid killing creativity and thwarting flexibility by putting partners into a straightjacket. Partners need to be given the space to innovate and grow within a framework that maintains the coherence of the ecosystem.

The initial roadmap for the ecosystem will need to be adapted and refined, without creating so much uncertainty that partners are dissuaded from making complementary investments that would help the ecosystem thrive. The ecosystem leader will need to shape the right kinds of interfaces between partners that create trust and smooth knowledge sharing so that transaction costs are reduced and the ecosystem becomes more productive. Flexible structures will need to be established to promote learning and innovation.

Getting this complex combination of things to happen coherently is a tall order. But, as we will see, successful ecosystem leaders have managed to pull it off.

Our first example is Amazon's successful scale-up of its Amazon Web Services (AWS) business.[1] It is an amazing story of how Amazon built a highly successful cloud-based infrastructure service by streamlining its own originally quite disparate IT infrastructure in response to the emerging needs of a few foundation customers. We will use this case throughout this chapter to show how Amazon and AWS developed a clear vision and roadmap to attract partners, explained the potential value proposition and set clear expectations for what they expected from a partner, lowered the barriers to entry into the ecosystem, and created an architecture for the ecosystem that made it clear to partners where they fit in. But let us start with a short description of what AWS is.

AWS, which provides cloud-based information technology services, has grown from being one of Amazon's relatively unknown divisions to one of its biggest—quickly. The idea dates back to 2000, when Amazon wanted to launch an e-commerce service called Merchant.com to help retailers such as Target and Marks & Spencer build online shopping sites atop Amazon's e-commerce engine. That was challenging. Like many start-ups, Amazon had not given much thought to standardizing IT infrastructure. Every business in the company focused on its own projects, with no thought to standards or scale. Amazon ended up with an IT mess that made it difficult to separate various services and make them available to third parties.

Amazon set about cleaning house, creating a portfolio of IT services that external partners could access over the internet through a set of documented application programming interfaces. That led Amazon, as Andy Jassy, the CEO of AWS, explained, "to pursue a much broader mission, which is AWS today. It allows any organization or company or any developer to run technology applications on top of our technology infrastructure platform."[2] Jeff Bezos, Amazon's founder and CEO, later added, "We didn't have that infrastructure. So, we started building it for our own internal use. Then we realized, 'Whoa, everybody who wants to build web-scale applications is going to need this.' We figured (that) with a little bit of extra work, we could make it available to everybody. We're going to make it anyway—let's sell it."[3]

Amazon launched the new ecosystem in August 2006 with Amazon Elastic Compute Cloud (Amazon EC2), a web service that provided resizable computing capacity in the cloud. Based on feedback from foundation customers, Amazon combined EC2 with its Simple Storage Service (Amazon S3), which enabled storage in the cloud, to create AWS, a scalable, low-cost, cloud-based infrastructure platform. AWS then grew quickly. By 2008, it had overtaken the amount of bandwidth being used by all of Amazon's retail businesses.[4]

Several well-known online businesses have been built on Amazon's Web infrastructure, including the video streaming service Netflix. Other high-profile customers included Yelp, Foursquare, and a variety of US government agencies including the CIA. The AWS ecosystem brings together tens of thousands of partners, over half of whom are located outside the United States. These partners are of two types: consulting partners and technology partners. Consulting partners are professional services firms that help customers design, architect, migrate, and build new applications on AWS. Technology partners are those that provide customers with software solutions, developer tools, and management and security systems that are hosted on, or integrated with, AWS.[5] In 2018, the AWS ecosystem's market share was estimated to exceed 33 percent of the global cloud infrastructure services market, much larger than that of the ecosystems led by Microsoft, IBM, and Google—combined.[6]

As it expanded, AWS made a significant impact on the group's financial results. In 2017, AWS reported sales of $17.5 billion, with an operating income of $4.3 billion. In fact, that year, AWS accounted for most of Amazon's total profits.[7] AWS achieved this record performance by first refining its vision and initial roadmap, and then by attracting large numbers of new and different partners.

Refining the Vision and Road Map

Many ecosystems begin life in a particular geographical region. Among our cases, athenahealth, Alibaba, and Amazon are examples of this. Geographic concentration has the advantage that partners tend to share a common cultural and business context. Proximity also makes communication between partners somewhat easier. But to gain the full potential benefits of an ecosystem, including access to the broadest range of diverse capabilities and knowledge, the ecosystem needs to attract partners and customers beyond its original geographic base. Both Amazon and Alibaba now benefit from the product, services, and know-how they have accessed by engaging with partners around the world. Expanding your ecosystem to attract dispersed and different partners and customers, however, also presents challenges. As an ecosystem grows and expands its boundaries, there is a danger that uncertainty and ambiguity will increase. New participants will bring their own objectives and cultures to the ecosystem. This diversity increases the risk that partners' investment decisions follow divergent, or even conflicting, paths. It is also difficult for partners to understand causality in the ecosystem and where it is headed. Confusion could reign. This in turn increases the risk that well-intentioned investments in the ecosystem may prove useless, or even contradictory and destructive.

The vision and the road map for the future remain the two most effective levers that an ecosystem leader can use to reduce this uncertainty, attract customers, and help partners productively engage with the ecosystem and make the right investments to support its future growth. A clear vision is essential in getting potential customers to understand the value proposition the ecosystem will deliver; while communicating a transparent road map helps partners converge on a coherent set of product and service offerings that customers will value.

Amazon started with a clear value proposition for potential AWS customers: get rid of time-consuming, expensive tasks; innovate at the speed of a start-up; and reduce risk.[8] AWS also enabled customers to purchase storage and computing capacity as and when needed, so they were charged only for capacities they used, sparing them large up-front capital expenditure. Deploying AWS allowed corporations, be they start-ups or established enterprises, to spend their resources on the features that differentiate their business rather than on servers or data-center operations.

Amazon also provided its potential partners with a clear vision for the kind of ecosystem that it wanted to create around AWS. Speaking to potential partners at a CloudTech meeting in San Francisco, Andy Jassy sketched out his vision for an AWS Partner Network (APN): "It would deliver all the potential of cloud computing by combining agility with breadth, offering a range of partner services from databases and computing power to applications services and management, continual innovation and iteration, and cost savings and flexibility."[9] Amazon described its vision as "a network of thousands of APN partners globally who are dedicated to taking cloud computing to the next level. The goal of the APN is to enable APN partners to successfully build their business on AWS by providing valuable technical, business, marketing, and go-to-market support."[10]

At subsequent meetings, Amazon laid out its road map, including how it saw cloud computing's future; the emerging roles it saw for partners in the ecosystem; the APN partner program involving training, certification, and partner learning plans; and its partner network marketing center, which was designed to disseminate best practices in marketing initiatives by AWS and its partners.[11] The clarity and appeal of its vision of why and how partners should engage, backed by a comprehensive road map of how the ecosystem could evolve globally, attracted large numbers of partners, helping the AWS ecosystem scale rapidly. In 2017 AWS reported that it had tens of thousands of partners. And more than 60 percent of the partners were located outside the United States.[12]

Attracting More Partners

Laying out a clear vision for what the ecosystem could deliver and what it might look like, along with a revised road map to help it evolve and scale, are the first steps in attracting the attention of new partners to augment the mass, capabilities, and knowledge provided by the foundation partners that got the ecosystem going. Thereafter, the ecosystem leader needs to communicate a strong set of partner value propositions, clarify their expectations and help equip them to fulfil different roles, and make it easy for them to engage with the ecosystem by removing barriers that stand in their way.

Explaining the Value Proposition to Potential Partners

For most ecosystems, an important part of the scaling process is attracting new partners, often in large numbers. As in the case of foundation partners and customers, attracting new partners requires a strong value proposition. However, it also needs to be simple so it can be easily communicated en masse. The kind of value proposition that needs to be explained in detail in face-to-face interactions creates a bottleneck that is almost certain to stifle growth.

An important contributor to the rapid growth of the AWS ecosystem has been its simple and attractive value proposition. It offers partners four advantages:

- AWS will help your company drive revenues by providing tools and resources.
- AWS will provide programs designed to support your specific business objectives.

- AWS will enable you to differentiate based on your areas of expertise.
- And the platform will connect you to customers and prospects.

Offered such powerful benefits, partners joined the AWS ecosystem in droves—for example, more than ten thousand in 2017 alone. However, attracting partners is not sufficient. They need to be the right kind: partners that can bring capabilities and experiences that the ecosystem needs in order to succeed. The ecosystem leader therefore needs to create incentives to attract partners that can play different roles, such as providing the components of a solution, operational capacity, sales channels, complementary products and services, and so on. They can act as market makers, as important sources of technology and competencies, or maybe providers of market and customer knowledge for the leader. But to attract the right partners, the ecosystem leader needs to identify the capabilities it thinks the ecosystem needs in order to drive its growth and then design a set of value propositions that will appeal to partners that can fill the gaps.

What did Amazon do to identify the partners it needed for AWS? AWS identified that it would need three key types of capabilities to drive its growth: software solutions, technical consulting, and sales support. First, it needed partners that could provide software solutions that would add value to customer data and could be hosted on, or integrated with, the AWS platform. This would include software for specific functions such as handling security, big data analysis, mobile interfaces, digital marketing or data storage, as well as solutions designed for specific industries such as health care, manufacturing, logistics, or government. These would be provided by technology partners. Second, it needed the capability to help customers of all sizes design, architect, migrate, or build new applications on AWS. These capabilities would be provided by a range of professional services and consulting partners. And the third type of partners needed to bring sales capabilities, which would be provided by dedicated channel partners or by professional services and technology partners seeking to grow their own revenues by leveraging AWS as part of a package supplied to customers.

Because ecosystems are dynamic organisms that evolve as they develop, it is almost impossible for an ecosystem leader on day one to be able to come up with a complete and accurate list of all the capabilities and roles required to enable the ecosystem to scale. Inherent uncertainties mean that growing the ecosystem is inevitably an iterative process and probably also involves an element of serendipity. So, while it is important to have a clear starting point for the capabilities you expect the ecosystem to require, having flexibility while learning from experience is also key. This also has an upside: Incentives to attract particular kinds of partners may draw in different ones, bringing with them valuable new contributions that were not originally conceived of.

Clarify Expectations of Partners and Help Equip Them to Take On Their Roles

In this drive to attract new partners, however, ecosystem leaders need to balance the openness of their network with the need for quality. An unbridled drive for growth could undermine the ecosystem if too many weak and unscrupulous partners are admitted. Therefore, setting the right expectations for new partners is important. From the beginning, AWS made it clear what it expected from its partners. Andy Jassy told a room full of partners on the first day of an annual event called AWS re:Invent:

> The reality is, we are going to direct business to those of our partners who are committed and who really understand the platform because our customers want partners who understand the details. . . . Those of you who get committed to understanding the details and the breadth and the depth of the platform, are going to be the ones that help our joint customers the most, and I believe will be the ones that have the most success as we go through the next couple of years where a lot of the playing field is going to be reshuffled.[13]

New partners may have to be developed and may need to be induced to improve the quality of their contribution to the ecosystem. Amazon offered to support committed partners by providing a variety of capability-building programs and marketing tools to help them strengthen their skills and acquire new customers. Based on the successful completion of these programs, as well as other factors such as revenue and customer references, partners could ascend through tiers, from registered through standard, to become advanced or premier partners. Partners could choose to focus on specific types of services or industry verticals such as Big Data or health care. Amazon would then validate a partner's competency in those specific areas based on customer references, AWS certifications, Amazon's evaluation of the partner's technical readiness, and its volume of business through the AWS ecosystem.

Such a combination of improvement programs and certification is not unique to AWS. ARM adopted a similar strategy through its "ARM Approved" program. The chip-designer described the objective of the program as the mechanism "through which we enable our ecosystem partners in specific technologies and activities, so that they can support you better. Every ARM Approved partner has been through a robust audit process, which allows us to recommend them to you in their specific field."[14]

Other ecosystem leaders have taken different approaches to maintaining quality during the growth phase. Alibaba, for example, admits new partners to its ecosystem without requiring payment of any kind of fees—which helps its ecosystems to scale quickly. Then, to incentivize quality improvements, ethical behavior, and good service, Alibaba publishes information to help customers and partners assess the capability and reliability of other participants. Alibaba.com, for example, contracted leading credit-rating companies in China to provide data for what were called Trustpass profiles. The Trustpass profiles displayed information about vendors' creditworthiness along with data on them from customers who had used Alibaba.com. In the B2C space, it took another route to ensure ecosystem partners delivered quality. It introduced Alipay. After agreeing to a purchase, the customer would pay Alipay, where the payment would be held in an escrow account. The payment would be released to the seller only after the customer had notified Alipay that it had received the goods and was satisfied with their quality.

Managing an ecosystem is analogous to running a club. There must be requirements to gain membership, the need to contribute an annual fee to maintain membership, peer pressure, and the threat of expulsion for inappropriate or poor behavior. There can be differentiated levels of membership and roles with some members accepting more responsibilities and making larger investments in exchange for certain privileges, while associate members may have more limited rights and responsibilities.

On the one hand, it is critical to attract the right kinds of partners, support them so they improve their capabilities, and encourage high standards and commitment by rewarding those who deliver in the interests of the ecosystem. On the other hand, an ecosystem leader that sets the bar too high risks stymieing the ecosystem's growth. If your ecosystem is to grow, it needs to be easy for the right partners to join. And there need to be mechanisms to induce and assist the partners to improve the quantum and quality of their contributions to the ecosystem.

Lowering the Barriers to Joining the Ecosystem

Another role of the ecosystem leader is to continue to remove unnecessary barriers to joining. That was an important ingredient in the rapid expansion of the AWS ecosystem. Jassy stressed how easy it was to join, "With our service, you read the documentation and you go." Jeff Bezos underlined the point, "AWS is self-service: you don't need to negotiate a contract or engage with a salesperson—you can just read the online documentation and get started."[15]

When Thomson Reuters wanted to scale the ecosystem it had started around crop data, it focused on making it easy to join for the farmers whose data it needed. To create value, it needed input from large numbers of farmers producing soy, wheat, and corn. Only at that scale would the ecosystem provide a reliable picture of supply and quality. Thomson Reuters created a simple mobile app that farmers could download. The interface enabled farmers to upload data about the acreage they had planted, and provide regular updates on the condition of their crops, likely harvest dates, and yields. In exchange, farmers received aggregate information and analysis of trends, along with weather reports, global supply forecasts, and other market data. As the ecosystem scaled, new opportunities for value creation opened up. Once Thomson Reuters had a sufficient number of observations to provide data region by region, it could help farmers anticipate local gluts and shortages, and the likely pressures on transport and storage capacities.

It is not enough, though, to attract the right partners, help equip them, and lower the barriers that might dissuade them from joining. The ecosystem leader also needs to provide some shape and structure to the ecosystem, so that it strengthens the network and helps potential partners develop viable roles in the ecosystem. Indeed, an inappropriate architecture can become a bottleneck in the management of an ecosystem and the evolution of its capability to innovate.[16]

Laying Out a Viable Architecture

The architecture of the network of an ecosystem can take various forms. Amazon's architecture for AWS, for instance, was based on a stack of infrastructure, products and customer services that could underpin a variety of customer solutions.

At the base of the stack was the AWS global infrastructure, which included forty-four Availability Zones consisting of one or more data centers, each with redundant power, networking, and connectivity, housed in facilities in sixteen regions around the world. The next level consisted of foundation services: computing, storage, database, and networking capacity provided by AWS. These

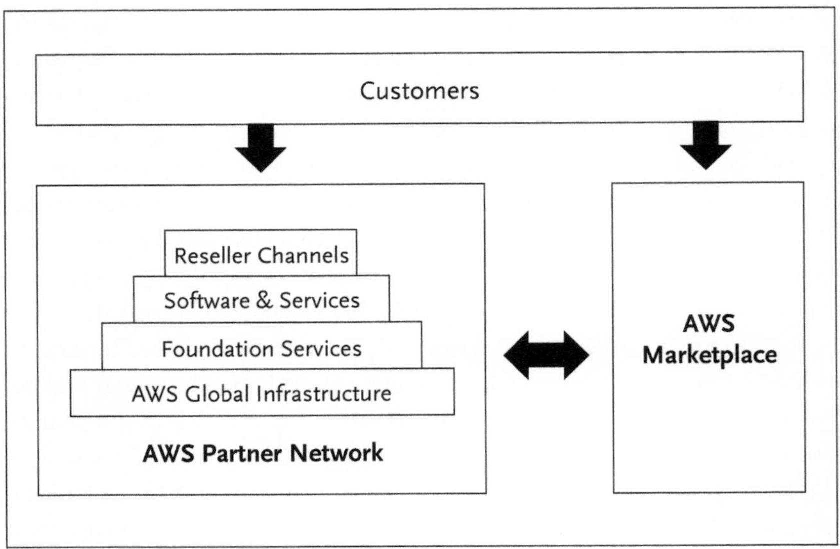

EXHIBIT 5.1. The AWS Ecosystem Architecture. Source: authors' research.

services were linked to a level that contains software and services, organized into five domains: client-side data, server-side data, network traffic, operating system and security, and applications. These domains could be provided by one or more external partners, with each element linked through the stack to the customer's data using standardized interfaces and protocols. The customer buys from some mix of the AWS marketplace, professional services, consulting or technical partners, or via a network of reseller channel partners (see exhibit 5.1).

Around the stack is the AWS Partner Network, described earlier, that provides business, technical, marketing, and go-to-market support to help partners profit from the ecosystem more effectively. Next to that sits the AWS Marketplace, an online store that helps customers find, buy, and start using the software and services they need. Visitors can use AWS Marketplace's 1-Click deployment to launch preconfigured software and pay for what they use, by the hour or month. AWS described its Marketplace as a structure that "complements programs like the Amazon Partner Network and is another example of AWS's commitment to growing a strong ecosystem of software and solution partners."[17]

The existence of a clear architecture enables partners to identify their optimal roles in the ecosystem and to connect with each other while helping

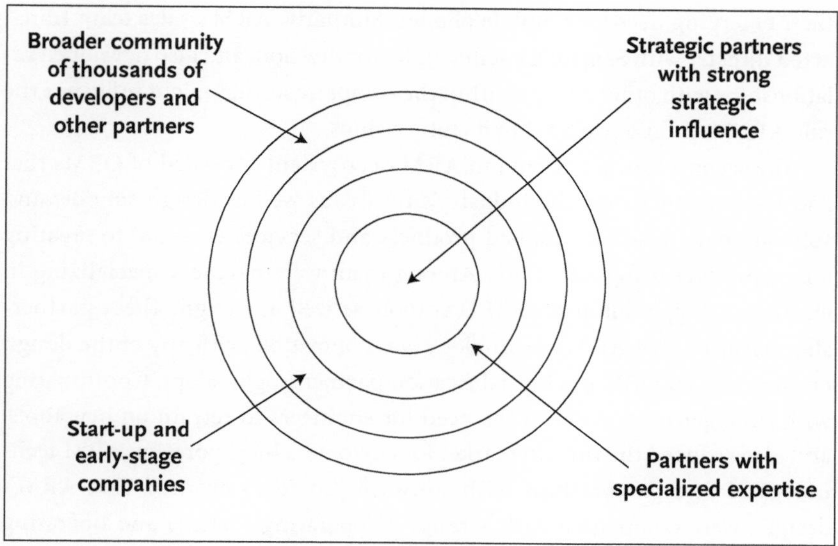

EXHIBIT 5.2. Architecture of ARM's Partner Network. Source: authors' research.

customers navigate the ecosystem to find the products and services they need. It is neither a hub-and-spoke network, in which AWS would sit at the center and orchestrate every move, nor a focused alliance, where AWS would specify roles and deliverables. In the AWS architecture, partners can come and go, reposition themselves and their relationships with AWS and other partners, even as they enable customers to assemble solutions à la carte.

But there is not just one architecture for ecosystem networks. An interesting alternative is that provided by ARM. ARM's ecosystem architecture was not a stack, but a series of concentric circles (exhibit 5.2). At its core were around twenty strategic partners that had the ability to influence the technological direction of the industry because of their market power or technological prowess. These were mostly OEMs, such as Samsung, and chip fabricators, such as TSMC. The quality of ARM's interactions with them were so important to the success of its ecosystem that it assigned one of ARM's top management team to manage the relationship.

The members of ARM's marketing team worked with each partner as a sort of super account manager. For example, ARM's marketing person for the mobile phones segment was responsible for building relationships with all the managers in different parts of the Samsung Group to develop a picture of their emerging needs for mobile phones. Similarly, ARM's sales team transacted directly with Samsung's semiconductor division, and also developed relationships with other groups within the company, as that might influence the role ARM technology played in its future chips.

The second concentric ring in ARM's ecosystem consisted of OEMs that had less influence over the industry's future, as well as design support and software partners that supplied products and services essential to creating a new product using ARM's IP. Among them were partners specializing in electronic design automation (EDA) tools as well as design. These partnerships ensured that ARM's technology was compatible with any of the design options that an OEM or chip-fabrication partner might adopt. Coordinating with these partners reduced the need for engineers to retrain on new tools, and also reduced the time to market for customers incorporating ARM technology. Other partnerships with software providers ensured that ARM's designs were compatible with a range of operating systems and operating environments. These partners had been slotted in the second ring of ARM's ecosystem because the knowledge that needs to be exchanged between them and the rest of the ecosystem was less complex, and simpler interfaces proved to be effective.

The third ring comprised partnerships with early-stage and start-up companies that were linked to the ecosystem through light-touch interactions, and was focused on providing them with the tools and other support needed to integrate ARM technology into their products. The primary role of these partners was to build new product prototypes that helped the ecosystem keep on innovating.

The final ring in ARM's ecosystem architecture was home to a broader community numbering tens of thousands of developers and other participants. Their links to the ecosystem were facilitated by the ARM Connected Community website. Managed by a dedicated ARM executive, the online community provided free access to extensive resources for developers; a forum for developers and engineers to exchange ideas and get support in the ARM ecosystem; and company and product listings classified by product category, market application, and ARM technology—all linked to partner sites.

Again, no one architecture is right for every ecosystem. The right architecture will vary with the specific needs of every individual ecosystem.[18] The architecture needs to mirror the technical challenge and complexity posed by the value that the ecosystem must deliver.[19] As a general rule the ecosystem leader should aim to promote an architecture for the ecosystem that combines several niches, each of which makes a different contribution to customer value and creates a virtuous spiral by generating new knowledge or additional demand as they interact. Of course, each "niche" may be large in terms of volume and revenues, and may also contain many partners. Competition within each niche may generate benefits for the ecosystem by encouraging rivals to improve efficiency or drive innovation.

The AWS architecture defined these niches in resale, consulting, technology, infrastructure, and so on. The point is that they defined areas in the ecosystem where partners with different types of capabilities can prosper. The stack architecture illustrated by the AWS case tends to be most appropriate when the customer needs to buy a bundled solution comprising a number of different components supplied by partners with different offerings. The stack provides a clear menu to help customers choose what they need. They can "pick and mix" to assemble the solution themselves, or rely on a single supplier who draws together the right combination of different partner offerings to satisfy the customer's needs. It also helps partners decide where to play and how they can best work with other partners with complementary capabilities.

The concentric circle architecture illustrated by the ARM case tends to work well when the ecosystem leader needs to interact in different ways with the partners (and possibly more intensively with some partners than others), in order to achieve the necessary knowledge sharing and co-innovation. By identifying an inner ring of a few strategic partners where messy, often tacit, knowledge needs to be exchanged, an ecosystem leader can focus on creating channels for the "high-touch" communication required by this group. The structure of outer rings, meanwhile, where the need for codified knowledge and prepackaged information can be exchanged with a larger numbers of partners, enables the use of more cost-effective communications technologies. Again, the architecture also helps partners decide where to play and how best to engage.

Whichever architecture you choose as an ecosystem leader, there are no doubt two important design considerations. First and as a general rule, one should avoid any overlap between the ways in which each niche contributes to the value that the ecosystem delivers. That is because the interfaces between the elements will become blurred if the niches overlap. Uncertainty and confusion will result. The ecosystem leader's aim, therefore, must be to develop a structure where each bundle of value-creating activities is clearly delineated from the next. A well-defined modularity may well be a precondition for an effective ecosystem.[20]

In addition, to enable the ecosystem to scale, the jigsaw of niches must be complete. All the tasks and capabilities that are necessary to deliver value to the customer need to be covered. This may seem obvious, but there is always a risk that critical gaps may be overlooked. For example, in businesses characterized by network effects—where the user benefits only when a critical mass of others adopt the same technology—market making is an essential ingredient for value creation. But since it may not be directly required to deliver the product or service, the need to attract partners with this critical capability is easily forgotten. AWS deftly avoided this trap by considering the role that different partners, even those supplying specific pieces of technology or software, could have in enhancing sales of the AWS package or in helping to make the market by expanding awareness of the benefits of cloud computing.

Protecting Partners' Turf

Having designed an architecture that opens up attractive niches for different partners to contribute to the capabilities and growth of the ecosystem, the ecosystem leader must refrain from intruding into the specializations or the businesses of its partners. If niches in the ecosystem turn out to be profitable and fast growing, the temptation for the leader to start competing with its partners can be great. A "land grab," however, is sure to undermine the credibility of the leader, and can cause growth of the ecosystem to stall. Potential partners are likely to be scared away if they have reason to fear that if they build a successful business, the ecosystem leader will try to take it over.

Ecosystem leaders also need to strike a balance between the growth of the ecosystem and short-term profit opportunities. Researchers Gawer and Henderson described how Intel, for example, had adopted different approaches to do so. It had chosen not to encroach on some of its partners' markets, while entering others that were becoming core to its own value proposition, even in the face of damaging its relationship with its partners.[21] Arguably, the latter has limited Intel's ability to expand its ecosystem.

Amazon rethought the balance between network growth and corporate profits as its ecosystem grew. After it opened its Amazon.com e-commerce platform to third parties and supported them by providing storage, shipping, payments, and customer service through its 'Fulfilment by Amazon' service, many retailers complained that once they tasted success, Amazon would enter the category and use its size and power to undercut prices and capture market share. That eroded the trust between Amazon and its retailer partners.[22] Amazon is much more careful now to avoid behavior that would create such conflicts; it recognizes that the benefits gained by attracting new retailers greatly outweigh the reductions in direct sales. AWS has taken this lesson to heart: it provides hosting and web-services capacity to Netflix even though the latter competes with Amazon's video streaming services.

ARM learned early to be careful about suspicions that it would encroach on its partners' territories. ARM's semiconductor customers were not happy to be bypassed when ARM increasingly talked to the OEMs directly. Some feared that joining ARM's ecosystem would end up commoditizing their products, lowering switching costs, and reducing their control over prices. Despite these risks, many semiconductor companies realized that they stood a better chance of winning business from the OEMs if they worked with them, rather than relying solely on their contacts. Despite being the leader of what became a huge and well-established ecosystem, ARM continued to take such partner concerns seriously.

To allow the ecosystem to scale, the ecosystem leader sometimes has to get out of the way. Recall the example of Taobao stepping back from various activities that we mentioned in chapter 1. Daniel Yong Zhang, Taobao's president, explained,

> Taobao used to organize a lot of small-scale, thematic promotional events to try to drive sales—even down to things like a special Spring-Festival promotion for red sweaters. Over time, the number of these new promotions grew, so new ones were launched three or four times per day. When Taobao was smaller, this part of the business used to count for 30% of our revenues. When Taobao's turnover increased, these promotional events became redundant, accounting for only 0.8% or 0.5% of the gross value flowing through the marketplace. They were enormously time consuming and complex to set up; the Taobao team had to find relevant products one by one, and negotiate participation with each seller individually. All this complexity was absorbing 80% of the time of Taobao's marketing staff. We had to stop these promotions because we were becoming the bottleneck. We had to understand that in an ecosystem, doing less can lead to exponentially more.[23]

Some of these decisions were relatively easy, he observed.

> It is very clear that Alibaba should not sell products, but the boundaries of the leader's role are not always easy to determine. Take software services. In principle, Alibaba knows it should leave them to partners although in the short-term, it would have been easier for Alibaba to provide this service. But that would lead to unsustainable complexity and fragmentation. The solution has been for Alibaba to provide the basic building blocks such as the exchange platform and a rudimentary CRM system for every shop owner on Taobao. Alibaba is clear that it will not provide anything that is useful only for a single seller or even a small group of seller—only things to be used by large numbers of participants.[24]

Making space for partners as the ecosystem scaled up was very much in Alibaba's self-interest. Explained Alibaba's Ming Zeng, "If there are problems, for example, failures in logistics, Alibaba is usually the last to be able to help. It is much better to rely on third parties to see the opportunity to profit by providing an improved service. Just like the government trying to manage the market is a disaster, if Alibaba tries to be smart and fix a problem, it usually messes up the system."[25]

Stimulating Partner Investments

The successful growth of an ecosystem also depends on partners investing to increase the capacity and capabilities available to the ecosystem. Indeed, one of the key benefits of an ecosystem strategy for an ecosystem leader is the ability to leverage investments made by partners. The benefits can be huge. For example, according to our estimates, developers have by 2018 invested over $440 billion to create the 2.2 million apps available on Apple's App Store.[26] As the ecosystem leader, Apple charges a small amount for listing every app and takes a commission each time one is downloaded. Apple generated over $9 billion of revenues from services in the quarter to March 2018, most of it from the App Store. This represented a 31 percent rise over the previous quarter, putting it on track to achieve its goal of doubling software and services revenue by 2020.[27]

To derive those benefits, the ecosystem leader needs to get partners to invest. The dependence of the ecosystem leader on its ecosystem to deliver value has a second implication: it is difficult, if not impossible, for the ecosystem leader to grow faster than its ecosystem. Therefore, the ecosystem leader must succeed in getting partners to invest at a rate that ensures both innovation and the desired expansion of the ecosystem.

High levels of uncertainty will of course dissuade partners from investing in the ecosystem. As we saw with kick-starting the ecosystem and attracting foundation partners, providing a clear vision and road map for the future evolution of the ecosystem is key. Not only does it encourage partners to invest, it also helps them make the right kind of investments. An important role of the road map is to reduce the uncertainty around the technologies the ecosystem will adopt as it grows. This is particularly important in industries with rapidly changing technologies, where a dominant design has yet to emerge.[28]

A shared road map for innovation, even if it is not highly specific, will enable partners to make sense of unforeseen events and induce them to keep making investments that scale the ecosystem. To see how this works, let us return to the case of Dassault Systèmes and how they encourage co-investment through a clear road map. Indeed the many partnerships in the DS ecosystem are coordinated by a clear and shared technological roadmap of how software platforms for computer-aided design, virtual production and testing, global collaborative working, and social collaboration will evolve. The road map contains information about which new industries DS wants to find applications for, how the company wants to address specific industry needs, what the role of 3D will be, what the timeline for development of enhanced platforms will be, and so on.

Another way in which ecosystem leaders can encourage partners to invest is through the provision of tools and training programs that will enable them to upgrade their capabilities. We have already described earlier in this chapter with the case of AWS the benefits of equipping partners to perform their roles in the ecosystem. Providing well-structured tools and programs makes it easy for partners to invest in improving their capabilities, as well as making sure they invest in the right capabilities—those that will be aligned with the needs of the ecosystem and the opportunities it is likely to provide in future.

The resources that AWS provides through its APN program have stimulated thousands of partners to invest in developing their capabilities to provide consulting or technology solutions built around AWS. The APN offers a large suite of programs that enables partners to invest in competences that help grow their businesses as well as the AWS ecosystem. These include online modules and assessments that partners can use to improve the skills of their executives in business development, relevant technologies, and cloud computing applications. APN also offers opportunities for face-to-face training in solutions, the use of Big Data, and tools for the delivery of professional services. These investments help the AWS ecosystem deliver more value to customers and attract additional buyers, growing the ecosystem and driving up Amazon's revenues.

Making it easy for ecosystem partners to invest in the right kinds of capabilities also helps Amazon avoid the threat of commoditization. This is a challenge that Amazon's cloud business faces, given the competition from powerful players such as IBM and Google. It would force Amazon to compete on volume and price, causing margins to collapse. That may still happen, but Amazon has so far managed to stay ahead of rivals, in part by encouraging its ecosystem partners to invest in raising their game, adding more value to AWS through the products and services they have built on top of its infrastructure.

It is clear that AWS takes the requirement for partners to invest seriously. Recall Andy Jassy's exhortation at the first AWS annual partner meeting, "The reality is, we are going to direct business to those of our partners who are committed." He could have added that those who failed to invest in the ecosystem probably wouldn't see too many leads coming their way. Thus, to stimulate the partner investment an ecosystem needs to grow and prosper, ecosystem leaders might need to use a mix of carrots and sticks.

The ecosystem leader also has to often encourage partners to invest in more than training. To enable an ecosystem to scale, they need to invest hard cash in everything from new infrastructure to redesigning their products and services. Stimulating those investments requires targeting the right partners, aligning with their incentives to invest, and making complementary investments of your own.

Alibaba's experiences with growing its Rural Taobao ecosystem shows how that can be achieved. Following its IPO in 2014, expanding e-commerce into China's rural areas was one of the three main strategies Alibaba announced (along with globalization and Big Data). China's rural regions presented enormous, largely untapped opportunities for the development of e-commerce. Around six hundred million Chinese citizens resided in rural areas, representing a huge pool of purchasing power as well as a source of distinctive needs. Most, however, had limited retailing options and suffered from the prevalence of counterfeited products. Fewer than one in three rural residents were connected to the internet, and in the first quarter of 2015, less than 10 percent of the online purchases made on Alibaba Group's retail marketplaces were shipped to rural areas. The low penetration of e-commerce, even among those who had internet access, was largely a consequence of limited marketing initiatives targeting rural customers, as well as the lack of local sales advice.

Catalyzing the growth of a new ecosystem to serve a potential market of six hundred million people was a massive challenge. Even for a company with considerable financial resources, it would not have been possible for Alibaba to do so had it not been able to get partners to invest in making it happen. To get the ball rolling, Alibaba had to make significant seed investments. In October 2014, it announced that it would invest RMB 10 billion (US$1.6 billion) over the next three to five years to build one thousand county-level Taobao Rural Operations Centers and one hundred thousand village-level Taobao Rural Service Centers throughout China. These outposts of e-commerce would provide villagers the facility to buy and receive goods from Alibaba Group's online marketplaces and, eventually, start online businesses. These centers would provide hardware, e-commerce training, technical support, and information about promotional offers on online marketplaces. Beyond facilitating the purchase and sale of products online, they would also be conduits for people living in remote villages to conduct a range of everyday activities, such as paying utility bills, topping up mobile phones, making travel bookings, and so on.

The opportunity looked attractive, but to get these rural operations and service centers up and running would require investment well beyond even Alibaba's means. In additional to physical space, each center would require a bundle of computer equipment including a large-screen display as well as a datalink with reasonable speed and capacity. Alibaba approached the provincial, county, and village administrations in China. And it found the key to getting them to invest buried in a central government press release. Following a directive from China's State Council, the focus on GDP growth in assessing local performance had been broadened to include social inclusion and the well-being of the local population. With an incentive to deliver on this new performance indicator, local governments enthusiastically embraced the opportunity, leading many provincial and county governments to include provision for co-investment in building local Taobao service centers (at an estimated cost of $7,000 to $15,000 per village) in their annual budgets. By the end of 2015, more than twelve thousand village-level service centers had been opened in over twenty provinces. In addition, 598 counties and municipalities in twenty-six provincial-level units had invested in e-commerce training for more than fifteen hundred local government officials.

The next challenge Alibaba faced was in staffing these centers with trained personnel—as important a requirement for success as equipping them with hardware. To facilitate this, it set up a network of county-level centers to train people from the local community interested in becoming qualified Rural Taobao Partners. Alibaba targeted young people familiar with the internet and online shopping, who were returning to their villages from the city. Located in each village-level service center, the Rural Taobao Partners helped villagers order and pick up what they needed—physical products, train tickets, mobile phone top-ups, and so on—and handle refunds on products returned. They would also sell local products online, handle delivery, and collect payments. The partners generated income primarily by charging service fees for the above. As of December 2015, there were 5,870 Rural Taobao partners in China, each earning between $300 and $450 per month. The more successful Rural Taobao partners earned up to $2,500 per month.

Alibaba also has to deal with some major constraints in growing its e-commerce ecosystems, such as the problem of fake and contaminated products, especially in food and beverages, such as "eggs" made of gelatin or rice containing a substantial proportion of plastic pellets. In 2008, an estimated three hundred thousand babies in China fell ill, and at least six died, because of consuming milk powder that was adulterated with melamine, a toxic industrial compound.[29] To deal with that constraint, Alibaba convinced dozens of brand owners including L'Oréal and chocolate maker Ferrero Rocher to attach a QR code–based ID tag to every item they produced. Alibaba's Blue Stars program constructed a database of these codes and made them available over the internet. When consumers scanned the QR codes on product packages in stores, they could view data from the manufacturer such as the origin of the product. As a result, online shoppers could verify the authenticity of goods and obtain refunds if they turn out to be fakes.

Getting Your Ecosystem to Scale

Having kick-started the ecosystem, you need to grow it by bringing in new partners, often in large numbers. In order to do so, the ecosystem leader needs to provide compelling value propositions to attract partners with different capabilities and reduce the uncertainty and other barriers that could deter new entrants. That requires coming up with answers to the following questions:

1. Are your vision and roadmap sufficiently clear in encapsulating the opportunity to create new value for customers, and helping reduce uncertainty and ambiguity that might scare off potential partners?
2. What is the simple and compelling value proposition that will encourage potential partners to engage with the ecosystem?
3. Do you have a clear view on what capabilities and roles you need to develop the ecosystem? And do you have a plan to attract partners beyond the foundation partners?
4. Do you have a good understanding of what barriers the new partners have to overcome to join the ecosystem? And can you reduce these barriers?
5. Can you design an architecture of your ecosystem with clearly defined niches in which partners can thrive? And have you ensured that you have clearly defined areas for value creation that do not overlap?
6. What mechanisms do you have to protect your partners' contribution and ensure you don't encroach on their business activities?
7. What incentives have you put in place to stimulate your partners to co-invest in the ecosystem?

6 Improving Ecosystem Productivity

SO FAR, WE HAVE CONCENTRATED ON THE BENEFITS TO BE gained from pursuing ecosystem strategies. But in chapter 2 we also cautioned that ecosystems are generally less efficient than hierarchical organizations at delivering customer value, once the opportunity has been identified and the offering scoped out.

It may be necessary to accept some loss of efficiency in exchange for the greater knowledge creation, innovation, and flexibility that ecosystems offer. But if the inefficiencies become too great, the ecosystem may collapse under its own weight. Thus, the efficiency with which the ecosystem delivers value needs to be "good enough" to ensure that its inefficiencies do not swamp the gains elsewhere. The productivity of the system matters, and ecosystem leaders can play a key role in promoting it.

Overcoming Ecosystems' Productivity Disadvantage

An ecosystem can never be as efficient as a vertically integrated company because bringing all activities under one roof allows a company to achieve the maximum alignment between activities; each one of them can be designed to dovetail seamlessly with the one that comes before and after it. Activities at different stages in the value chain can be synchronized, eliminating wasted capacity or bottlenecks that would undermine efficiency. One of the most important benefits of a vertically integrated value chain is that the capacity of each contributor can be matched to the others, and this so-called line-balancing is easier to perform because coordination is under the control of a single firm.

However, vertical integration and internal value chain optimization has a downside: it generally reduces flexibility. Some companies seek to address this problem by using internal marketplaces to coordinate their activities. Internal markets can achieve greater flexibility while maintaining efficiency because transactions inside a company seldom require the complex contracts that are otherwise necessary to guard against the failure to perform or price gouging by suppliers. The application of improvement processes such as Total Quality Management, lean management, and Six Sigma can ensure that all the units in an organization adhere to common standards. Transfer-pricing systems can be established to govern internal exchange. The effects of fluctuation in volumes and changes in the product mix can be handled by production planning and supply-chain management systems. Investments are coordinated by the company's capital-budgeting process. Therefore, with the appropriate structures and processes in place, vertically integrated companies can enjoy the benefits of low transactions costs and high productivity while remaining fairly flexible.

However, by its very nature, vertical integration constrains a company to perform most of its key activities in-house. And these in-house units may be less capable, less innovative and less efficient than external suppliers who are forced to compete in the open market. To deal with these limitations, companies have learned to generate many of the advantages of vertical integration by establishing tightly coordinated chains of external suppliers. Integration between these suppliers is often strengthened by creating sourcing hubs that enable the sourcing of components to be coordinated centrally.[1]

Given that ecosystems are usually at an efficiency disadvantage compared to vertically integrated or centrally controlled value chains, a key question for the ecosystem leader is how to reduce this handicap and at the same time preserve the advantages of ecosystems, including more learning, more innovation and the flexibility to cope with volatile environments and rapid growth that vertically integrated companies or traditional supply chains cannot match.

For instance, Alibaba's emerging ecosystem faced just this challenge when it decided to transition from being an information portal to an e-commerce website: it was both innovative and very flexible, but also hopelessly inefficient. It was difficult for Alibaba to ensure that payments would flow smoothly and securely from buyers to sellers. China's credit card system was still in its infancy. Potential customers were worried about the security of online payments as well as the delays involved in making payments by alternative methods such as checks and postal orders.

These problems were aggravated by the fragmented nature of China's logistics industry at the time, which comprised tens of thousands of providers. Their capabilities were weak, their services were unreliable, and their coverage was patchy. A delivery might pass through many hands, each representing a different level in a long transportation chain from the warehouse to a village, before it reached its final destination. In fact, Alibaba's Jack Ma used to lament in those days that the "terrible" logistics were crippling the growth of internet retailing in China. The promise of the new ecosystem was enormous, but it may never have gotten out of its starting blocks if Alibaba had not been able to tackle the inefficiencies in its delivery and payment system, often by creating systems like Alipay that customers and partners could use. In other cases, it relied on building relationships with creative partners in logistics like Huawei and Haier.

Solving these kinds of problems to improve efficiency and minimize the productivity disadvantage of ecosystems while protecting the benefits is a fine line to tread. Pursuing too much efficiency risks killing the creativity needed to cope with uncertainty and damages the process of learning and innovating. So the goal is to improve the ecosystem's productivity, rather than simply trying to maximize its efficiency at all costs. And there are some practical steps an ecosystem leader can take to address this challenge. First among these is to design a set of interfaces through which the partners can interact efficiently.

Designing Efficient Interfaces between Participants

Ecosystem leaders can play a huge part in addressing the productivity challenges their ecosystems face by designing interfaces between partners that reduce transaction costs.[2]

In a classic supply chain, most of the interfaces between parties are governed by contracts. That's appropriate, and efficient, when performance can be measured objectively (think of a situation where a component or service must be delivered in the right quantity at the right time). However, in an ecosystem the interaction between partners is seldom that simple. For an ecosystem to succeed in innovating, partners need to interact in a way that helps each party to learn. Instead of designing the interfaces around transactions where

1. **Write contracts that focus on high-level outcomes, leave room for flexibility, are perceived to be fair across the ecosystem, and are clear about dispute resolution.**
2. **Create portals to smooth the path of data exchange between the ecosystem leader and its partners, and among its partners, without trying to control all these exchanges.**
3. **Develop a set of systems and organizational solutions to manage the exchange of complex know-how.**
4. **Codify some of the complex and tacit knowledge so that it can be exchanged more efficiently.**
5. **Encourage mechanisms that help build trust between partners.**
6. **Agree on governance standards within the ecosystem.**
7. **Penalize bad behaviour.**

EXHIBIT 6.1. Designing Interfaces for Improved Productivity. Source: authors' research.

one party delivers something to another, the ecosystem leader needs to design interfaces that will facilitate the flow of knowledge and enable innovation. As the participants in an ecosystem learn, their roles and contributions will change, so the interfaces need to be flexible enough to allow the ecosystem to evolve continually.

What the ecosystem leader needs to design, therefore, are interfaces that enable diverse participants to efficiently, but flexibly, exchange products, services and information that are constantly changing. We propose seven principles that can be used to guide the design of such interfaces (see exhibit 6.1).

Writing Appropriate Contracts

Traditional contracts usually won't be up to the challenge of organizing the interfaces in an ecosystem. Recall that DS has more than eight hundred partners in its ecosystem, who continually update and develop their software solutions or development needs. Many of them do not even interact through DS but, instead, work directly with each other. Imagine trying to renegotiate contracts with hundreds and perhaps thousands of such partners in an ecosystem every time the products, services, information, or access provided to the ecosystem changes in unpredictable ways. Think about trying to re-price all the knowledge flowing between all the partners in an ecosystem and then, rewriting new contracts to govern the new exchanges. The ecosystem would drown in lawyers' fees and be paralyzed by delays in getting the contracts renegotiated.

Of course, there's nothing wrong with contracts per se. They are part and parcel of business interactions. But traditional performance contracts are insufficient to ensure effective collaboration between ecosystem partners.[3] Aligning behavior is difficult enough in traditional supply chains—but in innovative ecosystems, typically littered with unknowns and high uncertainty, trying to specify contracts with concrete actions and deliverables, and fixed prices, is likely to become a hopeless task. And when unexpected changes occur, partners in the ecosystem may be affected unequally. This could invalidate the premise on which carefully tuned contractual agreements were based, sowing distrust. Ecosystem leaders therefore need to encourage partners to draw up contracts that focus on high-level outcomes, while leaving room for flexibility. Additionally, these contracts must be perceived as fair when things change, and also clearly clarify how dispute resolution will be handled.

However, the rapidly changing requirements, cost uncertainties, and difficult-to-measure performance that characterize most ecosystems prevent the partners from drawing up contracts that include every possible contingency. Rather than specifying detailed actions and detailed outcomes, contracts between ecosystem partners should be written to capture the open-ended nature of the collaboration required. A good analogy is an employment contract that defines a job description but does not specify detailed tasks and outcomes. Such open-ended contracts between the partners in an ecosystem provide an element of de facto oversight and incentives for the parties to make decisions as if they were part of the same organization.[4] These kinds of contracts provide the ecosystem with the flexibility to respond to unforeseen situations.

Suitable contracts must also guarantee fairness. In an ecosystem, one partner rarely has complete information about all the others in the ecosystem. It is often difficult to judge whether changes in behavior by other partners are acceptable. The contract must ensure that decisions will be taken in such a way that they are demonstrably fair to all the partners in the ecosystem. In 2003, INSEAD's Chan Kim and Renee Mauborgne proposed that fairness in a contract requires three qualities to be present. One, clarity about the rules of the games and the purpose that must be achieved. Two, provisions to ensure the engagement of all the affected partners in decisions that concern them. This is a way for the ecosystem leader to communicate respect for all the partners.

Three, a transparent explanation of when and why the terms of agreement can be modified so as to avoid automatic suspicion and engender trust.[5]

However, to make these flexible contracts that focus more on the process of collaboration (rather than specifying precise tasks or outputs) work, partners must accept that they need to maintain a balance between the investments, risks, and rewards accruing to each party.[6]

Contracts also typically include clauses covering the mechanisms for dispute resolution—and this is essential in contracts between ecosystem partners too. But they need to take a different form than seen in most commercial contracts so that they can handle the high levels of innovation and flexibility characteristic of ecosystems. Rather than being a mere safety valve of last resort, they need to be cast as almost routine procedures for responding to a stream of contentious issues as they arise. Ecosystem partners need contract provisions that enable them to resolve the many inevitable differences that would arise between them simply, quickly, and collectively. The goal is not to break the deadlock of rare, and potentially terminal disputes, but instead to facilitate shared problem solving.[7]

An example of this kind of contract is the agreement that ARM and Vodaphone entered into in March 2019 governing their joint development of a product that integrates Vodafone's global network and Internet of things (IoT) platform with Arm's IoT software and services. It commits the parties to work together to develop a programmable, connected system on chip (SoC) designs that eliminate the need for traditional SIM cards like the ones used in mobile phones. But rather than detailing specific product features and deliverables, the contract captures the partners' commitment to develop interconnectivity capabilities, standards, and security protocols that will allow other partners in the ecosystem to develop single IoT products that can be shipped and reliably connected anywhere. The aim is to enable the end user to securely deploy and manage massive numbers of IoT devices across global markets at lower cost and with less complexity.[8]

Enabling Data Exchange

Our second recommendation for improving ecosystem productivity is for the ecosystem leader to develop interfaces that can smooth the exchange of data among the partners. This starts with the simplest case: where data needs to flow between the ecosystem leader and other participants in the ecosystem.

The kind of interfaces that need to be established and the benefits to the ecosystem are well illustrated by the experience of The Guardian, a leading British newspaper. (We will discuss this case in more detail in the next chapter, but here it is useful to focus on the data exchange between The Guardian and its partners.) The Guardian's open journalism ecosystem is an interesting example of how creating interfaces for the smooth exchange of data between an ecosystem leader and its partners can help an ecosystem develop and prosper. In the early days of the internet, The Guardian wanted to enable readers, free-lance journalists, and website developers to access its content, and also encourage them to integrate this into the applications and websites these independent users and developers would create. To enable this data exchange to happen efficiently, The Guardian decided to build an Application Program Interface (API) to facilitate the process. As we mentioned in chapter 4, APIs are sets of routines, protocols, and development tools that determine how software components should interact as data flows between them. Because the right APIs make interactions easy, they are the enablers of many successful ecosystems.

But this creates a potential problem for ecosystem leaders: leakage of valuable data to a mass of partners. The Guardian faced this problem. While it wanted to promote the goals of open journalism, it also wanted to limit the amount of information that its partners could access for free—a classic case of the trade-off between enabling partners and protecting its own interests that ecosystem leaders frequently face. To achieve the right balance, it needed a sophisticated API to manage its interactions with partners. The interface The Guardian came up with comprised two tiers. The For-Free tier was available to any website developer who registered, but it limited the number of calls they could make per second as well as the total number of calls every day from each application. It also restricted access to the amount of text in each piece, and limited access to a certain, albeit large (over 1.7 million in 2015) number of pieces of content. Additionally, the For-Free tier required developers to display the embedded advertising associated with the content they pulled from the newspaper's website. The Paid-For tier, by contrast, gave subscribers access to the full range of content available from The Guardian, including articles, video, audio, and images, at a fee that varied with the number of calls made each day and the amount of data pulled though the interface. This tier also allowed partners to display third-party advertising without sharing revenues with The Guardian.

Just supplying data to partners, however, sharply limits the amount of value an ecosystem leader can create. The Guardian recognized this constraint. It could create and capture more value in its ecosystem if it could go beyond simply supplying data efficiently to its partners. If it developed an interface that facilitated efficient, two-way flows of information with its partners, it would be able to access valuable learning from its partners' activities as well. So, it embedded in the interface an analytics code that allowed The Guardian to track the location and popularity of the content used by its partners, including any embedded advertising. Designing such an interface enabled the newspaper to draw data and accumulate learning from its extensive ecosystem, reaching beyond the activities in the ecosystem that it directly controlled.[9]

Because content and readership data are the lifeblood of the newspaper business, it made sense for The Guardian to design an interface that enabled it to keep strong control over the data that flowed between it and its partners in the ecosystem. But ecosystem leaders don't always need to tightly manage the exchange of information, or even track who takes what and contributes how much. In the DS ecosystem of more than eight hundred business, education and software partners, it would be almost impossible to try to track information exchanges between the partners at a reasonable cost. Nor is this necessary in order for DS to create and capture value in the ecosystem. By creating the 3DSwYm interface, similar to a social media platform where partners can share information and exchange concepts and models, DS was able to help partners become more successful and promote its own products and services without controlling the data flows.

Is there a risk in not controlling such data exchange? Could there be leakage of important data outside the ecosystem? That risk exists. But it may be less important than one imagines. As we know from research on R&D collaborations, a lot of information-sharing between scientists and engineers takes place in an informal know-how trading market, similar to what one finds in an ecosystem.[10] Engineers develop informal knowhow trading networks, and make judgments about who they consider to be an expert in a particular field. They build personal "rolodexes," and when they have a problem, they seek out the relevant expert—even if the expert works for a rival—and seek his or her advice. If they know that the information is critical to the rival's competitive advantage, the expert will not share much. However, in many cases, experts are willing to share considerable information because they expect to need, and receive, reciprocal help in the future. Engineers are actually quite good at estimating the value of the information they share, and the exchange of information proves to be effective. In fact, among experts in any field, the obligation to return a favor in a fair way is felt quite strongly.

The message for ecosystem leaders is clear: these informal exchange mechanisms can be harnessed to drive the ecosystem forward by putting in place interfaces and platforms that facilitate self-organization. Rather than creating a constraining set of structures and rules to manage knowledge and data flows in an ecosystem, the ecosystem leader might most effectively promote the success of its ecosystem by organizing conferences, creating private social networks, and setting up loosely organized joint development teams that help promote informal sharing and exchange of know-how. The value created through the vibrant exchange of knowledge among partners within the ecosystems of ARM and DS are testament to this approach.

Managing the Exchange of Complex Knowledge

Within an ecosystem, the flow of data between partners becomes particularly challenging when highly complex knowledge needs to be exchanged. More often than not, this complex knowledge is not written down, but resides in the heads of individuals. It also tends to be fragmented between different parts of an organization. As a result, it is especially difficult to assemble and transfer. This leads to our third recommendation to ecosystem leaders as they seek to shape interfaces that will make the ecosystem more efficient. To make sure complex knowledge flows smoothly across the ecosystem, the ecosystem leader needs to deploy an armory of approaches that include putting in place systems, tools and organizational structures that facilitate its own knowledge capture as well as the necessary flows between partners. The nature of complex knowledge, however, means that it is almost inevitable that the interfaces will require high levels of human interaction.

Accessing the complex knowledge embedded in the unfolding technological and product roadmaps that ARM needs to understand from its original equipment manufacturers and semiconductor fabrication partners is a case in point. This process involves more than collecting blueprints from each partner. ARM often has to piece together the future directions of a partner's technologies and products from snippets of knowledge locked in the heads of employees in different departments. Worse still, that knowledge tends to be unclear, tentative and incomplete. As a result, the interfaces that an ecosystem leader such as ARM has to create to smooth the flow of complex knowledge across the ecosystem needs to be very different from those designed to share data.

As we saw earlier, ARM's solution was to deploy specialized employees, in the form of partner managers, to act as an interface with those partners with whom it had to exchange large quantities of complex, tacit knowledge. Initially, each partner manager was assigned to a handful of partners, or in some cases, just one. The partner managers were responsible for piecing together an understanding of the product and technology road maps of its OEM partners (its "customers' customers") as well as the semiconductor partners to whom ARM licensed its designs. Their job description included: "developing sound, professional, long-term relationships with management, technical, and marketing personnel at the partner [firm] as a key role as well as creating, reporting, and executing on account strategies."[11] Another important part of the job was to "represent a partner to ARM, and provide feedback to ARM business units, engineering, marketing, and management regarding partner technical and business requirements," and "identify and capture insights on the competitive landscape, trends, projections, and other relevant information."

Relying on dedicated and experienced staff to access complex knowledge from partners makes a lot of sense when this knowledge is highly valuable to the ecosystem leader. Certainly, ARM's use of partner managers as the primary interface with its collaborators in the ecosystem worked well at first. But as ARM's ecosystem grew to include more than four hundred partners around the world, this approach to partnership management had to be modified. It wasn't efficient or practical to dedicate expensive and scarce partner managers to every partner in the ecosystem. So ARM began to vary its interfaces according to the type of knowledge the partner could provide, the partner's size, application segment in which it worked (such as mobile phones or automotive), type of technology involved, and the partner's degree of influence on the future direction of its industry.

These actions reflect the classic trade-offs between value creation, flexibility, and efficiency that all ecosystem leaders have to make. As we saw in chapter 5, the first step ARM took to improve the efficiency of its interactions with its partners was to identify a small set of strategic partners who would be critical to the future success of its ecosystem. The top twenty strategic partners were assigned to one of ARM's directors—the CEO and his direct reports—to manage the relationship. This ensured that even where the relationship was sales oriented, and a large ARM marketing and sales team was involved, top management could balance the short-term objective of ensuring revenues with the longer-term interests of sharing forthcoming technology roadmaps that would guide the future direction of the ecosystem.

The second step to improve effectiveness and efficiency was to split the traditional job of the partner manager into distinct roles performed by dedicated staff. A segment marketing organization was created for each end-use applications area. ARM grouped its activities into eight applications segments: Wireless, Storage, Imaging, Automotive, Consumer Entertainment, Networking, Security, and Industrial. These segment marketing teams had the task of working out, as ARM's chief technology officer, Mike Muller, put it, "who are the players, who matters, and what do they want."

ARM's experience illustrates the need for ecosystem leaders to think carefully about the different types of interactions they need to have with partners within their ecosystem, and how the interface might need to vary between different divisions of the same partner. And a knowledge exchange designed to shape the future direction of technology or a product road map should use different channels and interfaces than those where the purpose is to secure sales or source products or services. Creating distinct channels to handle different types of interactions reduces the risk of damage to relationships as a result of mixed motives colliding or impeding the flow of knowledge by forcing it through an unsuitable or inefficient interface.

Codifying Knowledge

A fourth recommendation for ecosystem leaders to keep in mind when designing interfaces with partners is to recognize that some data and information is difficult to articulate and share. In such cases, the ecosystem leader may develop a system that codifies the knowledge. Codification can enable the knowledge to be universally shared or may render it accessible only to technical experts within the ecosystem who are familiar with the jargon used. In either case, it will facilitate the transfer of knowledge that would otherwise be imprisoned in one corner of the ecosystem.

The benefits of codification are well illustrated by the solution Thomson Reuters came up with when faced with the problem of providing information to support its customers trying to navigate the legal system. The information buried in legal documents is often difficult to share, partly because the implications of court proceedings are hard to extract and communicate. As a result, the productivity and efficiency of the legal system may be undermined. Thomson Reuters recognized that if it could better codify the patterns and implications of large amount of legal cases across the world, it could make it part of the information it provided to professionals in financial services, insurance, legal, taxation, and accounting. In chapter 4, we described the partnership that Thomson Reuters set up with CodeX, the Stanford Center for Legal Informatics. That is an example on how Thomson Reuters developed a codification system in collaboration with its ecosystem to improve productivity.

But codification of knowledge within the ecosystem can do more than improve productivity. It can also open up new opportunities to fuel innovation and create new value. The next step Thomson Reuters took shows how this potential can be realized. In 2015, Thomson Reuters sponsored the Legal Tech Open Innovation Challenge at CodeX, which was "an open call for legal professionals, programmers, entrepreneurs, data scientists and any other interested parties to develop new applications that improve the efficiency of the legal system by providing high-value analytics."[12] Participants were given access to federal court docket data, outside data, and Thomson Reuters's open-source company identification system, PermID. The winner developed an application that used court data to create a model that predicted the likelihood that motions to dismiss would be successful before specific judges in US federal civil courts. As a result, Thomson Reuters was able, as Tim Baker, its director of innovation, put it: "To combine our proprietary content and domain expertise with a broad range of leading technologists to further fuel innovation and advance the practice of law."[13] This new model contributed to facilitating the exchange of complex legal data across the network of Thomson Reuters's partners.

Hence, by making it easier to access, interpret, and exchange complex information, thereby improving the productivity and efficiency of practicing law, Thomson Reuters was able to strengthen its ecosystem and better serve its customers, who were "increasingly looking to the next generation of technology solutions to build and advance a better functioning legal system." Enabling codification to help knowledge flow more easily throughout the ecosystem is thus a key contribution that the ecosystem leader can make to promote the network's efficiency.

Encourage Building Trust

Our fifth recommendation for how ecosystem leaders can enhance productivity is to find ways to nurture trust—between the ecosystem leader and its partners, as well as among all the partners in the ecosystem. When the participants in an ecosystem trust each other, expensive safeguards become unnecessary and transaction costs fall. Trust thus makes the ecosystem more productive. Trust is indeed a key coordinating mechanism in any hybrid form of organization in between markets and hierarchies.[14]

The kinds of trust that can make the interactions in an ecosystem more efficient depend on the type of risks associated with what they are jointly trying to achieve. Two sources of risk are particularly important. One, the extent to which one party depends on the other, and two, whether or not the quality of what each party delivers can be objectively assessed.[15]

To understand how these two types of risk can be handled in an ecosystem, think about a very simple everyday analogy. Suppose you are engaging a painter to paint your home. People don't choose a painter they have never used before, give her or him the keys to their house, and let him or her finish the painting when they are on vacation. Most will get the painter to start in a small, secluded part of the house, and then hurry home at the end of the day to assess the quality of the work. If the painter has done a poor job, they will fire him. And how do they ensure that the painter doesn't take on another job and delay theirs? They withhold payment until the job is complete and may offer a bonus for finishing on time.

Some interactions in the ecosystem are much like those with a house painter. The relationship is asymmetric; one party depends on a partner's performance, but the latter's success does not depend on interaction with the former. In that case, contracts with performance measures and incentives are likely to provide the most efficient way of managing the interaction and ensuring trust, as long as the partner's responsibilities can be precisely defined and performance is observable. Apple's Apps Store and Amazon's marketplace use this approach by requiring buyers and sellers to enter into contractual relationships, sometimes backed by incentives to encourage good performance.

However, as we have already flagged, it is rarely possible to detail all the tasks and responsibilities of each partner in an ecosystem and write these into contracts. In the process of creating new value, ecosystems typically involve partners in poorly defined and emergent processes of learning and innovation. Partners' roles and interactions will change over time as the ecosystem evolves. Moreover, the performance of partners is often difficult to observe and measure. This is especially true when they contribute knowledge, capabilities and access to the process of building a complex interdependent ecosystem, where the causes of success or failure are hard to trace. It is in these situations that trust becomes extremely important to underpin smooth and efficient engagement between partners.

There are basically three ways to build trust: through one's reputation based on competence, consistency, integrity, and so on; through repeated interaction gradually building familiarity; and through norms that create predictability and trustworthiness.

It is hard to build trust based solely on objective measures or simply through observation. Therefore, reputation almost always plays an important role. Take the example of an ecosystem leader wishing to attract a partner to stimulate the demand for the product or service that the ecosystem delivers by acting as a market maker. If the new partner fails to generate demand, was the company an untrustworthy shyster? It is impossible to tell. The ecosystem's products might have been such a poor fit with the needs of potential customers that even the most competent and committed partner would not have been able to help it succeed. How do you solve this dilemma? The best way to develop trust is to focus on partners who enjoy an established reputation because you know that if they don't do their best to stimulate demand in the market, their reputation will suffer.

For many of the interactions that are necessary for an ecosystem to deliver value, partners' reputations can therefore play a key role. Attracting reputable partners will foster the trust required to reduce transaction costs in the ecosystem and make it productive. Ecosystem leaders need to make sure that when partners join the ecosystem, they put their reputations on the line. A good way to do this is to require that in order to join, key partners lend their brands to the products and services the ecosystem delivers, and prominently communicate their involvement in the ecosystem. This is particularly important in the outer reaches of an ecosystem, where performance is less observable and hard to measure. Here the ecosystem leader has to rely on attracting partners with strong reputations and helping others to build their reputations.

Recall that AWS, for example, fostered the growth of a trusted global partner ecosystem by setting criteria for entry into its AWS Partner Network (APN). That network also provided mechanisms by which partners could build their competence and reputation through a series of certifications.[16] AWS maintained a partner directory that allowed potential customers to find trustworthy partners, where customers and approved software-and-service vendors could connect.

In other interactions between the partners in an ecosystem, performance may be more easily observable and objectively measurable. Consistent and repeated interactions will build familiarity and ultimately trust. Even then, success will depend on the quality of the interactions as well as the inputs. In these cases, dependence and trust in the relationship is symmetric. Symmetric relationships in an ecosystem, where success depends on understanding and coordination between partners, can only be developed by experimentation and learning by doing. The ecosystem leader therefore needs to find ways of promoting interactions between partners that provide opportunities to learn from each other and to experiment with joint activities. One way the ecosystem leader can do this is by sponsoring pilot projects where partners can explore and test ways of working together.

Alibaba, for example, when confronted with the need to improve logistics in China, had to identify seed partners who were willing to build trust by embarking on a journey of co-learning. It identified a small group of partners who believed that by working together, they could dramatically improve the ecosystem's logistics capabilities. This required sustained effort with an uncertain result. And, as Alibaba's Ming Zeng noted, the company then "worked almost day and night with these seed partners to get a prototype up and running as soon as possible. Once it was operating, learning and competence could be accumulated."[17]

Contrary to early expectations, Alibaba found that the partners who joined weren't industry leaders—these were often too wedded to their traditional models and even complacent—but up-and-coming companies that believed in the future of e-business, could see the upsides of the ecosystem, and were willing to build trust over time by working together.

Trust is often also a consequence of a calculated approach, via a sober assessment of the costs and benefits to the partners of exploiting each other's vulnerability. The risks involved in committing to an ecosystem will only be acceptable to partners when they trust that the ecosystem as a whole is working to create mutual benefit as well as serving individual interests. It will fail if partners suspect that the ecosystem is riddled with hidden agendas working against them. The ecosystem leader, therefore, has an important role to play in building trust in the ecosystem as a positive force that treats participants fairly.

Just as with corporate leadership, communication has a key role here. Ecosystem leaders need to keep reminding participants of the benefits of being part of the ecosystem it is delivering. They need to celebrate partners who make investments or perform extra activities for the benefit of the ecosystem as a whole, to promote its prosperity in the longer term. They must promote forums, both online and face-to-face, where partners come together, listen to each other's opinions, understand the implications of their decisions on specific partners and the wider ecosystem and potentially modify them, help develop a common view of events as they unfold, and look for opportunities for mutual benefit. Fostering this understanding of partners' shared destiny and promoting these types of interactions helps reduce transactions costs, improves the ecosystem's productivity, and creates a self-reinforcing cycle of commitment and adjustment that will help partners through the inevitable crises and hiccups that the ecosystem will experience.[18]

Agreeing on Governance Standards

Trust is also based on good norms that create predictability and trustworthiness. Therefore, our sixth recommendation is that the ecosystem leader should develop norms and standards that all of the parties in the ecosystem must subscribe to. An ecosystem will be more productive and efficient if customers, users, and partners don't have to check each other's credentials, because they know that the ecosystem leader ensures that they all abide by a set of minimum standards. Apple's App Store, for example, insists that every offering meet certain minimum standards in five areas: Safety, Performance, Business, Design, and Legal. Safety, for example, covers standards for the exclusion of objectionable content, prevents outside links in apps designed to appeal to kids, and specifies requirements for the ways by which customers can get questions answered and access support. In the area of performance, meanwhile, Apple sets standards relating to completeness, hardware compatibility, and the rate at which the app can drain battery power or generate heat in a device.[19]

In creating its More Disruption Please (MDP) marketplace, athenahealth has taken standard-setting a step further to complement trust and facilitate interactions between partners in its ecosystem. Services sold on athenahealth's platform must conform to the company's privacy and security standards, and any solution accepted for the MDP marketplace must either lead to an increase in client revenues, reduce inefficiencies, or improve health outcomes.

To check that these requirements are being met by partners, it has established a system for tracking performance metrics in real time.

As we saw in our discussion of APIs, standards covering the way product modules are designed, or the manner in which data is packaged and exchanged, help to smooth interactions between participants, and make the ecosystem work more efficiently. The ecosystem leader can also play a role in developing standardized interfaces to smooth the interactions between different partners. As we saw in in chapter 3, for example, DS developed a portal where all of its partners can access road maps for the different sectors to which it offers PLM solutions. Within its customized social network, DS then established standard protocols to enable the easy exchange of complex, three-dimensional designs. These standard interfaces and protocols helped reduce transactions costs, eliminate uncertainty, and increase flexibility. They helped partners avoid the need for developing complex agreements each time they altered their activities or roles. And when a situation was too complex to fit the standard protocols, and so required a nonstandard agreement, DS helped its ecosystem partners focus on crafting a contract that promoted collaborative activities and encouraged shared problem solving.

Penalizing Bad Behavior

Not every participant will live up to the standards that govern its ecosystem, so our final recommendation is that ecosystem leaders need to find ways to penalize those whose behavior threatens to undermine the ecosystem's integrity, productivity and efficiency.

The problem is illustrated by Alibaba's Taobao ecosystem. In its early days, it suffered from misrepresentation by sellers that deliberately misclassified their products in an attempt to get greater exposure. A seller of a computer mouse, for instance, would list it in a high traffic category such as men's clothing to gain more visibility. To work efficiently and fairly, products and services must be properly categorized, so buyers can make purchase decisions from a comprehensive set of alternatives. Initially, Alibaba lacked a process for correcting categorization errors, and frustration and confusion built up among sellers. Alibaba needed a way of correcting errors and preventing unscrupulous sellers from gaming the system. Explains Taobao's Zhang Yu: "The difficulty is that everyone in the ecosystem is trying to maximize their own interest, sometimes at the cost of others, which damages the fundamental principle of a healthy ecosystem, co-create and share. Therefore, there is a need for police, who can fight for the public interest."[20]

Instead of dealing with the problem itself, Alibaba decided to leverage the ecosystem by recruiting new partners that could help. It introduced a categorization feedback-and-dispute resolution process, whereby a Market Judgement Committee would make all categorization decisions. Members of the committee were selected from qualified representatives of both buyers and sellers, and decisions were made by voting. By choosing this approach, Alibaba was able to enhance the effectiveness of each party and help the ecosystem become more robust.

Another type of destructive behavior that can plague ecosystems is free riding. Partners often need to make irreversible investments or other kinds of commitments based on the expectation that they will reap benefits in the future. The participants therefore face the moral hazard that some of their partners will try to ride on the backs of others, renegotiating the relationship after partners have already committed capital, effort, or technology.[21] The ecosystem leader needs to control the risk of moral hazard by promoting transparency in interactions, and by imposing sanctions on, or even excluding, those who refuse to play fair. For example, one of the companies we studied had to exclude a significant development partner from the ecosystem after it found out that the latter had been consciously using software code from one of the other partners without having the permission to do so.

Balancing Innovation and Flexibility with Efficiency

In order to secure the competitiveness of your ecosystem against vertically integrated rivals and traditional supply chains, and to make sure that the benefits only an ecosystem can deliver aren't outweighed by extra costs, you need to focus on creating efficient interfaces between the partners. This means answering the following questions:

1. Where it is appropriate to use contracts to govern relations in the ecosystem, are these sufficiently flexible, targeting high-level outcomes and performance standards rather than specific deliverables and actions?
2. Are these contracts perceived to be fair and do they facilitate shared problem solving, rather than simply acting as a safety-valve of last resort?

3. Have you constructed interfaces to enable efficient exchange of data between you and your partners as well as between partners? How much control do you need to exert over the data being exchanged?
4. When complex, tacit knowledge needs to be exchanged, have you put the tools, systems and structures in place to enable this, including mechanisms for high-touch human interaction where necessary?
5. Have you helped boost the efficiency of the ecosystem by putting in place mechanisms that help build trust between partners, including attracting reputable partners and encouraging them to put their brands and reputations on the line?
6. Have you established a set of minimum standards that all partners agree to abide by as a way of reducing risk and reducing the costs of transacting within the ecosystem?
7. What mechanisms have you put in place to penalize free-riders or other forms of bad behavior in the ecosystem?

7 Unleashing Ecosystem Learning and Innovation

ONE OF THE MOST IMPORTANT ADVANTAGES OF AN ECOSYS-tem is its exceptional ability to foster co-learning and catalyze innovation. The ecosystem leader can play a pivotal role in turning that potential for learning and innovation into reality.

New knowledge is the lifeblood of innovation in an ecosystem. Consequently, the ecosystem leader's role starts with the actions it can take to bring new knowledge into the ecosystem or to ensure that fresh ideas are generated from the ecosystem's day-to-day activities. Once that knowledge is captured, the ecosystem leader must harness that knowledge to trigger innovation. Sometimes it is the ecosystem leader itself that innovates, using knowledge it has accumulated by virtue of its pivotal position in the ecosystem. But equally important, the ecosystem leader can also encourage its partners to innovate, individually and jointly. To facilitate such innovation, ecosystem leaders must disseminate knowledge so that both explicit and tacit knowledge gets to those who can effectively use it to innovate.

At the same time, ecosystem leaders need to keep proprietary some of that new knowledge their ecosystems generate. Proprietary knowledge underpins a leader's soft power and, as we will see in the next chapter, can be critical to ensuring they can monetize their contributions to the ecosystem. Deciding how much knowledge to share with partners in order to stimulate innovation, and how much knowledge to keep proprietary, is one of the most fundamental calls an ecosystem leader needs to make.

Encouraging Inflows of New Knowledge

Ecosystem leaders infuse new knowledge into the ecosystem by deploying strategies to engage with a wide variety of partners, each of whom brings distinctive capabilities and experiences to the network. The benefits of a strategy that is carefully designed to stimulate fresh inflows of knowledge is well illustrated by the example of The Guardian, one of the UK's oldest and best-known newspapers, and a case we already touched upon in chapter 6.

Started as the *Manchester Guardian*, a regional newspaper in England in 1821, for the first 178 years it was a newspaper, initially thriving, and, more recently, struggling like most of its rivals as advertising and content increasingly moved to the internet. Even so, the ecosystem that The Guardian has built since 2000 has made it the fourth-most-popular news portal in the world, attracting over 270 million unique visitors in February 2019. Almost two-thirds of them came from outside the United Kingdom, 26 percent from the United States alone.[1]

Central to The Guardian's success has been the decisions taken by its top management team during the early 2000s, aimed at harnessing the knowledge and capabilities of its partners. This led to a business model different from its rivals. Rather than producing and distributing content for which readers are willing to pay, and selling advertising alongside that content, The Guardian built an ecosystem that is able to continually access new knowledge from readers, advertisers, and other news outlets. In this way, the ecosystem was continually refreshed with diverse flows of new content.

Initially, this idea faced a lot of internal resistance. As The Guardian's former editor, Alan Rusbridger, observed in 2010: "We had to get over the arrogance that only journalists are figures of authority in the world. If you let other voices in, you will create a Website where authors and readers are more engaged, more involved, and, I think, journalistically better."[2] Any newspaper that remains closed, by contrast, is "going to have to generate everything itself," according to Rusbridger, and that, quite simply, is no longer possible in today's connected world.[3]

The first move that The Guardian made to create a more open ecosystem was to make its online content freely available, not only to readers, but also to third party websites. The newspaper launched an open platform application programming interface in 2009 that allowed Web developers to create links to Guardian content and relay it to their viewers. Initially free to all users, the platform later transitioned to a two-tiered pricing model giving limited access for free and charging for wider access, as discussed in chapter 6.

But if it were to continually fuel innovation within its ecosystem The Guardian would also have go beyond maximizing the reach of its stories and establish an inflow of new content. To achieve this, it would have to change the way it interacted with its partners in the ecosystem. This meant relinquishing some control over how its content was used. Rather than simply allowing other websites to link to its content, it created, as we mentioned in the previous chapter, an open and flexible platform that allowed The Guardian's content to be embedded into partners' sites. This enabled The Guardian to start engaging with innumerable partners in a new way without the costs of searching them out. Many of these partners were journalists, publishers and websites that The Guardian was not previously even aware of. Its open platform allowed The Guardian's content, in the words of Digital Content Director Emily Bell, "to be woven into the fabric of the internet."[4]

These moves might look like an act of extraordinary benevolence on the part of The Guardian. But they also had an upside for the company: as its content was distributed around the world by its partners the Guardian was able to track how that content was being used and when and where it was being consumed. The result was access to a massive stream of new data, way beyond anything it could generate in-house. It would subsequently use this treasure trove of data to further innovate its business model. Precise information on when and where its content was being used allowed The Guardian to understand the relationship between content and where and when users accessed it. Having captured this new data, it was later able to precisely tailor its content and advertising to the specific contexts of its users, as we explain below.

The obvious next step in the quest to use its ecosystem to generate innovation was for The Guardian to open up the way it sourced and created content. Again, this required it to cede a degree of control, this time over how it produced some of its content. In 2011, it launched "n0tice.com," a platform for self-generated content that was an amalgam between a message board and a social media platform. It became a mobile publishing platform that resembled a community notice board.

Using the locational tools embedded in mobile phones and web browsers, n0tice.com displayed to users Guardian content relevant to their current locations. It also allowed them to post on its website content tagged with their location.[5] Therefore, while the platform was free, it enabled The Guardian to generate revenues through location-specific classified advertising, optimized using algorithms derived from the data it had garnered from its original open-access platform. Although anyone could list things for sale for free on n0tice .com, they were also offered premium services such as featured positions on the screen, larger sized advertisements, and extended duration on the website for which they paid fees.

A year later, The Guardian unveiled an open API for n0tice.com that allowed businesses, journalists, and other developers to use the full complement of information available on the platform. All content published on n0tice.com was covered by the Creative Commons Attribution Share-Alike standard, so that it could be used commercially elsewhere.[6]

n0tice.com and the moves that preceded it, show how an ecosystem leader can stimulate an increased flow of knowledge into its ecosystem. For The Guardian this had the advantage, in Matt McAlister's words, that: "When you let go a bit, and let a community run with the space you've created, amazing things start to happen."[7] Over the next few years, n0tice.com was spun off into a separate subsidiary, called Contribly, transforming itself from a location-specific message board into a broader platform that provided media companies with the tools to access, moderate, and curate user-generated content.[8]

The Guardian leveraged Contribly to expand its ecosystem further into user-generated journalism, when it launched GuardianWitness, in April 2013. GuardianWitness allowed readers to submit images or stories to The Guardian, either through a smartphone app or over the internet. Contributions appear on the GuardianWitness website, and a selected few features on The Guardian's main website or its print edition. The platform encourages users by setting weekly news 'assignments' (essentially investigative questions) that readers are asked to respond to. From time to time, The Guardian also invites readers to contribute to breaking news stories, which, in addition to appearing on the GuardianWitness app and website, could be incorporated into the newspaper's articles. Readers can also submit unsolicited content and ideas. These are then reviewed by The Guardian's editorial team to see if they are fit for publication.

The Guardian's leadership rightly saw GuardianWitness as a culmination of its longstanding strategy of creating new opportunities within its ecosystem by drawing in massively more data and knowledge from a wide variety of sources. As Joanna Geary, The Guardian's social and communities editor, noted in 2016: "At The Guardian, we have a long history of getting our readers involved in our journalism. In the last few years, our readers have helped us to review MPs' expenses documents, follow the UK riots, gain real-time insights into the Arab Spring as events in the Middle East unfolded, and challenge the government's employment schemes. GuardianWitness further reinforces our recognition that journalism is now a two-way conversation, and will open up our site, as we never have before. Not only will this make it even easier for our readers to get involved in our journalism and form both local and global communities of joint interest, it will also provide our journalists with a fantastic new tool, providing them with insights and views that we don't yet have access to."[9] Thus the quality of The Guardian's content and its ability to identify and leverage scoops ahead of its rivals were greatly enhanced as a result.

The Guardian's experience aptly illustrates how an ecosystem leader can stimulate innovation in its ecosystem by engaging with more and different partners, and attracting strong inflows of new knowledge from diverse sources. By creating platforms that provide readers and local media organizations with the opportunity to contribute news and content, The Guardian found a way to open the floodgates of new knowledge into its ecosystem. It developed effective and user-friendly tools, as well as incentives, that encourage contributors to engage afresh with a trusted institution. The mass of new information its ecosystem was then able to access and absorb fueled innovations, both by The Guardian and its partners. These delivered a richer experience for its customers and opened up new revenue streams.

In the same way, many of the ecosystem leaders we studied for this book have found novel ways of stimulating flows of new knowledge into their ecosystems that benefit themselves and their partners. For example, when a new industry partner joins the DS ecosystem, it brings fresh knowledge about the design challenges, the behaviors of materials and products, and customer requirements in their industry. DS offers tools to encourage its new software partners to capture this expertise and fresh knowledge into software applications. These applications then become fully integrated into the DS platform and service offering, enabling it and its ecosystem to generate more value for customers. ARM's partners, including OEMs and semiconductor fabricators, continually bring knowledge about new technologies, product needs, and manufacturing processes into its ecosystem. This new knowledge is then incorporated into ARM's chip designs and the tools, as well as software and services offered by other partners in the ecosystem, allowing it to deliver more functionality and greater value to customers.

In the case of e-commerce ecosystems such as Amazon and Alibaba, the data continually created by day-to-day activities is an even more important source of knowledge. Every transaction generates new data about the behavior of the parties involved, as well as their characteristics such as location, service performance, and timing. With the right analytics, this data can be turned into new knowledge and insights, ranging from likely consumer preferences and consumer psychology, to the credit worthiness of suppliers and the risks they might pose, allowing Amazon and Alibaba, and their respective ecosystems, to create more value for customers and generate more revenue for themselves.

In each of these examples, however, the benefits could only be reaped once the ecosystem leader had engineered a significant, and sometimes difficult, change in mind-set. Its own staff, and its partners, had to embrace the conviction that, far from destroying value or risking it leaking away, opening the gates to flows of information from outside the ecosystem is fundamental to generating new opportunities for value creation.

Innovating as the Ecosystem Leader

One way to utilize the new information and knowledge flowing into the ecosystem is for the leader to use it to fuel its own innovation (the results of which, as we will see, it may or may not choose to share with its partners).

Generating insights from data aggregation is one of the easiest ways for an ecosystem leader to innovate. At athenahealth, data from around one hundred million patient encounters each year provided near real-time insights into clinical trends."[10] athenahealth used that data to create its annual Payerview ranking, which ranks payers (insurance companies) on a variety of financial, administrative, and transactional metrics. These metrics include the average time taken by a provider to receive reimbursement, the percentage of claims resolved on the first submission, how long it takes a payer to respond to an enrolment request, the administrative burden related to provider enrolment in electronic transactions, and other aspects of the quality and reliability of insurers.[11] Sharing these rankings enables patients to make better informed choices, encourages competition, and indicates where the potential for improvements are greatest. Hence, by simply aggregating data from across the ecosystem and sharing it with partners in an easily digestible form, athenahealth was able to stimulate innovation that created more value for customers and partners alike.

ARM has gone a step further to become one of the key innovators in its ecosystem. Drawing on complex information about the emerging directions of key technologies, products, and services among its partners, it uses this data to guide the design of innovative chip architectures. The importance that ARM places on this flow of data from its partners is so great that whenever it grants a license for the use of its technology, it also insists on a reciprocal relationship with the licensee. The aim is to ensure that it gains insights into the licensee's process technology road maps and potential applications that are emerging.

By developing strong relationships with several OEMs, ARM could gain an early indication of the requirements for new products. Likewise, its relationships with semiconductor partners and other players provided a window on the way hardware technologies would evolve. ARM combined the knowledge it accessed from its partner network with its own views to identify the emerging trends for new products and technologies. As Mike Muller, ARM's former Chief Technology Officer, explained to us, the key innovation challenge then for ARM as the ecosystem leader was: "How do you integrate and communicate the multiple strands of information coming from the OEMs and partners?"

Part of the answer lay in keeping the ultimate objective in mind: To develop architectures that embodied the highest common denominator as the best compromise between different partners' requirements. Initially, this kind of thinking did not come naturally to many of ARM's partners, particularly large high-tech companies that are extremely protective of their intellectual property. However, once they saw the upsides for innovation within the ecosystem and were convinced that ARM could be trusted to keep their proprietary knowledge confidential, they were willing to engage in two-way knowledge flows. Thereafter, the new architectures that rapidly emerged benefitted the entire ecosystem, so partners had to forgo designs customized specifically for them—but in exchange, they enjoyed more cost-effective solutions. By pooling knowledge from across the ecosystem and designing innovative architectures that multiple customers could use, ARM was able to spread the development costs. Some of the resulting scale economies were then passed on, offering better value to customers.

These examples underline the key role of the ecosystem leader's own innovation in enabling the ecosystem to create new value for customers. Ecosystem leaders can fuel this innovation by designing structures and processes that enable the ecosystem to keep on sucking in new knowledge from partners, customers, and its broader environment, and using this to innovate. But they can also go much further in helping to realize their ecosystem's innovation potential by stimulating innovation among their partners.

Encouraging Learning and Innovation between Partners

Beyond using the information generated by the ecosystem to fuel its own innovation, the ecosystem leader can also catalyze learning and innovation between the partners in its ecosystem. Opening up the ecosystem to new partners and encouraging them to share information are first steps, but they don't go far enough. The leader also has to create the channels, tools, and interfaces through which information can be shared between partners so that joint learning can take place.

In the AWS ecosystem, for example, Amazon doesn't control all the communications between its partners and customers. AWS maintains a directory to help potential customers find partners they can work with, and the AWS marketplace facilitates direct connections between customers and software or service vendors. Amazon works hard to turn these connections into more than sales opportunities for existing products. As it explains to its partners, Amazon provides tools and training to help "invite the customer to innovate and to be proactive in their IT development while creating more opportunities for your firm."[12] Amazon also facilitates linkages between the partners in its ecosystem to foster innovation by including the partner's information and search functions within the APN partner network so that it becomes easy to identify others with complementary capabilities.

In a similar vein, The Guardian promoted joint learning between partners by enabling them to share data about the preferences of their customers under the auspices of its Pangaea Alliance. Pangaea brings together data from Reuters, CNN International, *Financial Times*, *The Week*, *Fast Company*, and others. As a group, these well-known media brands reach over two hundred million of the world's most affluent and influential people. Their readers tend to consume multiple media, and travel globally. It is therefore difficult for any publisher working alone to develop accurate profiles of these readers. Pangaea offers a solution by enabling pieces of information on any individual customer to be shared between all the partners in the ecosystem. This allows readers to be segmented in innovative ways and advertising to be targeted more precisely. As Tim Gentry, the global revenue director at Guardian News & Media and the leader of the project, explained, "We share first-party data with each other, and create compelling audience segments."[13] For instance, subscription information from one publisher is combined with behavioral data from other publishers to create an innovative reader profile for which an advertiser pays handsomely.[14] Advertisers can thus target readers who are frequent travelers, often reading content from multiple publishers.[15] In addition to promoting that kind of innovation, Pangaea enabled companies to target the combined audience of all the partners by purchasing advertising space on all their websites in a single transaction on a shared platform. By connecting the major publishers in its ecosystem and providing the infrastructure necessary to share and analyze their respective data, The Guardian was therefore able to catalyze innovation among its partners in a way that helped its ecosystem unlock new value.

Designing the right kinds of structures and interfaces to connect partners, and help them identify productive opportunities to exchange data and knowledge as we saw in chapter 6, can be an effective way to promote innovation by partners. Where innovation is impeded by difficulties in sharing information, the creation of standard interfaces, protocols, and codification of knowledge allows for better coordination, reduced transactions costs, and reduced uncertainty. This can help remove the barriers to shared innovation, just as we see in the trading of commodities and in financial markets.

Beyond the volume of data and knowledge accessed by partners, successful innovation often is driven by the quality of their interactions. This is particularly true when innovation requires experimentation. In this case, rather than one party simply relying on the other, dependence in the relationship is symmetric. As we saw in chapter 6, that implies the interactions between partners need to be designed to provide adequate opportunities to experiment with joint activities in ways that develop trust and allow the partners to learn from each other. By facilitating these kinds of interactions, ecosystem leaders can play an important role stimulating innovation.

DS facilitates high-touch interactions between groups of cutting-edge partners and its own employees in its quest to develop innovative solutions and create the ultimate user experience. For example, it has brought together groups of leading manufacturers of virtualization devices, including partners with knowledge of virtual reality, augmented reality, virtual training, and gaming, to work with the DS certification lab and R&D teams to apply these new technologies to industrial design. By initiating these kinds of new collaborations, DS enables partners to verify the compatibility and performance of their respective technologies and align their future technology road maps. DS continues the learning and innovation process by hosting demonstrations for customers along with joint marketing and business development activities that help expand its partners' reach into markets they are jointly targeting.[16]

In other cases, the ecosystem leader may need to invest in new ways for customers and partners to interface with the ecosystem in order to stimulate innovation. When Amazon launched the Kindle Fire in 2011, for example, it was entering a tablet market dominated by Apple and some Android devices. However, the company's intention was not to make money on the devices themselves. Instead, it sought to create a channel through which customers could interact with the Amazon ecosystem differently. That opened up new opportunities to sell content, and for its partners to develop innovative offerings. As technology writer Steven Levy wrote: "When you pay $199 for Fire, you're not buying a gadget—you're filing citizen(ship) papers for the digital duchy of Amazonia."[17]

Amazon has continued to invest in the same way, launching the Amazon Echo, a smart speaker connected to the voice-controlled personal assistant service Alexa. The Echo has stimulated a wave of partner innovation across its extended ecosystem as partners have developed for Alexa what Amazon calls "skills." These third-party applications have added several new capabilities to Alexa, including the ability to play music; check for delays on your daily commute by train, bus, ferry, or car; answer general questions; set an alarm; order a pizza; call an Uber; and control connected devices such as lighting and thermostats. Amazon helps its partners to innovate around its Echo-Alexa platform by providing them with The Alexa Skills Kit, a collection of self-service APIs, tools, documentation, tutorials, and code samples that make it quick and easy for any company to develop new skills for Alexa. All the code is in the "cloud"—not on any device—making innovative upgrades seamless.

Meanwhile, athenahealth has encouraged innovation in its partner ecosystem by establishing a start-up accelerator. The accelerator has been designed to provide additional resources to start-ups with well-developed products so that they can scale. The start-ups get workspaces, seed funding (from $250,000 to $2 million), and access to the ecosystem's client base. More importantly, athenahealth channels expertise drawn from its employees, clients, and partners to help the chosen start-ups innovate and grow.

ARM has taken a different approach to nurturing start-ups. It found that start-ups interested in using ARM technology for their products would make contact with each other. Using a light touch, ARM provided them with the tools and other support necessary to integrate its technologies into their products and link them with others using ARM's designs. It also offered flexible licensing on a per-use basis, recognizing that building a product prototype is the partners' primary focus. This reduces the hurdle to using ARM technology, even while allowing fledgling companies to focus their resources on innovation. By using proven technologies, design tools, and supporting software from ARM, the start-ups enhance their credibility. Encouraging innovative start-ups to attach themselves to the ARM ecosystem in this way has the potential to pay handsome dividends when these companies open up new applications for ARM's designs, or provide superior tools and software for use by its other partners in the ecosystem.

These examples show how, as an ecosystem leader, you can stimulate innovation among partners, which benefits the ecosystem and, importantly, if indirectly, your own business. You choose the mechanisms, ranging from bringing new groups of partners together through to investing in a new platform on which you could innovate or launch an incubator. You don't need to control every aspect of that innovation process. The trick is to step back, let your partners' creativity and drive for success do their work, and enjoy the benefits.

Sharing Ecosystem Learning

Once an ecosystem leader has successfully stimulated learning and innovation in the ecosystem, there are additional benefits to be gained if the results get shared across the ecosystem. Sometimes the ecosystem leader or its partners may want to keep some of their learning proprietary so that only they can profit from it. But in many other cases, sharing what has been learned will be what we like to call an "ecosystem good." This is akin to what economists term a public good. It is a good from which the entire ecosystem can benefit without disadvantaging anyone else. The improved reader segmentation that The Guardian's Pangaea ecosystem has created, for example, is a "good" that helps all the partners in the ecosystem more successfully target content and advertising. By using it, everyone can gain and nobody needs to lose.

Most companies actively spread the word about their insights and innovations across their markets and supply chains through controlled "broadcasting" in order to encourage the uptake of new products, services, and technologies. They might also offer training to selected distributors and service providers to ensure their innovations are properly supported. However, to unlock the full potential of their ecosystem, an ecosystem leader needs to go much further. Their aim should be to stimulate partners to innovate, not just inform or equip partners to support innovations that already exist. To achieve this, they need to find ways to make sure that whatever new knowledge is generated flows smoothly in many directions and to multiple partners so that it reaches every corner of the ecosystem where it might be valued.

Amazon, for example, encourages innovation in its ecosystems by constantly fostering the sharing of information among its partners. The benefits of this strategy, and Amazon's role in generating them, are aptly demonstrated by its experience with 2nd Watch, one of its partners in the AWS ecosystem. Now one of AWS's cadre of premier consulting partners, 2nd Watch provides cloud migration and management services to help customers "maximize [their] value from AWS" by designing, deploying, and managing their cloud-deployment strategies. When Coca-Cola realized that a digital marketing campaign was generating more traffic than its internal systems could handle, it needed a solution—quickly. In just two months' time, 2nd Watch worked closely with Coca-Cola to develop an innovative way of migrating all its North American sites to AWS.[18] Amazon communicated this case to all its other partners and customers by publishing a best practice case study on its partner network, APN. Doing so helped 2nd Watch win new customers. It also enabled the ecosystem to figure out how to innovate and improve cloud migration services for the benefit of other customers. That, in turn, helped grow the ecosystem and its capabilities, driving more business to AWS.

Another case in point of a smart ecosystem leader that helps its partners share experiences and disseminate new learning is DS. By staging an annual partner forum, the 3DEXPERIENCE Partner Executive Summit, DS brings together partners from around the world to interact with its senior executives and specialist engineers, discuss vision and strategy, participate in workshops, and network face-to-face with peers. The opportunity to share learning across the ecosystem is augmented by dozens of more specialized knowledge-sharing events each year that bring its ecosystem partners and customers together. Examples include user-group meetings around the world, technical meetings, and customer-led seminars describing experiences, such as how

Finnish engine-maker Wärtsilä Marine used the ecosystem to develop innovative products, systems, and services to meet its customers' needs.[19]

ARM exhorts its partners: "Jump-start your concept-to-compute journey with ARM processor designs, rich development resources, and a diverse partner ecosystem. You'll be joining one of the world's largest, most prolific and creative communities of product innovators."[20] ARM had set up eleven communities to discuss, among several topics, innovations in graphics and multimedia, the Internet of Things, security, embedding ARM-based processes in machinery and equipment, and one in Mandarin to help its Chinese partners.

These examples underline the point that while ecosystem leaders have a role in promoting innovation in the ecosystem by making it easy to share information and learning across the ecosystem, they can also put in place mechanisms that encourage partners to develop "ecosystem goods" that can be shared. Because they leverage the innovation capacity of large numbers of partners, these mechanisms may prove to be the most effective way to stimulate innovation within the ecosystem that benefits all and drives value creation forward.

The Dilemma: Proprietary versus Shared Learning

Given its pivotal role in the ecosystem, the ecosystem leader is often in a position to absorb a great deal of fresh data and new knowledge generated by the ecosystem. Sharing this knowledge can clearly help promote innovation across the ecosystem. But sometimes sharing this knowledge isn't in the ecosystem leader's best interest. Ecosystem leaders therefore have to make what might turn out to be one of their most important and difficult decisions: How much of the new knowledge should it share with its ecosystem partners? And how much should it keep proprietary to bolster its leverage over the network and its capacity to extract profits?

This dilemma is real. The performance of the ecosystem leader depends on the health and vitality of its ecosystem and its ability to discover and generate new value through innovation. The leader therefore has an incentive to share knowledge across the ecosystem in ways that help its partners and the ecosystem create more value, innovate, and grow. This was aptly demonstrated by The Guardian's ecosystem, wherein sharing news, analyses, opinions, and even customer-behavior data was fundamental to its success. The Guardian ecosystem developed because it recognized that the traditional stance of using news collected exclusively by its own journalists would constrain its access to information, impede learning, and narrow its appeal. By sharing its knowledge, The Guardian could stimulate its partners to access, analyze, and share new knowledge. By sharing its customer data with other media outlets, The Guardian could better understand the behavior of readers, improve segmentation, and create better value propositions for advertisers.

Likewise, we saw that ARM, DS, and AWS were able to help their ecosystems create more value, grow, and enhance their productivity by sharing the knowledge they had gleaned about everything from customer needs to technology advances. They developed a set of tools, training programs, and workshops, often making them freely available or at a low cost, to enable the knowledge to be disseminated to partners that could make the best use of them.

Yet there are some types of new knowledge that many ecosystem leaders need to keep to themselves or within a small circle of a few, close partners. That is either because sharing the new knowledge would damage the partners who provided it or stymie the ecosystem leader's ability to make profits. ARM, for example, cannot share the knowledge it has about OEM and chip-fabrication partners' future product and technological road maps. Broadcasting the details of its partners' crown jewels across the ecosystem of partners that sometimes compete with each other would result in the immediate termination of ARM's partnerships. At the same time, ARM's engineers integrate the knowledge that the company accesses from its partners to create a picture of each industry's future technological requirements. These data are a critical input in ARM's design process. It underpins its ability to create chip architectures that meet the competing needs of its partners. That knowledge plays a key role in ensuring that ARM profits from its contributions to the ecosystem. Clearly, it is not something ARM would be able to share with its partners without impairing its revenues and profitability. By keeping the knowledge to itself, ARM can develop and sell designs that earn it handsome returns.

To help make this decision about what knowledge it should share with partners and what to keep proprietary, the ecosystem leader needs to work out whether or not the new knowledge and innovation is what we termed an "ecosystem good." Recall that the key characteristic of an ecosystem good is that all partners can benefit from using it without reducing the benefit that another partner can gain by doing so. Much of the knowledge, learning, and innovation that an ecosystem generates falls into this category. In fact, its use by other partners might even have advantages, enabling the whole ecosystem to create additional value and become more productive. In this case, it makes sense for the ecosystem leader to facilitate the dissemination of that knowledge across the ecosystem as much as possible.

The decision whether or not an ecosystem leader should share particular pieces of knowledge is not always so clear cut. The potential benefits of sharing knowledge in the hope of improving the performance of the ecosystem as a whole will need to be weighed up against the advantages of keeping it proprietary and allowing the ecosystem leader to capture the benefits itself. And these trade-offs don't apply only to the leader; the partners in the ecosystem will also be making similar decisions about when it makes sense to share their innovations with the ecosystem and when to keep it for themselves.

Recall how 2nd Watch shared some of its innovations about how to migrate IT functions to the cloud with its partners in the AWS ecosystem. It could be argued that 2nd Watch should have kept the knowledge proprietary; by publishing it, it may have helped its competitors in the ecosystem. However, 2nd Watch adopted the view that the benefits of sharing outweighed the disadvantages. Sharing its innovations helped popularize the idea of moving the IT function to the cloud and demonstrated that it could be done quickly. That accelerated the growth of the market for cloud migration services. Potential competitors may have benefited, but so did 2nd Watch. Besides, publishing the new ideas first helped establish 2nd Watch as one of the pioneers in the field. Exhibit 7.1 lays out these trade-offs for the ecosystem leader and also its partners Each of the parties in the ecosystem can potentially generate new knowledge, but then need to decide whether they will benefit more by sharing that knowledge or keeping it proprietary. In arriving at a decision, they must take into account the fact that the ecosystem is a dynamic system. As we will discuss in chapter 10, ecosystems may evolve, and thus the choices may also evolve over time. What seems proprietary today may become a common good later.

As exhibit 7.1 illustrates, knowledge shared by one partner may enable innovation by others, which can stimulate further learning and innovation in the ecosystem. Sharing new knowledge can thus ignite a spiral of innovation across the ecosystem, helping it grow faster and create new value, benefitting all the participants. On the other hand, if the ecosystem leader or the partner decides to keep the knowledge proprietary, it may be able to use it to improve its own business and extract more profits.

If this process is managed well within the ecosystem, it can create a powerful, virtuous cycle of sharing and additional knowledge creation. When

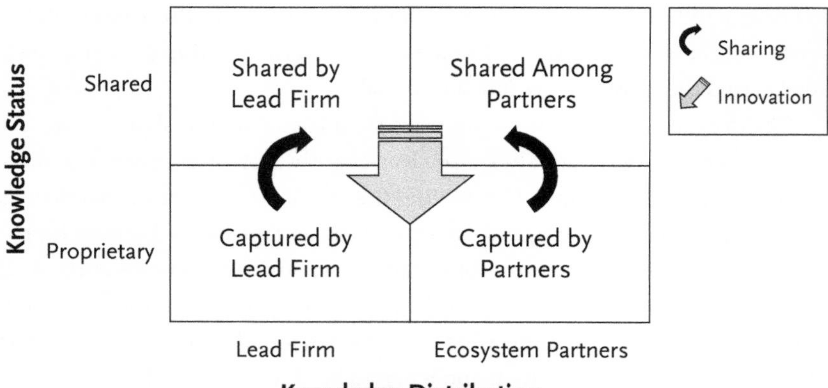

EXHIBIT 7.1. Proprietary and Shared Knowledge in an Ecosystem. Source: authors' research.

Alibaba, for example, shares knowledge about demand patterns with its logistics partners, it encourages them to invest in new IT systems and algorithms to optimize distribution. That helps improve the efficiency of distribution partners as well as customers' satisfaction-levels. The logistics partners' innovations also generate better data about the sellers' performance in terms of how quickly and reliably they had an item ready to be picked up as well as data about customer returns. Alibaba then accesses that data on the sellers' service levels, and uses it to create proprietary indicators of their competitiveness and health. These indicators can be combined to produce unique credit scores that are much more accurate than those relying on standard financial measures. They can also be continually updated in real time.

By leveraging the data generated by its ecosystem in this way, Alibaba has built a highly profitable new business, Sesame Credit. Its competitive advantage is the ability to generate reliable assessments of creditworthiness of small- and medium-sized borrowers who lack a credit history, which it can sell to potential lenders who would otherwise struggle to assess the likelihood that they would be repaid.

This cycle of new knowledge creation, sharing and innovation in any ecosystem can act as a powerful driver of new revenue and profit opportunities for partners as knowledge moves back and forth between them. One of the unique strengths of an ecosystem is precisely its capacity to have a higher level of sharing of the ecosystem goods, because ecosystem partners realize that the potential for innovation for all is enhanced through this sharing.

Unleashing Innovation in the Ecosystem

The success of an ecosystem ultimately depends on its ability to innovate. The diversity of partners, in terms of their capabilities, activities, and the different environments in which they operate an ecosystem, creates the potential to generate greater and faster innovation than is possible for any company acting alone. The ecosystem leader can play a critical role in helping realize this potential, both for its own benefit and that of the ecosystem. To achieve this as an ecosystem leader, you need to answer the following questions:

1. What kind of mechanisms do I create to encourage the flow of new knowledge into the ecosystem that would enable innovation?
2. How do I use the data and knowledge coming from the partners in the ecosystem to enhance my own innovation?
3. What structures, processes and incentives do I need to set up to facilitate innovation among my ecosystem partners?
4. How do I promote sharing of the knowledge the ecosystem generates to stimulate even more innovation in the ecosystem?
5. How do I convince my ecosystem partners that by sharing information they can create "ecosystem goods" that can be used to benefit the whole ecosystem without disadvantaging themselves?
6. Have I got the right balance between the knowledge I share with partners in order to benefit the ecosystem and the knowledge I keep proprietary to reinforce my power in the ecosystem and my ability to generate profits?

8 Monetization

Working Out How and Where to Take Your Profits

MOST OF OUR DISCUSSION SO FAR HAS BEEN FOCUSED ON the key question of how you can go on creating new value by catalyzing, fostering, and shaping the development of your ecosystem as its leader. That might be a worthy goal in itself. But for your shareholders to benefit, finding a way to monetize your ecosystem is obviously also essential. In this chapter we explain how and where you can draw a growing stream of profits from your ecosystem and how to profit from an ecosystem in a sustainable way, nurturing your monetization engine rather than choking it, so that profits keep flowing.

The first point to recognize is that successfully developing your ecosystem and creating value is a necessary, but not sufficient, condition for delivering profits. You can lead the creation of a huge and vibrant ecosystem and still not earn a cent from it. In the world of ecosystems, leadership is no guarantee of riches. This cruel fact is nowhere better illustrated than in IBM's experience with the personal computer (PC) business. We can avoid this trap by understanding how and why IBM fell into it.

Before IBM launched its first PC in 1981, the market for home computers was chaotic and competitive. Over the preceding twelve months, more than fifty companies had launched home computers, each with its own standards, protocols, and operating systems.[1] IBM's entry started transforming the industry almost immediately. Its reputation and relationships with American business ensured that the IBM PC became an instant hit.

For several years, there was, in fact, a shortage of IBM PCs because the company was unable to keep up with demand. Other computer-manufacturers, such as Columbia Data Products, Eagle Computer, and Compaq, stepped in to fill the breach by offering the next best thing: machines that were more or less IBM compatible.[2] There were other suppliers too, like DEC, HP, and Olivetti, but all soon moved toward compatibility with the combination of IBM PC architecture, Microsoft's MS-DOS operating system, and the Intel processors that had begun to emerge as an ecosystem. Less than a year after IBM chose Microsoft's MS-DOS as its operating system, Microsoft had licensed MS-DOS to over seventy other companies.[3]

Over the next few years, start-ups flocked to join IBM's ecosystem, along with more established players. Some, such as Tecmar, Quadram, and AST Research, are long-forgotten names. However, other partners in the ecosystem like Compaq, which was subsequently acquired by HP for $25 billion, and of course Microsoft, grew in size and importance.[4] By mid-1984, 75 percent of all the software being written for home computers was for IBM PC- and DOS-compatible machines.[5] The IBM-compatible architecture had established itself as the "dominant design" in the PC industry and the ecosystem around it had become the most powerful force in the market. In fact, IBM's ecosystem became so dominant that *Creative Computing* magazine observed, "You don't ask whether a new machine is fast or slow, new technology or old. The first question is, "Is it PC compatible?"[6] Within a few years of the introduction of PC clones, almost all rival PC architectures had disappeared. Only a few home computers, such as the Apple II series, survived. IBM had established itself as the undisputed leader of the PC-compatible ecosystem.

In many ways, IBM, working in partnership with Microsoft and Intel, was an exemplary ecosystem leader. Just as we recommended in chapter 5, it provided a framework within which the ecosystem could improve its efficiency and grow. This covered everything from the choice of the chip through to the interfaces (such as the system bus), right down to the video controllers—as well as the operating system. Initially, this kind of leadership of the ecosystem seemed to be enough to deliver profits: IBM was making good money on its sales of PCs. However, by 1985, the PC shortage ended.[7] A wave of inexpensive compatible machines, and in some instances even clones produced by American and Asian companies, flooded the market, causing prices to plummet. By the end of 1986, it was possible to buy a PC that matched the performance of a $1,600 IBM PC for as little as $600—or almost a third.[8] IBM's profit margins collapsed. IBM may still have been leading the ecosystem, but it had no ability to successfully monetize it. It was a cruel irony that at least two of its major partners, Microsoft and Intel, remained highly profitable while continuing to rely on IBM's leadership for many aspects of the ecosystem.

IBM's ability to profit from its PC ecosystem never recovered. Fifteen years later, in 2001, IBM lost $397 million in the PC business. Its losses continued in 2002 and 2003, and after losing $139 million on PC sales of $5.2 billion in the first half of 2004, it decided to get rid of the PC business. On May 1, 2005, IBM sold its PC business to the giant Chinese computer manufacturer, Lenovo Group, for $1.25 billion. In the Securities and Exchange Commission filing associated with the sale, IBM was forced to disclose that "the [PC] business has a history of recurring losses, negative working capital, and an accumulated deficit."[9]

IBM's experience is a powerful reminder that successful leadership of your ecosystem does not necessarily result in a profitable business. Despite leading the development of a PC ecosystem that created enormous value for customers and partners, a firm was unsuccessful in finding sustainable ways to monetize its position as an ecosystem leader. Monetization is one of the toughest challenges that faces any ecosystem leader.

Three Keys to Successful Monetization

Ecosystem leaders need to take specific measures to secure sustainable profit streams from the ecosystems they help create. After analyzing several ecosystems in different industries—some sustainably profitable, others chronically loss making—we have identified three keys to unlocking the profits in ecosystems. See exhibit 8.1.

One, as we analyzed in chapter 3, the ecosystem must be able to create offerings that deliver more value to the end user than any company can single-handedly provide. If the ecosystem cannot deliver additional value at a price that customers are willing to pay, there will not be any surplus to share. Ecosystems must create and grow the proverbial pie before carving it up. Therefore, you need a vision of the unique value the ecosystem can create, and a strategy to realize this vision, with the help of partners.

All the successful ecosystems we have described until now delivered new types of value to customers. Amazon and Alibaba delivered value in the form of greater convenience, more choice, and competitive prices. ARM's

1. Your strategy must ensure that the ecosystem delivers more value to the end user than any company can single-handedly provide.
2. You need to identify a keystone: some element of or activity in the ecosystem that you can own and control, on which the ecosystem's ability to create value for customers depends.
3. You must set up the right tollgates in the right places, through which you can collect a share of the customer value that the ecosystem creates.

EXHIBIT 8.1. Monetizing Value. Source: authors' research.

ecosystem delivered a flexible, lower-cost, lower-risk solution to the needs of mobile handset makers than Intel alone could offer. For athenahealth, it is a software bundle offered to doctors and medical practices at a price that no other company can. DS created customized PLM systems for a wide range of very different industries.

Two, to extract profits from your ecosystem, you need to find what Iansiti and Levin in their early, influential book on ecosystems called a "keystone." This is some element of, or activity in, the ecosystem's value creation system that you can own and control, on which the ecosystem's ability to create value for customers is dependent. Without that element, the ecosystem cannot satisfy its customers—just as a dome would collapse without its keystone.[10] The keystone ensures the ecosystem will continue to need you. Part of the reason for IBM's inability to sustainably monetize the PC-compatible ecosystem was its lack of such a keystone. While IBM provided many elements that helped the ecosystem to thrive, including the overall architecture and the specifications for many of the interfaces between components, it lacked a proprietary component that other participants would need to buy in order to serve their own customers.

To provide a sustainable flow of profits, the keystone needs to satisfy certain conditions. These are the same four conditions strategy theorist Jay Barney concluded that a resource must satisfy before it can underpin a sustainable competitive advantage: it must be valuable, rare, non-substitutable, and hard to imitate.[11] Only then can you use the keystone to extract profit reliably.

As we saw, ARM's chip intellectual property (IP) satisfies these conditions for a viable keystone. It is an important contributor to the value the ecosystem provides to the customer, it is rare, and there is barely an alternative for it. Switching to an alternative would entail participants reinvesting heavily in training and tools and processes, which makes substitution an expensive proposition. In that sense, the participants in the ecosystem are held hostage by ARM's chip designs. For that profit to keep flowing, the ecosystem leader's keystone must also be hard to imitate. If it could be easily copied, other companies able to provide an adequate imitation would soon supplant a profitable ecosystem leader. Here again, ARM's IP scores. To imitate ARM's chip designs would require access to a large stock of accumulated knowledge, and access to complex knowledge about the technological road maps of handset makers and semiconductor manufacturers. These are only available from close and trusting relationships, which are typically slow and costly to build.

Three, you need to set up tollgates through which you can collect a share of the customer value that the ecosystem creates. To be profitable as an ecosystem leader, you need to create a mechanism that will allow you to charge for the keystone you contribute to the ecosystem. That mechanism—think of it as the design of a tollgate—may take the form of license fees, royalties, commissions on transactions that take place in the ecosystem, or a share of the profits on sales of products or services the ecosystem partners supply. The tolls need to be efficiently collected. Participants should hardly notice they are paying them. This will reduce the likelihood of them trying to bypass the tollgates.

Tolls based on the activity in the ecosystem give the ecosystem leader an inbuilt accelerator to grow its profits as the ecosystem expands. For instance, ARM monetizes its contributions to the ecosystem through one-off license fees paid by ecosystem participants as well as customers who want the right to its proprietary IP. ARM also charges a royalty on the sale of every unit of the devices embodying its designs. Thus, ARM derives a double benefit as the ecosystem expands: Its revenues and profits grow when new participants join the ecosystem, as well as when as existing partners grow their sales.

Now compare that with IBM's original PC ecosystem. IBM laid out the ecosystem's architecture, interfaces, and protocols, but it lacked an effective tollgate through which it could capture a share of the profits generated by the ecosystem. Its leadership and contributions clearly created value for all the participants, including users, but it was difficult for IBM to collect a license fee for its contributions. The architecture, for example, was difficult to capture in a single bundle that IBM could license to participants. When IBM tried to protect its IP and designs, the IBM-compatible makers found substitutes that allowed them to bypass IBM's tollgates. Both Intel and Microsoft, by contrast, contributed IP that could be bundled into discrete components: the central processing unit and the operating system, respectively, which were essential to the system's functionality. Intel's CPU and Microsoft's MS-DOS were perfect for tollgates; it was almost impossible to navigate around them. Consequently, IBM led the PC ecosystem, but Intel and Microsoft collected billions of dollars of tolls from the other participants.

Focus on Growing the Size of the Profit "Pie"

In our experience, when executives start thinking about monetization in the context of an ecosystem, they focus on carving up the profit pie. They worry about who is siphoning profits out of the ecosystem, how they can increase their shares, and where they should focus to maximize profitability.

That logic makes sense in the context of a traditional supply chain, where prices and volumes are set by the market, making monetization a zero-sum game. That is, if one participant gets more, someone must get less. However, these are the wrong questions in the context of an ecosystem, where companies choose to align with partners in order to create more customer value and expand the potential for profits. As we have seen throughout this book, successful ecosystem leaders try to attract more customers, encourage more investments, and stimulate more innovation in the ecosystem. Those dynamics generate more customer value and increase the size of the ecosystem's profits pool. Therefore, the first step in successfully monetizing your ecosystem is to make sure that you focus relentlessly on increasing the size of the pie. This should be the primary consideration in every decision you take.

Indeed, the focus on creating additional value should be so single-minded that it must exclude worrying about the distribution of the value between partners. That seems counterintuitive, but think again. Does it harm ARM's prospects of monetization if it takes a decision that will increase the profits that semiconductor manufacturers earn? Will Amazon's ability to monetize shrink if it finds a way to reduce the costs and increase the profits for the online sellers on its platform? The answer is a resounding "no." On the contrary, these actions are likely to encourage partners to invest more in, and expand, the ecosystem. In the process, ARM and Amazon will create the opportunity to capture additional profits from their ecosystems, which will become larger and more robust. Moreover, the ecosystems will be more attractive to partners and more competitive against rival ecosystems. As a result, their possibilities for monetization will be further enhanced.

Ecosystem leadership is about creating the conditions for a positive-sum game, where the sum of the winnings and the losses are greater than zero. It does not matter how much your partners benefit from any action you take as leader. The factor that decides whether any initiative makes sense is simple: Will it benefit the future monetization engine by making the ecosystem larger, more competitive, or more valuable to customers?

In the world of ecosystems, a strategy that focuses on the division of the pie risks the network being stillborn. Trying to restrict the amount of money partners make is only likely to discourage them from joining the ecosystem or, if they are already partners, investing and innovating in it. Instead, ecosystem leaders must want them to be as successful as possible in creating value for the consumer.

There is however an important caveat. As the leader of an ecosystem, you cannot tolerate partners that milk the ecosystem of more value than they generate. If they did so, they would be squeezing the lifeblood out of the ecosystem. One of the leader's roles, as we saw in chapter 6, is to weed out free riders who are damaging the ecosystem by siphoning off disproportionate amounts of value compared to what they are creating.

Securing Your Keystone Role

The next prerequisite for successfully monetizing the value that an ecosystem creates is to secure your keystone role so that you can go on extracting profits, year after year. To put it another way, you need to find a site for your tollgate that cannot easily be bypassed. That usually starts with one or more proprietary pieces of IP or other assets that the ecosystem needs in order to create value for customers: the initial keystone. To see in practical terms what that keystone looks like, it is worth revisiting the qualities a keystone needs to underpin a sustainable stream of profits.

The ecosystem leader needs to identify a keystone asset that helps the ecosystem generate value and is embodied in something that other participants in the ecosystem have to buy: a component, a design, or a service. It cannot be a public or ecosystem good that anyone can access without paying for it. Ecosystem leaders may need to provide ecosystem goods to facilitate the working of the ecosystem, such as interface protocols or shared knowledge—but if they want to monetize the ecosystem, their keystone contribution needs to be something they can own and sell to others.

We also saw that the ecosystem leader's keystone—the core component, design, service, or other form of intellectual property that it contributes—needs to be something that is hard to copy. For instance, Amazon contributes excellent logistics infrastructure and software to its ecosystem. ARM offers its proprietary, low-power reduced instruction set chip architectures. For athenahealth, it is cloud-based billing and practice-management software. And DS has a number of very powerful proprietary algorithms that enable fast design and simulation. All of these four different types of keystone contributions are essential for the ecosystem to deliver value to customers and are difficult to copy. They are underpinned by proprietary IP and, importantly, years of accumulated knowledge and experience.

Even when backed by proprietary IP, however, no keystone can sustain an attractive flow of profits forever. Any contribution to an ecosystem can eventually be copied or substituted, given enough resources and time. Therefore, you need to update and evolve your keystone so that it can generate new and unique sources of value that participants in the ecosystem will continue to pay for.

Remember the case of Nokia, the leading supplier of mobile phones in the 1990s and 2000s. It contributed a number of key elements—such as expertise in wireless antennae, signal processing, and high-resolution camera technology—during the rise of its mobile phone ecosystem after 1990. Nokia and its ecosystem became so dominant that by the fourth quarter of 2008, it accounted for over 40 percent of all the mobile phones sold in the world.[12] However, Nokia's key contributions had been imitated or bypassed by then. That is why its newly appointed CEO, Steve Elop, wrote to the company's employees in his very first memo: "I have learned that we are standing on a burning platform. And we have more than one explosion—we have multiple points of scorching heat that are fueling a blazing fire around us."[13] Nokia missed the boat on smartphones after Apple launched its iPhone in 2007, when it had the technical capabilities to produce smartphones. In fact, it had designed some precursors to smartphones in the late 1990s, but it never fully understood the need to renew what it offered to its ecosystem. Another shortcoming in Nokia's strategy proved just as critical: its failure to recognize that, because app developers were by then powerful potential partners in its ecosystem, it had to create a keystone these developers would need to pay for if they were to continue to participate. Apple created such a keystone in the form of its App Store. Without this vital element, through which it could control app developers' access to the ecosystem and collect a toll, Nokia no longer offered the ecosystem with something unavailable from elsewhere. In a few years, Nokia almost completely disappeared from the market, and what was left of its mobile phone business was sold to Microsoft in April 2014.

Having a keystone that enables you to "charge a toll" is clearly essential. However, no keystone will last forever. Thus, you need to be constantly updating and extending the value proposition on which your keystone is based.

The Role—and Limitations—of Scale in Sustaining Your Profit Stream

The larger the scale of the ecosystem that you as ecosystem leader can catalyze around your keystone, the greater will be the size of the profit pool available to you. As in any business activity, greater scale results in lower costs. ARM can amortize the costs of designing a new architecture more effectively than any other company can because its designs became the global standard. Amazon has achieved such massive scale that it gets the best prices—and more—from its suppliers. The scale of its ecosystem enables it to support warehouses around the country, spread the fixed costs of state-of-the-art automation, invest in advanced software that optimizes its logistics, set inventory levels, and enable the prediction of customer orders so that stock can be locally positioned in advance.

Scale also makes the ecosystem more attractive to customers and partners because of network economies, as we have shown in earlier chapters. These include a greater choice of products and services and a lower risk of being stuck in a dead-end technology. By making it more attractive to stick with the ecosystem, rather than defect, the advantages of scale help protect the ecosystem leader's monetization engine. For instance, no mobile telephone OEM would take the risk of using a competing RISC-chip architecture as long as the license fees and royalties that ARM charges remain reasonable. Doing so would reduce that OEM's choice of semiconductor fabricators; necessitate investments in nonstandard development tools and training; and run the risk of disappearing into a technological cul-de-sac not supported by complementary hardware, software, or services. Likewise, even if Amazon chose to charge a premium, customers in the United States would continue to use it to enjoy the wider choice and greater convenience Amazon's scale allows it as compared to other e-commerce ecosystems. Ecosystem scale thus underpins higher margins and a flow of profits for the ecosystem leader.

However, even scale cannot guarantee the sustainable monetization of an ecosystem. Netscape's Navigator rose to become the biggest ecosystem in internet search with a market share of over 86 percent by May 1996.[14] Just two years later, Microsoft's Internet Explorer ecosystem had decimated Netscape's leadership, bagging an estimated 96 percent share of browser usage. A key factor in the decline of Netscape's ecosystem was a technological disruption in the form of Cascading Style Sheets (CSS), which enabled visually engaging webpages to be downloaded more efficiently compared with JavaScript. Internet Explorer was also helped by the fact that it was bundled into every copy of Microsoft's Windows operating system, which had a 90-plus percent share of the desktop operating system market at the time.

This pattern was repeated in the second round of the browser wars. Scale again proved ineffective in protecting the dominance of the established ecosystem, when, this time, Internet Explorer was dethroned. A new business model disrupted its ecosystem and monetization processes when Google introduced its free Chrome browser in December 2008. Google pioneered the concept of rapid releases, launching seven versions of Chrome over the next year. The result was a relentless hemorrhaging of Internet Explorer's users and partners. By May 2012, Google's Chrome had overtaken Internet Explorer, and has since gone on to capture almost 60 percent of web browser usage while Internet Explorer has declined to less than 20 percent.[15] By 2018, Microsoft had pretty much killed Explorer, and replaced it with Edge in Windows 10.

Using Your Position in the Ecosystem to Accelerate Innovation and Renew Your Keystone

If cementing a keystone and reaping the benefits of ecosystem scale are insufficient to maintain a stream of profits for the ecosystem leader over the long run, what else is required? In every case we have studied where the ecosystem leader has been able to sustain its profit stream, it has done so by using the ecosystem to accumulate fresh knowledge that allows it to renew its keystone asset. As ecosystem leader, you have a unique perspective on what is going on inside it. That enables you to learn from developments right across your ecosystem. Capturing and redeploying what you can learn from the ecosystem enables you to keep on innovating faster and more effectively than rivals, as well as any would-be usurpers among your partners.

However, this does not happen without effort. As the ecosystem leader, you need to focus relentlessly on how you can leverage the ecosystem to accumulate a rich haul of new data and knowledge. You then need to make sure you have the processes in place to act on what you have learned, using it to innovate, renew your keystone contribution, and strengthen your position in the ecosystem.

In e-commerce ecosystems, such as those led by Alibaba and Amazon, the flow of transactions provides the ecosystem leader with a treasure-trove of information about everything from the behavior of buyers and sellers to variations in prices, volumes, and geographic hotspots across a range of products and services. The key to sustainable monetization lies in using this knowledge generated by the ecosystem to innovate faster and more effectively than others do.

We have already seen numerous examples of how ecosystem leaders can do this. As we mentioned earlier, Alibaba's Taobao Ke uses data from over five hundred thousand websites to adjust the advertising and offers that a user would view when logging in, depending on their location, time of day, and previous purchase history. Alibaba leveraged what it had learned from Alipay about the sellers on its sites, which covered everything from their revenues and returns to discounts and customer satisfaction ratings, in order to develop a new business through Ant Financial. Based on the same data procured from sellers' e-commerce operations, Ant Financial extends loans to small- and medium-size businesses that lack credit histories. From its network of health care clients and partners, athenahealth was able to draw data that helped it to establish the MDP Accelerator, which assists start-ups with expertise and market intelligence to overcome the barriers in joining its marketplace, thereby fueling the growth of revenues and profits in its ecosystem. Similarly, Thomson Reuters used the data it accumulated from the farmers to develop more accurate forecasts for crop volumes and prices.

All these innovations were only possible because of the ecosystem leaders' unique position as data and knowledge aggregators. As we discussed earlier, some data and knowledge must be shared with partners in order to maintain the health and vitality of the ecosystem, while some of it needs to be kept proprietary so that the leader can play the keystone role that underpins its flow of profits from the ecosystem. Making the right decision starts by developing an understanding of the keystone role, and understanding precisely which proprietary data and knowledge are necessary to preserve that role.

When making the decision of what data to share, a useful rule of thumb is to share information that flows through the interfaces in the ecosystem but keep proprietary the data and knowledge gleaned about the behavior of your partners. It is the latter that will enable you to innovate and renew your keystone contribution to the ecosystem. Alibaba, for example, has massive amounts of data about the identity of particular shipments and their whereabouts at any point in time. They readily share this with their partners, be it the logistics providers, insurers, or the suppliers and end customers. What they do not share, though, is information on the behavior of buyers and sellers. Keeping this proprietary helps Alibaba maintain their unique contribution to the ecosystems, ranging from ensuring website optimization to evaluating credit worthiness, and innovation in these ongoing keystone contributions enables them to sustain their profit stream.

Designing Your Tollgates

The right type of tollgates will be different for every ecosystem leader, but there are a few principles that can help you design effective and efficient tollgates and work out where to site them in the ecosystem. The most common menu of alternatives the ecosystem leader can choose from includes license fees, royalties and transactions fees, selling data value-added services, and using data and knowledge to create new profit streams. In what follows, we look at the pros and cons of each.

License Fees

The most obvious tollgate mechanism is to charge a fee from companies that wish to join the ecosystem. ARM, for instance, charges a license fee for the use of their chip designs. However, a joining fee has one disadvantage: It acts as a barrier to new entrants that may impede the ecosystem's growth. So, while it is appropriate to charge a license fee when the benefits they gain are immediate and easily identifiable, doing so may dissuade potentially valuable partners from joining the ecosystem if they perceive the benefits to be less immediate. ARM has dealt with this challenge by charging a lump-sum license fee from its semiconductor partners, but at the same time providing tools and information for free to help developers that can use the ARM chip architecture. As we saw earlier, it licenses early-stage and start-up companies differently, recognizing their potential to become important partners. That reduces the hurdles to using ARM's technology even as it allows fledgling companies to conserve their resources.

In most e-commerce ecosystems, the leaders, such as Alibaba and Amazon, provide access to sellers, buyers, and service providers free of any license or sign-up fees. That is because scale is critical for competing with e-commerce ecosystems. These ecosystem leaders, therefore, have located tollgates elsewhere to minimize the entry barriers. Apple is the sole exception; it charges $99 a year to list an app on the Apple App Store.[16] Its strong, if not dominant, market share of the smartphone market no doubt provides it with the power to do so.

Royalties and Transactions Fees

Positioning the tollgate so that the ecosystem leader can profit from the volume of activity in the ecosystem by charging royalties or transaction fees has the added advantage of aligning the leader with its partners' success. Royalties, and other transactions-based monetization engines, embody a simple, but powerful proposition: the more the partner earns, the more the ecosystem leader earns. ARM, for instance, collects a royalty on every chip that uses its architectures (sixteen billion chips in 2016), in addition to the license fees it charges.[17] Likewise, athenahealth has moved its tollgates from selling software as a service to charging a commission on transactions, such as health insurers' reimbursements, flowing through its ecosystem.

Amazon's tollgates also work on the volumes of activity in its ecosystem. It makes a profit on all the products it sells from its inventory and collects a percentage of the sales price as a transaction fee on products sold by other retailers through its portal. Its Amazon Web Services ecosystem levies a fee for each byte of data transferred to and from its services, as well as a monthly fee for every gigabyte of storage used.[18]

Alibaba's tollgates work differently. On its Taobao marketplace, which is designed for small merchants, no fees are charged from the sellers or buyers, as the objective here is to attract as many of them as possible and encourage them to transact frequently. However, on its Tmall e-commerce site, set up to appeal to major brands and larger retailers, Alibaba charges annual listing fees as well as sales commissions. That reflects the value that brands get in terms of exposure and sales from appearing on the site. As the Tmall ecosystem accounts for 56 percent of online shopping in China, brands have little option but to have a presence there.

The main potential downside of royalties and fees based on transaction volume is that customers and partners may extrapolate the total amounts they would end up paying in the future if their businesses grows, and take fright. The solution here for an ecosystem leader is to reinforce the point that the amount they are paying will only grow large if they are wildly successful, in which case they should be happy to reward the contribution made toward their success.

Selling Value-Added Services

The tollgate does not have to be situated at the entry to the ecosystem, nor does it have to depend on the activities that flow through it. Some ecosystem leaders monetize their investments by selling value-added services to participants; attracting customers and partners opens up the potential for additional services that they are willing to pay for. For example, Taobao's over ten million sellers may well want to pay fees to improve their rankings on Taobao's search engine. Similarly, The Guardian's n0tice enabled users to place classified advertisements free, but The Guardian earns revenues by selling value-added services such as featured positions on the site or bigger advertisements.

Selling value-added services has the added advantage of helping potential partners to keep down the costs of their initial engagement with the ecosystem. However, this type of tollgate may make partners loath to deepen their engagement with the ecosystem, thereby limiting the potential opportunities for it to create new value.

Using Data and Knowledge to Create New Profit Streams

One of the most fertile sources of new profit streams is the data and knowledge that a leader is uniquely placed to capture. As we described earlier, Thomson Reuters developed an important new revenue stream by providing traders with improved forecasts based on the real-time, granular crop data it incentivized farmers to provide to the ecosystem.

Alibaba went a step further when it created the Taobao Ke revenue stream. It agreed with owners of third-party sites, ranging from social clubs to those providing transport schedules, to carry a link that would direct potential customers to Taobao stores. By aggregating and analyzing user data from websites that were part of the ecosystem, Alibaba was able to distil unique insights about how, when, and from where buyers arrived at sellers' virtual shopfronts. Alibaba then suggested optimal links to both Taobao storeowners and websites. In exchange for improving the quality and volume of click-throughs, the owner of the shop paid Alibaba a commission of 10 percent of the gross sales revenues when a lead came from the website. Of this commission received, 90 percent was passed on to the owner of the website through which the customer originally entered the ecosystem, with Alibaba retaining the remaining 10 percent (or 1 percent of the gross sales revenue). The toll on sales may have been low, but with five hundred million to one billion users clicking on Taobao Ke every day, Alibaba was receiving a substantial new revenue stream.

An ecosystem can also provide its leader with a wealth of insights, other than data, that can be monetized. ARM's business, for example, consists primarily in designing chip architectures for mobile phones. However, in the course of working with partners such as Qualcomm and Freescale, ARM learned about the emerging demand for tablet computers. Using that insight, complemented by what it had learned from other partners and some internal know-how, ARM was able to design new chip architectures for tablets. When the market took off after the release of Apple's iPad (which included ARM chips), a fresh revenue stream opened. ARM has since entered a series of new application markets such as chip designs that can be used in cars and in health care, infrastructure, and wearable devices. Its next goal is to use the knowledge it draws from its existing ecosystems to become a major player in the Internet of Things (IoT) that is starting to connect billions of devices and machines around the world.

Using data and knowledge to create new profit streams is mostly pure upside. The only downside risk is the potential competition with partners who are looking to pursue similar profit opportunities, which may cause friction within the ecosystem.

Nurturing Your Monetization Engine

The final consideration when designing ways to best monetize your position and investment in the ecosystem is the need to capture profits without damaging its future. The temptation to maximize profits today at the risk of jeopardizing future profitability is an ever-present danger. As an ecosystem leader, you must always remember that companies join ecosystems out of their own self-interest—not because of a fiat. They too need to earn acceptable returns; otherwise, they will leave the fold.

As we highlighted in chapter 5, it is essential that the ecosystem leader encourages partners to invest in enhancing the ecosystem so that everyone in the system benefits. All the ecosystem leaders we have studied have had mental approximations of how much profit they could draw without impairing their ecosystem's effectiveness and constraining its potential, and with it, their own. In some cases, their guidepost was a ceiling on the percentage of commissions, royalties, and transaction fees they thought it would be possible to charge without choking their monetization engines. In other cases, the ceiling was subject to precise analysis, such as working out exactly how much a partner would be willing to pay per unit based on the projected volumes, before it would become more economical to leave the ecosystem and take the work in-house. In yet other cases, the boundaries were drawn based more on informed guesswork.

Given that most transactions, activities, and partnerships where the ecosystem leaders erect tollgates are subject to some kind of ceiling, the leaders must diversify their revenue sources. That means designing multiple tollgates at different points in the ecosystem. Each one can then levy a smaller toll. Many of the ecosystems we analyzed, such as Alibaba, Amazon, ARM, and Thomson Reuters, generated profits from their ecosystems without inflicting too much pain on partners or customers by using multiple tollgates that they positioned at different points, each collecting a small fee.

Designing your monetization engine so revenues and profits grow as the ecosystem prospers and expands is also a good principle to adopt. Doing so avoids burdening the ecosystem with large fixed costs, which is especially important when it is small and underdeveloped.

Another rule of thumb is to vary the charges between participants, subsidizing some and demanding a higher proportion of the value created from others. It is in the interest of the leader to collect lower tolls from those who contribute enormously or those who derive less value, but nonetheless play a useful role in contributing to the health and success of the ecosystem. Alibaba, for example, invites small sellers on Taobao to join for free, with the option to buy value-added services, while large retailers on Tmall pay a substantial listing fee as well as commissions.

Questions You Should Ask Yourself When You Design a Monetization Strategy

Although the ecosystem leader needs to focus first on enabling the ecosystem to create value for its customers and engage with a growing number of diverse partners, the end-goal is to establish a sustainable stream of future profits. The leader faces a major challenge in finding ways to reliably monetize the contribution it makes to the ecosystem while maintaining its health and vitality.

In coming up with a viable monetization strategy, you need to answer the following questions:

1. Have you developed a credible strategy to enable the ecosystem to create more value than a company working alone by focusing on initiatives to grow the size of the value pie, rather than prematurely deciding how that pie is to be divided up?
2. Have you identified your "keystone" contribution to the ecosystem that is valuable, rare, non-substitutable, and hard to imitate, and so can enable you to extract a sustainable stream of profits in exchange for leading the ecosystem?
3. Once you have identified your keystone, how do you make sure it remains relevant by continually renewing the sources of value it generates, leveraging knowledge, and learning from across the ecosystem?
4. Have you put in place the right mix of tollgates through which to extract profits, including license fees, royalties and transaction fees, sales of value-adding services, and leveraging data and knowledge produced in the ecosystem?
5. Do you have the right balance between profiting from the ecosystem, investing in it, and damaging the ecosystem by "milking it dry"?

9 Leading an Ecosystem

How You and Your Organization Need to Change

NEW STRATEGIES, STRUCTURES, AND SYSTEMS ARE ALL NECESSARY to build ecosystem advantage, but people, particularly the CEOs who inspire, motivate, and direct them, make it all happen. Business leaders, such as Alibaba's Jack Ma, Dassault Systèmes' Bernard Charles, and ARM's Robin Saxby, galvanized their people as well as their partners to build profitable ecosystems. They guided their ecosystems from uncertain beginnings through the process of scaling up, and, in the face of a rapidly changing environment, innovated, flexed, and evolved their way to success. Their styles differ, but they share a number of common approaches and traits that we will describe in this chapter. In this way we will identify the essential characteristics of a successful ecosystem head.[1] We will also see how an ecosystem leader's organization needs to change and suggest how executives seeking to lead ecosystems need to rethink the way they measure success.

Leading an Ecosystem Begins with a Change in Mind-Set

Most management books extol the virtues of a leader who can define a clear mission for his or her company and unveil a strategy made up of detailed initiatives to achieve that goal. However, one of the powerful benefits of an ecosystem strategy is its ability to break free from the limitations of a well-defined goal and, instead, help realize an uncertain vision that creates value for customers and partners alike. Indeed, ecosystem CEOs seek to launch their businesses on another trajectory, going beyond what anyone in the company can imagine. Traditional leadership approaches based on command and control and traditional planning systems are therefore ill equipped for that challenge. A different approach is required.

Gaining ecosystem edge requires a radical change in mind-set of all, from the CEO down. In our interactions with dozens of ecosystem builders, we found that all, despite their different industries and starting points, shared four key beliefs (see exhibit 9.1) to a greater or lesser extent.

One, all had an unshakable conviction that there was an opportunity to create new customer value by creating an ecosystem. One of the most outspoken ecosystem heads is perhaps Jack Ma, Alibaba's cofounder and executive chairman, who was certain there was an opportunity to offer China's growing middle-class the benefits of greater convenience, more choice, and the ability to seek out the best prices by using e-commerce. Robin Saxby believed that ARM could save its customers money, offer them a wider choice of suppliers, and provide technical innovation faster, if it created the de facto global standard for RISC chips. Having revolutionized the book retail industry and then US retailing with Amazon, Jeff Bezos was convinced that there was an opportunity in offering companies infinitely scalable computing capacity and related services on a pay-only-for-what-you-use basis—an idea that became AWS. Like other entrepreneurs, these ecosystem builders were certain in their minds that they could create value even if the path to doing so was shrouded in fog. Despite numerous uncertainties, they pursued their vision with both eyes focused on the main opportunities.

The second belief the ecosystem builders share is an ever-growing conviction that no company acting alone can unlock the opportunity. All the CEOs we studied were certain that the challenges they faced could only be met by identifying, attracting, and harnessing the knowledge, capabilities, and innovation potential of partners. They also felt that the solution couldn't be found by slotting potential allies into well-defined roles in conventional supply chains.

Such a mind-set doesn't come naturally to most CEOs, especially in large, well-established companies. Their preference is to "do it ourselves" so that control and returns are assured. However, conventional thinking limits the benefits of the diverse mix of capabilities and knowledge that partners can bring to an ecosystem. It also squanders the opportunities for learning and innovation that are created when partners with different strengths interact with one

1. **Belief that there is an opportunity to create new value for potential customers**
2. **A deep conviction that no single company can unlock the value opportunity acting alone**
3. **A focus on attracting, engaging, and motivating people who are not necessarily their employees**
4. **A relentless focus on growing the size of the overall ecosystem pie**

EXHIBIT 9.1. Four Elements of the Mind-Set of a Successful Ecosystem CEO. Source: authors' research.

another. Even in a young company like Alibaba, the unexpected benefits of engaging with partners have brought Jack Ma and his leadership team to the point where, rather than asking how they can do something, they now instinctively pose the question: "Who out there can help us achieve our goal?"[2]

The third dimension of the mind-set of successful ecosystem builders is an unrelenting focus on attracting, engaging, and motivating people who aren't their employees. Every seasoned leader knows how to communicate a vision and a mission that their employees will buy into and motivate them to achieve it. However, the difference when leading an ecosystem is that most of the people you have to motivate and inspire don't work for you! Those who aspire to lead an ecosystem must always keep in mind that their role involves leading and motivating people across the network—not just the employees of their company. Leaders building and operating an ecosystem must invest a considerable amount of time to engage with, educate, and motivate people working for their partners (a task that we will discuss a little later in this chapter). It isn't surprising, then, that each of ARM's executive directors has been assigned the task of working with the leaders of one of its critical partners.

The fourth, and final, belief of those successfully leading an ecosystem is their undiluted focus on growing the size of the pie. Getting the best deal for their companies from customers and suppliers helps most executives rise through the ranks. Their approach is that business is a zero-sum game: for us to get more, others need to get less. Such a mentality hinders the successful creation and operation of an ecosystem. Ecosystem builders must stay focused first, and foremost, on how to create a positive-sum game, where no one has to win at someone else's expense. Maximizing the value that an ecosystem creates for all its participants needs to be the priority all the time.

As we mentioned several times now, the biggest benefits of ecosystem strategies are their ability to deliver more value, quicker innovation, and greater flexibility to respond to fast-changing environments than any company could attain by acting alone. The CEO needs to ensure that everyone understands that making that happen is "job one."

As we saw in the last chapter, if you grow the size of the pie, it doesn't matter if partners benefit even more than your own company does. In fact, that may well be a positive thing; the more success partners taste, the more you will benefit as the ecosystem leader. And there are measures you can track to judge the health, vitality, and success of the ecosystem, and the benefits your company gains as you build it. Those parameters can help develop a leadership style that looks beyond the performance of a single company and recognizes that the achievements of the ecosystem—in terms of the value it generates and the rate at which it is innovating and developing—are critical to future success. This is particularly true as the nature of competition shifts from rivalry between companies to competition between ecosystems, as we will discuss in chapter 10.

From Command and Control to Collaborative Leadership

Leadership styles that work when leading a company or a traditional supply chain, may prove to be unproductive, at best, or disastrous, at worst, when applied to an ecosystem comprising a complex network of different kinds of partners. This is because leadership is usually associated with power over people, as opposed to power *with* people. In traditional hierarchies, that's achieved by formal command-and-control structures backed by a charismatic leadership style, where the leader may attract followers to execute orders as per his or her wishes. Charisma may continue to play a role, but command-and-control isn't consistent with the fact that ecosystem builders have to rely on large numbers of people whom they don't employ.

To master the art of leading an ecosystem, CEOs have much to learn from Mary Parker Follett, the early twentieth-century social worker and management guru avant la lettre. She described management as the art of getting things done through people, and essentially believed in the power of people working together, as a community. She distinguished between bringing about change in a coercive fashion and a co-active manner, and saw leading a community as a creative process that could advance the group by constantly reframing the issues it faced.[3]

Follet's sage approach holds important lessons for ecosystem builders as they think about the challenges they face. Managing an ecosystem, quite clearly, demands collaborative leadership: a combination of the ability to work together, to listen, to influence, and to adapt flexibly rather than depending on commands and controls.[4] Leadership in an ecosystem is different from leading through power, expertise, charisma, or dogma. A leader in an ecosystem is often perceived to be the peer of those whom he or she leads, and must achieve results by stimulating collaboration with and between the company's partners in the ecosystem.

In our view, there are four key leadership skills required to lead an ecosystem: listening, adapting, influencing, and collaborating (or LAIC, for short).

Listening

Leaders practicing collaborative leadership recognize that they are not perfect. They need a team with complementary capabilities. Such capabilities may not always be very explicit, and the leader needs to make an effort to solicit team members to come forward. So, a collaborative leader needs to monitor his or her peers, whose signals may be weak and not codified. Ecosystem builders must watch out for these weak signals, so that they are aware of what's going on across the ecosystem.

Only leaders who take the time to get under the skin of their peers, respond quickly to their needs, and stiffen their partners' resolve in the face of uncertainties will succeed in guiding and building ecosystems. Collaborative leadership requires the capacity to build relationships, so that partners' CEOs can trust you, and each other, to take entrepreneurial actions in the face of change. All that requires enhancing the capacity to listen, empathize, and feel for those within the organization as well as partners in the ecosystem. The capacity to listen and hear other CEOs must be underpinned by the willingness to learn, and the confidence to accept that what others have to say may sometimes be more valuable than your own opinions.

Adapting

As we have argued earlier, companies build ecosystems because the world is becoming more uncertain and doing business is getting riskier than it used to be. There's relatively less protection now in the form of government regulation or information asymmetries. At the same time, innovation has become more complex because sources of information are getting more dispersed. The environment in which ecosystems need to be led has therefore become less predictable.

Leading an ecosystem thus demands the ability to adapt rapidly to changing circumstances. That is why ecosystem builders must rethink the very nature of the risks they face. Most CEOs regard ecosystems, which are in a continual state of flux and evolving in unpredictable ways, as a risk that must be mitigated. However, the flexibility to respond to an uncertain environment is one of the key strengths of an ecosystem.

Leading an ecosystem, therefore, is all about encouraging and nudging the network to respond flexibly, and not always demanding an adherence to established processes or norms of doing things. The major risk that leaders needs to tackle is the ecosystem's loss of vitality, which may cause it to stall. Effective ecosystem heads must accept the system's capacity for self-organization and coordinate investments to successfully create and capture value.

Influencing

Given the severe limitations of command-and-control systems in a business ecosystem, CEOs need to excel at influencing people, deploying the "soft power" that comes from vision, credibility, and evidence, to bolster their cases. Like peers in social networks and most knowledge workers, ecosystem partners usually want to be convinced about what they should do, and not told what to do. Partners often have their own insights, expertise, and entrepreneurial drive, so they want to be treated as equals. By dint of size or market position, ecosystem partners often expect to be a lot more powerful than the ecosystem leader. For example, many of the OEMs in ARM's ecosystem, such as Apple and Samsung, dwarf the company. If ARM tells them what to do, they may have good reason, data, and knowledge to disagree, especially in a world where the information that exists outside an organization is as valuable as internal data. Effective leaders in an ecosystem thus need the skills to influence partners without manipulating them, as that is bound to arouse resentment. By doing so, they can bring together a more diverse set of capabilities and experiences than exists in any company.

Collaborating

Finally, in an ecosystem, leadership is all about getting things done through a community of peers. Moving forward requires collaborating with partners to identify and unlock value, and to implement change. To be effective, CEOs must be able to promote continuous collaboration and learning between partners. They should convey an attractive vision of the opportunity that the ecosystem can grasp. Ecosystem builders cannot afford to act as brokers or go-betweens; they must put in place the structures and incentives to encourage their partners to work closely together.

These requirements mean that ecosystem CEOs must be willing to invest significant amounts of their own time in networking and promoting collaboration between other partners to create a virtuous cycle of engagement. Every engagement should stimulate and facilitate further collaboration. Collaboration is not always a natural act. Under pressure and confronted by shortages of time and budget, business leaders often prefer to isolate themselves from their networks, and implement initiatives themselves. Collaborative leadership demands that CEOs constantly guard against the temptation of going it alone.

Going beyond the Limitations of Collaborative Leadership

Listening, adapting, influencing, and collaborating (LAIC) are key leadership attributes required in ecosystems, but executives should not be blind to its inevitable limitations. Classic collaborative leadership also has downsides: listening may become dithering, influencing may become manipulation, collaboration may turn into procrastination, and adaptation may render the organization anchorless.

To complement principles of classic collaborative leadership in an ecosystem, four other leadership capabilities need to work in tandem: taking responsibility beyond your organization's borders, building consensus, developing social networks, and confronting the dilemmas that will inevitably arise in the ecosystem.

Responsibility beyond Borders

Smart ecosystem heads understand that their domain of responsibility doesn't stop at the boundaries of their organizations. In an ecosystem, organizational boundaries are fuzzy in terms of both authority and accountability. When an ecosystem fails to live up to the expectations of a consumer, he or she doesn't much care which nodes in the network were at fault. Like ministers in a cabinet or directors on a board, everyone shares responsibility equally. Consequently, ecosystem leaders become accountable for not only what happens inside their organizations, but also for how their partners behave and communicate. Ecosystem leadership requires CEOs to put in place the communication channels; monitoring systems; and, when necessary, the sanctions that enable them to lead an extensive hinterland of partners beyond the boundaries of their organizations.

Build Consensus

Acting through ecosystem partners requires getting most, if not all, of them to agree and take ownership of decisions before decisions can be implemented. Listening and influencing will come to naught unless consensus is achieved. Successful ecosystem heads put levers in place that enable them to build consensus in the ecosystem on everything, from the nature of the opportunity, through behaviors and values, to key initiatives.

However, the process of building consensus carries with it a risk: it can lead to the acceptance of the lowest common denominator, and suboptimal decisions.

Building consensus in an ecosystem is rendered difficult by one of its inherent strengths: diversity. Diversity typically enhances the quality of decision-making as long as executives accept and take on the cultural and contextual differences.[5] It's not effective to cover up the differences between individuals or companies out of a misplaced sense of respect or political correctness. Hence, leaders that enable their employees to confront and address their differences perform better than monocultural groups, as they benefit from the differences that diversity offers.

Those leading an ecosystem need to build consensus in ways that bring out the differences and the tensions in their networks. That will enhance creativity, innovation, and complementarity that is the raison d'être of every ecosystem.

Develop Your Social Networks

Effective ecosystem heads must be effective networkers. Developing a wide network will significantly enhance their ability to perform; it allows them to know better what is going on in, and beyond, their ecosystem. Jack Ma, Bernard Charles, and Robin Saxby are consummate networkers, who know how to build perceptions about themselves, how to manage status and relationships in the network, and how to develop the capabilities to spot information outside the ecosystem and link it back to their networks.

To sustain ecosystems, leaders need to contribute to their social networks as well as draw from them. Becoming a trusted source of knowledge and information builds their credibility, and acts as a quid pro quo for the benefits they gain from their relationships.

Confront Dilemmas

As we have already seen in previous chapters, leading in an ecosystem is fraught with dilemmas.[6] Should I keep the knowledge I learn from the ecosystem proprietary or share it with partners? Should I try to catalyze a new initiative myself or leave it to partners? When should I abandon an existing profit stream to partners and look to create a new one? The best approach is usually not "either-or" but "and-and." Both, the ecosystem leader and its partners, must protect their intellectual property and also conform to the group while thinking out of the box. To lead an ecosystem requires a mix of formality and informality. CEOs must heed experience and, at the same time, challenge it through experimentation. They must want to make money for their own organizations, but they need to be fair in sharing value among their partners, who will compete and collaborate.

Sure, it's uncomfortable to live with dilemmas, but there's no choice in an ecosystem. To lead effectively, CEOs must emulate some of the characteristics of the ambidextrous CEO.[7] They must embrace inconsistency by setting multiple and conflicting goals, maintain the tension between the demands for innovation and delivery efficiency, and develop an overarching identity and goal for the ecosystem while respecting the identity of every individual partner.

These characteristics add up to a very different leadership approach compared to what most business leaders are accustomed to. Not everyone can remake himself or herself in this new image. Some characteristics can be learned, developed, and amplified, based on existing leadership capabilities. Others may need to be hired into the organization so that a team that has the capabilities to lead the ecosystem forms around the CEO.

A final word of caution: the transaction costs of collaborative leadership can be high. Managing the relationships with partners often becomes a role for the ecosystem CEO. People like Robin Saxby of ARM or Bernard Charles of DS have to spend significant time on the quasi account management of the major partners in the ecosystem. That is why they need to be completely committed to the conviction that capturing the ecosystem edge is the best way to building their companies' success. Given the amount of time you will need to invest in the ecosystem, you have to know, as the saying goes, if "the game is worth the candle."

- **Ruthlessly focus the organization on what it does best:**
    - **Keep in house the knowledge or information that the lead company needs to keep proprietary in order to maintain its power in the ecosystem**
    - **Keep in house those activities where the cost to monitor and ensure the performance of your partners becomes too high**
    - **If the investments required to equip the partner to reliably conduct an activity in the ecosystem become too high, keep the activity in-house**
- **Building an organization that can interface effectively with external partners**
- **And readying employees for effective co-opetition**

EXHIBIT 9.2. Restructuring the Organization. Source: authors' research.

Restructuring the Organization

Traditionally, businesses have been designed to support a vertically integrated set of activities ranging from R&D to sales or to fit into a supply chain. Structures, processes, and even culture are honed for that role. However, that may not be the ideal organizational structure for playing the leadership role in a business ecosystem.

Our analysis points to three things that ecosystem heads must do to prepare the internal organization for the ecosystem (see exhibit 9.2). First, ruthlessly focus the organization on what it does best; second, build an organization structure that can interface effectively with partners; and third, ready employees for co-opetition decisions, such as separating the knowledge that must be shared from that which has to be kept proprietary.

Ruthlessly Focus Your Organization on What It Does Best

Business leaders routinely make decisions about what activities along the value chain should be performed in-house and what should be outsourced. The make versus buy decision is usually based on one well-defined criterion: who can do the job at the right quality for the lowest cost? That criterion to make a decision remains—what are the activities a company must keep in house, and what should it leave to its partners in the ecosystem. However, in the case of leading an ecosystem, other criteria too need to be taken into account.

Beyond the issue of whether a partner can deliver the right quality at a lower cost than your company, three additional considerations need to be weighed in an ecosystem. First, the ecosystem builder must assess whether it is important to keep an activity within the organization because it promises to be a source of knowledge or information that it needs to fuel its innovation or maintain power in the ecosystem. That is often critical to maintaining the tollgates that generate a sustainable profit stream (as we discussed in chapter 8). ARM provides us with a good example on how to make such choices. It doesn't leave interactions with OEMs to its partners; those interactions are key to understanding customers' road maps, which in turn guides the design of its RISC chip architectures. In the same way, AWS maintains its server infrastructure in-house partly because it can then track customers' demand patterns and price services accordingly. At the same time, it leaves the customer acquisition, the on-boarding, and the provision of services to partners, as those activities are not core to maintaining its role in the ecosystem and its profit streams.

One potential problem that ecosystem leaders face here is that almost every unit or department in their firm is likely to claim, for one reason or another, that its activities are part of the core. To surrender that, as they see it, would tear the heart out of what makes the company great. However, an ecosystem head must rise above the internal arguments, lobbying, and pleading, and work out the activities essential for the organization to maintain its leverage and profits. That calls for a certain ruthless objectivity.

Performance measurement adds a second criterion. An ecosystem builder needs to consider how much it will cost to monitor the performance of its partners for all the activities it will require them to conduct. While performance will be relatively easy to assess in the case of some activities, others will entail significant costs in the form of employee time and effort. If the monitoring costs keep rising, a point will be reached where it may be more cost-efficient and effective for the organization to perform the task in-house.

Third, getting ecosystem partners up to speed may require a significant investment by the organization. That will depend on the capabilities and knowledge that partners already have, as well as the difficulty in coordinating their contributions with the tasks the ecosystem leader performs. To ensure effective coordination, the employees of the ecosystem leader would have to invest their time to educate partners. Again, the setup costs of partnering will rise, as will the risk of proprietary knowledge leaking from the partner. When the investments needed to equip partners to conduct an activity in the ecosystem rise above a point, performing it in-house becomes more attractive.

In deciding which activities to focus on and which to leave to partners, ecosystem builders should look for the best compromise among four opposing forces:

- Partners' capabilities to perform the activity at an attractive cost as well as being able to innovate.
- The desire to keep the activity in-house to accumulate knowledge that can provide leverage and generate profits.
- The costs of monitoring performance if the activity is left to partners.
- The investment required to bring the partner up to speed to perform the task reliably and consistently.

Many of these costs and benefits are difficult to measure. However, the advantages of in-house control must be carefully weighed against the myriad benefits of leveraging partners. Failing to ruthlessly focus the ecosystem leader on what it is best at and needs to do to maintain its profitability in the ecosystem will result in squandering the benefits of an ecosystem strategy.

Building an Organization to Interface Effectively with Partners

An ecosystem's productivity depends on how effectively and efficiently partners can exchange knowledge, coordinate activities, and cocreate. Having the right interfaces in place is therefore critical to its functioning. However, most organizations do not have interfaces that are suitable for orchestrating an ecosystem. In a vertically integrated company or a traditional supply chain, the roles and responsibilities needed to benefit from an ecosystem are not needed. Hence, putting them in place is a priority for most ecosystem builders.

Let us return to the case of ARM to illustrate how they built an organization that was able to manage the interfaces effectively. For them, that meant splitting the sales roles from partner management and appointing dedicated executives to engage with partners, as we discussed in earlier chapters. The precise restructuring required in every company will, of course, depend on the nature of the engagement needed to ensure the smooth working of the ecosystem.

It is useful to keep in mind some rules of thumb when thinking about how your organization needs to change. Wherever mostly tacit knowledge needs to be exchanged between the ecosystem leader and its partners, it will be necessary to set up a dedicated team. Each member will have to spend a significant amount of time every day working with partners. The team may need to be large so that each member can focus on working with a small number of partners and building a trusted relationship with each of them over time. If differences in culture or context with a partner seem likely to threaten communication, the manager responsible for engaging with that company must be co-located with it for a specific period of time. When industry-specific knowledge is key to effective engagement, the partner-management team will need managers with experience in those industries.[8]

Sometimes, shared experience is sufficient to facilitate effective engagement. ARM, for example, found that when it had to exchange complex, technical knowledge with its partners, staffing the interface with engineers who shared the same educational background and training as the partners; people worked well. In fact, as long as they shared similar backgrounds and ways of working, even setting up remote partner-management teams was sufficient. Similarly, in the case of partners, where it was possible to codify and document knowledge, ARM found that a light touch organization to manage them was sufficient. So, in these cases, it set up a small team to work online with partners rather than focusing on face-to-face engagement.

Readying Employees for Co-opetition

Engaging with partners in ecosystems entails elements of both cooperation and competition. It involves, for instance, sharing some knowledge with partners while keeping other data proprietary; performing some strategic activities even if this encroaches on a partner's business; working together on an innovation, but competing to market it; and so on. The implications of co-opetition are not always easy to perceive, and even more difficult to incorporate, in decision-making. It is therefore essential that ecosystem heads who wish to gain an ecosystem edge take the time to ready employees to make the right calls in an ambiguous environment.

It starts with clearly communicating the message that cooperation and competition can go hand in hand. Surrendering potential profits to a partner or limiting the encroachment on their business, for example, might make sense if it helps the ecosystem to prosper. Faced with such choices, the ecosystem builder's role is to help executives and managers always keep the big picture in mind.

In applying that thinking to routine decision-makings, managers are likely to need the support of guidelines and processes. Part of the organization's internal restructuring so that it can lead an ecosystem effectively, will entail revising processes and procedures. That should include establishing "Chinese Walls" within the organization, so that information confidential to one partner does not leak to others. Similarly, it will be necessary to agree with partners in advance about how the ownership of any collaboratively developed intellectual property will be shared. Procedures for anonymizing and aggregating sensitive data may also be required.

Monitoring Ecosystem Performance

Effective leadership always requires feedback and monitoring of performance. The benefits your ecosystem delivers will ultimately show up in traditional measures of your company's performance: revenues, profits, cash flow and shareholder value. But as an ecosystem head, you also need forward-looking measures that track the health, vitality, and success of the ecosystem. These can help you execute on a leadership mind-set that looks beyond the performance of the company alone, and recognizes that the achievements of your ecosystem in terms of the overall value it generates and the rate at which it is innovating and developing are critical to future success.

Unlike a traditional strategy, where milestones can be clearly defined, ecosystem strategies are harnessed to realize an uncertain vision. So, while the organization's understanding of the business opportunity may remain the same, the structure and evolution of the ecosystem necessary to realize it may change quickly. It is difficult to measure ecosystem performance by confirming whether particular elements of it, as originally envisaged, are in place; the ecosystem's evolution along a different path may well be an indicator of its success in responding to a changing environment. That is why successful ecosystem builders focus on other measures of health and vitality. If learning, innovation, or growth in the ecosystem show signs of slowing, or rigidities begin to emerge in those processes, that should trigger red flags. If the ecosystem begins to stumble in its pursuit of the opportunity, or fails to keep adapting to change, those are warning signals too.

Three sets of indicators can gauge the health and leverage available from an ecosystem (summarized in exhibit 9.3).

Partner Attraction and Churn

The simplest indicator of the attractiveness of an ecosystem to the ecosystem leader and its partners is how many companies have joined and left the network in specific time periods. If new companies are not signing up, and existing partners are withdrawing, the ecosystem leader needs to figure out why. It is of course possible that all is well with the ecosystem; strong partners may be displacing weaker ones.

However, the churn could also indicate that the ecosystem is in a state of decline. New partners bring fresh capabilities, ideas, knowledge, and relationships, and they drive scale and positive network effects that are key to sustaining the vibrancy and competitiveness of an ecosystem. If the number of partners in the ecosystem is falling, the ecosystem leader should be extremely concerned. It suggests that the partners perceive that the leader is not delivering adequate value propositions, and prefer joining an alternative ecosystem.

Interestingly, rather than working out why more companies are not interested in joining or staying, ecosystem leaders often see it as a sign that they must exert more control over the ecosystem. Doing so is likely to worsen matters. A classic example of that trap is the evolution of the well-documented Symbian ecosystem.[9] In June 2008, Nokia announced the setting up of an independent, not-for-profit, Symbian Foundation, in order to catalyze an ecosystem around Symbian OS, Nokia's operating system for mobile phones. At the network's core was a royalty-free, open-source software platform based on code contributed by Nokia and its partners such as NTT DoCoMo, Samsung, Sony Ericsson, and Motorola. Initially the ecosystem thrived, with Symbian getting installed as the operating system in almost two-thirds of mobile phones worldwide. However, over the next few years, Nokia's partners, such as Samsung and Sony Ericsson, started to desert the ecosystem. Nokia hadn't caught on that its partners didn't feel their requirements were being listened to and incorporated into new generations of the product. Nor did it realize just how fast the demands on the operating system were rising as partners added considerably more functionality to their new mobile phone designs. The Symbian had fallen behind, as it simply wasn't tracking the right measures to assess whether the ecosystem was in good health. When, by 2010, Nokia did acknowledge the ecosystem was in severe trouble, its response was to take over the stewardship of the Symbian ecosystem.

That might have seemed like an altruistic move by the leader to save the ecosystem. In fact, it made things even worse. Nokia's control of Symbian made collaboration even less attractive, both for existing partners as well as potential new adopters. Symbian's global market share continued to slide, plunging below 30 percent by the end of 2010. Consequently, Symbian's application developers began to drop out of the ecosystem rapidly. By April 2011, Nokia had ceased to source any portion of the Symbian software from the ecosystem, and had shrunk its ties to just a small group of partners in Japan. Meanwhile, Google's Android ecosystem was developing, attracting at first forty-seven, and then eighty-four, partners, including hardware manufacturers, software developers, and applications creators into its orbit. By the end of 2010, Android had overtaken Symbian's market share and has today become one of the two dominant ecosystems in that market.

Another way to track the health of ecosystem partners is to monitor their revenue growth, profits, profitability, and cash flows. When partners are performing well on those parameters, it is a sign that the ecosystem is in good health. Some executives, drawing on traditional supply-chain thinking, may argue that the leader has left too much profit on the table. However, ecosystem CEOs need to see the bigger picture: partners that thrive are more willing to invest, innovate, and cooperate to improve the ecosystem's capabilities. Certainly, the ecosystem leader must ensure that its tollgates are effectively capturing a share of the profits, but the fact that partners are doing well is a sign that it can improve its own performance.

Wherever possible, it is worth tracking measures of the ecosystem's turnover, market share, and customer stickiness. A net inflow of new customers, especially if they are loyal, is a sign that the ecosystem is delivering value.

Indicators of Learning and Innovation

The second dimension of ecosystem health is the pace at which partners are learning and innovating to enable the ecosystem to create new sources of value. While performance in learning and innovation is difficult to measure, ecosystem leaders can track some proxies. It starts with collecting statistics on the IP generated by the ecosystem, such as the number of patents approved, and the number of trademarks and copyrights registered. The key is to compute that data across the ecosystem—or the partner network—rather than the ecosystem leader alone. These indicators will be more valuable if they enable comparison with competing ecosystems.[10]

Other quantitative measures of ecosystem health are the different types of data generated, the insights from the analysis, and how the ecosystem leader is using the data and insights. To gain a realistic picture of the learning and innovation taking place in the ecosystem will require qualitative assessment of the knowledge being generated by it, and also captured by the ecosystem leader. Measurement will require a system that regularly assesses what the organization is learning from its interactions with ecosystem partners. That is an inexact science, but continually asking how much the ecosystem is innovating and how well the ecosystem leader is leveraging that innovation is a useful discipline.

Indicators of the Flexibility and Development of the Network

A key advantage of ecosystem strategies is their ability to continually flex and evolve with the changing market environment, so ecosystem CEOs must keep their finger on the pulse of its development. That is not always easy. The process is more art than science. Still, four qualitative indicators may help:

- The extent to which new linkages between partners, and with the ecosystem leader, are being forged.
- The extent to which engagement between partners is deepening.
- The extent to which new clusters of cooperation between partners are forming.
- The extent to which the ecosystem leader is stepping back from activities it has catalyzed, and allowed self-organization to take over.

At Alibaba, as we saw earlier, these indicators were monitored. The fact that all these indicators were trending upward by 2005 was a sign of success. After seeding the development of China's logistics capabilities by working with partners, the company saw that logistics providers were picking up the baton, forming new linkages, improving data exchanges, and investing in new capabilities. Alibaba was therefore able to step back, and focus on its role as an enabler. Tracking these indicators also flagged areas where the ecosystem's development had been inadequate. Hence, in the delivery of white goods such as washing machines and refrigerators, for example, Alibaba found that its partners often fell short. It then intensified its efforts in this area, forming a partnership with China's largest appliances-maker, Haier, to develop the requisite logistics capabilities.

Gaining visibility into the dynamics of an ecosystem is more difficult than doing so in the case of a single organization, however large it may be. But

- **Attractiveness to Partners:**
  - **Partner numbers joining and leaving**
  - **Partners' financial performance**
  - **Customer stickiness**
- **Learning and Innovation**
  - **IP creation and knowledge generation**
- **Flexibility and Development of the Ecosystem Network**
  - **Creation of new linkages**
  - **Deepening of existing relations**
  - **Development of new clusters**
  - **Degree of self-organization**

EXHIBIT 9.3. Measuring How the Ecosystem Is Performing. Source: authors' research.

despite the challenges, investing precious leadership time in constantly monitoring the health of an ecosystem will always pay dividends.

A Blueprint for Ecosystem Leadership

To ensure that a CEO is ready to embrace the challenge of leading an ecosystem, he or she must answer five questions:

1. *Am I approaching the challenge with the right mind-set? Do I believe that:*
   - There is an enormous opportunity to create new value
   - No company acting alone, including mine, can unlock this opportunity
   - The key is to engage and motive people who don't work for me. The focus should be on growing the size of the ecosystem pie, not my company's share alone.
2. *Have I honed the skills needed to successfully lead an ecosystem? These include:*
   - Listening
   - Adapting
   - Influencing
   - Collaborating

3. *Am I ready to go beyond the limitations of classic collaborative leadership by:*
    - Taking responsibility for decisions taken beyond the borders of my organization
    - Building consensus
    - Investing in developing my social networks
    - Constantly tackling dilemmas such as what knowledge I should keep proprietary and what I share with partners.
4. *Have I restructured my organization to equip it to lead an ecosystem? This can be done by:*
    - Focusing it only on what it does best (or needs to do to maintain its leverage over the ecosystem)
    - Establishing interfaces with partners
    - Equipping employees to embrace co-opetition.
5. *Are we able to monitor the ecosystem's performance by using metrics? These would be:*
    - The number and significance of partners joining and leaving the ecosystem
    - The rate of innovation in the ecosystem
    - The flexibility and evolution of the ecosystem, including the quantity, quality, and density of the linkages between partners and with the ecosystem leader
    - The ability of the company to step back into an enabler role over time

10 Looking Back, Looking Forward

The Power and the Potential of Ecosystems

WE ARE CONVINCED THAT IN THE FUTURE, HOWEVER UNPREdictable it may be, all three trends that have come together since the early 2000s to make ecosystem strategy attractive today, are only likely to become more powerful. Customers, be they in consumer or business-to-business markets, will continue to shift to demanding solutions that no one single company has the capability to provide. As data and knowledge become more widely available, an increasing number of industries will face commoditization, so the pace of learning and innovation will become decisive for survival. And opportunities to connect and collaborate anywhere in the world will expand as information and communications technologies continue to improve. It is therefore a central thesis of this book that building ecosystems, rather than supply chains, will gain ground as a way of arranging competitive formations.[1] As a corollary, ecosystems will increasingly go head-to-head in tomorrow's markets.

Competition between Ecosystems Will Become the Norm

It is already happening. The AWS ecosystem is fighting for leadership of the fast-growing cloud computing market, with competing ecosystems led by Microsoft, Google, IBM, and Verizon. Another case in point is Amazon's emerging ecosystem for autonomous delivery that seeks to pioneer the use of drones for package delivery and self-driving food-delivery vehicles that are being developed in partnership with Toyota, Pizza Hut, Uber Technologies, Mazda, and China's Didi Chuxing, among others. This has taken on rival ecosystems led by Google's parent, Alphabet, and others including Waymo, nuTonomy, and Lyft. It also faces Baidu, China's largest search engine, which has built the Apollo ecosystem that has over ninety partners including Udacity, Microsoft, Infineon, TomTom, Daimler, Ford, and Volvo.[2]

In the coming era of extreme competition between ecosystems, it is not only customers who will enjoy more choice. Potential partners increasingly have a choice about which ecosystem they should join. Some may be in the fortunate position of being able to straddle competing ecosystems, placing a bet on more than one horse. That's often difficult, though. If a partner is to invest in and integrate into an ecosystem, in order to benefit from the opportunities for shared learning and innovation that will result, it will need to choose a single ecosystem to align with.

The rise of ecosystems will also rewrite the rules of competition and strategy as we have come to know them, encapsulated in the seminal work of Michael Porter.[3] The classic cost-leadership strategy based on growing the volume of products and services a company produces to reap economies of scale that drive down costs below competitors, will be replaced. In a world of competing ecosystems, cost advantage will come from aggregating the scale of your entire partner network to spread the fixed costs of investments in everything from design and innovation through to production and distribution. Your ability to reap network economies will become decisive. Witness the cost leadership that ARM achieves when it designs and supplies RISC chip architectures that go into over 95 percent of every mobile phone sold on the globe.

The classic differentiation strategy, based today on how much a company spends on R&D, the productivity of its scientists and engineers, and the acuity of its marketing staff in building its individual brand, will also have to be rewritten. As we have seen, competing on innovation in a world of ecosystems is all about your ability to leverage learning generated right across the ecosystem to fuel your own innovation and facilitate innovation by your partners. The power of your own brand will still be important. But how well you harness the halo effect of your ecosystem partners' strong brands will become critical, especially in the early stages of developing your ecosystem. Alibaba's Tmall, for example, has a huge advantage given that it is able to borrow the brands of nearly a quarter of the world's luxury brands that have official shop-windows on the platform. It is now moving to leverage this further by establishing Luxury Pavilion, a virtual app within Tmall, focused solely on luxury brands. To reinforce its aura of exclusivity, only those selected as VIP members will be able to access it.[4]

Porter's traditional "focus" strategy meant targeting a narrow segment of the market and tailoring the offering to serving its needs to the exclusion of other segments.[5] This involved streamlining the offering to the unique features that segment was prepared to pay for, or pruning the product range back to include only those products that appealed especially to them. These moves would allow a company to differentiate itself by satisfying customers with unusual needs, or cut its costs. Ecosystem strategies, by contrast, enable you to achieve many of the advantages of focus while still appealing to a wide range of customers with different, and often complex, needs. This is because, while you stay focused, you can rely on a diverse set of partners to serve the needs of different customer segments with tailored offerings that dovetail with your own core contribution. The fact that partners have complementary capabilities and experience, combined with network economies, enables the ecosystem to offer a wide range of tailored offerings while still keeping costs down.

More recently, many companies have sought to combine classic competitive strategies with increased agility. Management literature is replete with advice on how this can be achieved, with suggestions ranging from change management programs through to the creation of ambidextrous organizations.[6] Ecosystem competition, however, calls for a very different perspective on agility. Flexibility comes, in large part, from the fact that ecosystems are capable of self-organization, as partners adapt and evolve their strategies out of self-interest as the environment changes, much as do buyers and sellers in a market. Rather than simply struggling to make their own organizations more agile, ecosystems leaders take advantage of the capability of their ecosystem for self-organization to enable offerings to customers, as well as the value network behind it, to become more fluid.

Exhibit 10.1 summarizes the above considerations.

As competition between ecosystems grows, rewriting the rules of competition in the process, the demands on ecosystem leaders are only set to increase. The pressure to discover new sources of value for customers and to craft unique and attractive offerings will intensify. Partners will evaluate whether joining an ecosystem can deliver benefits, as well as how one ecosystem's value proposition compares with that of another network. A potential ecosystem

Competitive Advantage	Corporate Competition	Ecosystem Competition
Cost Leadership	Internal economies of scale	Network economies among and across partners
Differentiation	Innovation based on R&D and internal capabilities; the power of your marketing and brand building	Innovation based on learning generated across the ecosystem; magnifying your brand using the halo effect of partners' brands
Focus	Focus by streamlining the offering and product range	Focus by co-opting partners to broaden the offering
Agility	Organizational change management and restructuring	Harnessing the ecosystem's self-organization capabilities

EXHIBIT 10.1. Ecosystem Strategies Are Rewriting the Rules of Competition. Source: authors' research.

leader's value proposition to partners will need to be top-notch. In the competition between ecosystems, the speed with which a leader kick-starts a virtuous spiral of cooperation and the rate at which it can scale its ecosystem are both critical. Those that get ahead because of network economies will surge forward in what could easily become a winner-take-all game. However, to sustain the ecosystem leader's competitive position, the amount of learning and innovation generated by the ecosystem, and its ability to capture that learning, will be critical. Ecosystems that are less productive and efficient will be unable to compete. Mastering the strategies and capabilities we described earlier will become even more essential tomorrow than they are today.

When catalyzing the development of ecosystems, however, business leaders must bear in mind that ecosystems continually evolve, following a natural cycle of evolution that must be carefully anticipated and managed.

Riding the Wave of Ecosystem Evolution

Most ecosystems go through three stages. At first, the ecosystem leader identifies an opportunity and attracts lead partners and customers, kick-starting the virtuous cycle by which the ecosystem can discover new sources of value that it can deliver to customers. In the second stage, the ecosystem will start to scale, with new partners and customers joining the network. Different capabilities will be brought together in new ways, and exchanges of knowledge, experimentation, co-learning, and innovation will reach their peak. In the third stage, the different roles in the business ecosystem will become clearer. Partners will begin to specialize in activities or niches, and the interfaces and information flows between partners will become more formalized. That's when the quest for greater efficiency will become a priority, with innovation in the ecosystem likely to taper off. The most successful partners in the ecosystem will start winning market share and influence from less successful ones, and gradually go on to dominate their niches.

Throughout that cycle, the ecosystem leader's priorities and investment priorities, will need to change. In stage one, the focus will be on attracting partners, working with potential customers, recruiting and supporting market-makers, and encouraging partners to develop complementary products and services. In stage two, the ecosystem leader must provide a road map that will help the network scale, facilitate connections and knowledge exchange between partners, invest to encourage innovation, and set about developing a governance process.

As the ecosystem advances to stage three, the ecosystem leader will arrive at a critical point. An ecosystem's advantages as a way of organizing a competitive formation may begin to fade when partners' roles become more stable, the interfaces between them become more structured, dominant technologies and architectures emerge, and the market matures. All that will reduce the need for flexibility and adaptation. The ecosystem could persist. But in stable environments with little uncertainty and only incremental innovation, ecosystems are less efficient than supply chains. So, it may well make sense for the ecosystem leader to turn the network into a traditional supply chain, create a joint venture with key ecosystem partners, or acquire as many of its partners as it deems necessary to create a vertically integrated organization.

Moving toward a Traditional Supply Chain

Once the roles and responsibilities for activities in the ecosystem become clear, and specialized partners emerge in each of them, moving toward a traditional supply chain may make coordination more efficient. The way the traditional e-commerce business of Amazon has developed provides an interesting example of what happens. Uncertainty is reduced and supply contracts and service level agreements (SLAs) can be put in place to ensure that partners perform. This has the added advantage that it reduces the risk of freeloading that's inherent in the relationship between the partners in an ecosystem. Information exchange processes between partners can be formalized, allowing the deployment of a seamless IT system to monitor and coordinate the chain of activities required to deliver products or solutions to customers. Introducing demand planning systems and capacity coordination along supply chains will iron out unnecessary bottlenecks and reduce uncertainty.

All those structures and processes would not have been suitable to support the development of the ecosystem during the first two stages of its lifecycle. With the entry of new partners altering roles and relationships, contractual relationships would have been impractical. Given the ever-changing flows of information and knowledge that are generated during the co-innovation process, standardized interfaces and hard-wired IT systems would have acted as straitjackets. However, when the ecosystem has matured, and its optimal structure becomes clear, formalizing relationships and introducing standard procedures and repeatable processes will enable significant efficiency gains. The ecosystem leader may decide, therefore, that the time is right to transition the ecosystem, or at least major parts of it, to a classic supply chain.

Redefining relationships with ecosystem partners to approximate more closely a traditional supply chain requires careful transition management. Three issues, in particular, must be addressed. First, the ecosystem leader as well as its partners must accept the redefinition. Ideally, redefinition should be by mutual agreement, with all the parties in the ecosystem understanding and accepting that the new relationship is a better arrangement.

Second, as in any major change process, key personnel have to support the new arrangement. That requires demonstrating that employees will not only have new roles, but also, that they will enjoy the opportunities for career development and higher rewards. Failure to do so will result in employees defecting from both the ecosystem leader and its partners, which will damage the business.

Third, the new relationship must respect the heritage of the ecosystem. During the emergence of the ecosystem, several promises would have been made and expectations created. The new competitive formation needs to respect those. Informal arrangements that have grown over time need to be restructured and formalized. The ownership of the intellectual property developed through co-innovation, for example, will need careful handling. Even the perceived lack of fairness, along with ambiguity and confusion, risks undermining relationships based on which products and services must be delivered to customer.

Converging on a Joint Venture

An alternative approach for the ecosystem leader is to consolidate the key partner relationships into a joint venture that will operate at the core of the network. Forming a joint venture to integrate loose relationships can offer more benefits than forming a traditional supply chain. A joint venture binds all the parties tightly together into a long-term relationship. That reduces the risk of key partners defecting to a competing ecosystem. Likewise, entering into a joint venture is a chance to negotiate exclusivity, ensuring that key partners don't work with rivals.

A joint venture is better than a supply chain at handling contingencies for which it is difficult to specify a contract or SLA. When it is unclear, for example, what each party will contribute to the relationship in the future or how performance metrics will need to change, joint ventures offer a way to side-step those contingencies. In its essence, a joint venture agreement can be characterized by the statement that the parties share a common, well-defined goal, will do their best to contribute to the achievement of that goal, and will share the resulting profits. Unlike the early stages of an ecosystem, when the goals are less clear because of the need to discover new value, this approach is effective once the ecosystem has matured.

However, transforming the key partner relationships in a mature ecosystem into a joint venture has one major downside: it becomes difficult to replace a partner with an alternative collaborator, should the need arise. Joint ventures are notoriously difficult to unwind or even restructure. If the needs of the business change such that one partner no longer feels it needs to rely on the others, they can quickly descend into acrimony. A negative spiral of commitment loss, decision-making paralysis, declining performance, and wasted managerial effort on tackling internal disputes can ensue. If there is a possibility that different partners may be needed, or existing partners' relevance might decline in future, maintaining the ecosystem or moving it to become a supply chain is a better option.

Acquiring Your Partners

The last option that ecosystem leaders can consider for restructuring a mature ecosystem is to acquire some of its partners. To see this in action, let us return once more to the case of Dassault Systèmes and how they acquired CST, a software developer for the simulation of the behavior of electromagnetic equipment. In 2016, almost fifteen years after it began developing its ecosystem for multiphysics simulations, DS acquired one of its partners, the German company CST. Electromagnetism is an essential part of a multiphysics simulation for the development of smart and connected products, and IoT devices—from their complex design, to ensuring the performance, reliability, and safety of their interactions with their surrounding environment. In 2015, CST explained that it was merging with DS to understand better the changing trends in simulation technology. It went on to say that these trends had become more visible in recent years, and could be boiled down to just two key ones: "increased customer requirements for multi-physics capabilities, and efficient solutions covering the entire design flow." The partnership had led to "a closer relationship between the two companies, along with a confirmation that DS and CST have similar cultures: a focus on delivering leading technology, robust solutions, and strong technical support to best ensure our customers' own success. It became clear that joining forces was the natural next step."[7]

After having been part of the DS ecosystem for fifteen years, CST seems to have concluded that the flexibility the ecosystem afforded was much less important. Customers' value was now well defined, as was how it needed to interface with DS. Having learned through experience that their organizational cultures and management styles were compatible, DS and CST agreed to the acquisition rather than remaining separate entities. Offering to acquire CST made sense for DS because of ecosystem maturity. CST's role in supporting DS's product line was clear, while the interfaces with DS technology had become well defined. Tight integration and a close working relationship were required to deliver the benefits of cooperation. There was no need to retain the flexible engagement model that had applied when CST first became a partner.

DS's experience illustrates why acquiring key partners may make sense for the leader of an ecosystem that has reached maturity. It makes it easier to control its strategy, and its future direction. Its investments in innovation can be better focused, and it is possible to learn more easily than when it was an independent partner. Integrating CST with DS's systems and reporting brought more stability and predictability to the relationship.

Acquiring partners is also a way of ensuring that their products and services will no longer be available to competitors. Amazon's acquisition of Kiva Systems is a case in point. Influenced by its desire to differentiate its logistics capabilities from those of its rivals, Amazon acquired Kiva, a maker of robots that serviced warehouses, in 2012. Many retailers such as The Gap, Staples, and Saks were also using Kiva's robots. However, Amazon immediately snapped up Kiva's relationships with those companies so that it could deploy Kiva's technologies to build a competitive advantage for itself.[8]

A related reason for an acquisition is that the partner's knowledge and capabilities could become critical to the ecosystem leader's future. Alibaba's acquisition of UCWeb, which developed China's most popular smartphone web browser, illustrates this well. In 2009, Alibaba bought a small stake in UCWeb with the aim of creating ties with it. By the end 2013, Alibaba increased its stake in the company to 66 percent because it was becoming clear that mobile web browsing would be critical to attract and retain new e-commerce customers. In 2014, Alibaba bought 100 percent of UCWeb, and combined it with its own operations to form a new mobile technology division that would oversee Alibaba's browser, mobile search, location-based services, mobile gaming, app store, and mobile reader operations. UCWeb's capabilities had become so critical for Alibaba's business that it felt it should integrate it more closely than the loose relationship that an ecosystem would allow.

However, before moving quickly to acquire ecosystem partners, an ecosystem leader must be careful not to unintentionally jettison the advantages of maintaining flexible relationships with them. Partners in an ecosystem can usually draw on resources and knowledge from other companies, often a larger parent company that may not be available once they are acquired. Partners might therefore be more agile and innovative when they are in an ecosystem than after they are integrated into the company's structures and systems. An ecosystem allows companies to engage with, and benefit from, many more partners than it would be possible for them to acquire. Relationships are also more flexible in an ecosystem, with new partners free to join and existing ones allowed to leave. Ecosystem builders should be careful, therefore, not to undermine the advantages of having partners in their own networks by abandoning an ecosystem too early.

Spawning Your Next Ecosystem

Ecosystems will move through their lifecycle, and their advantages may be blunted as they mature, but that doesn't mean they will stop generating profits. The danger is that as an ecosystem evolves, its ability to deliver rapid innovation and exponential growth will decline. In order to keep innovating, grabbing new opportunities, and growing, ecosystem builders need to be continually on the lookout for chances to spawn new ecosystems. These new ecosystems may provide ways of unlocking value for new or existing customers, pioneering new business models, or entering other businesses.

Many of the companies we studied have maintained the growth and vitality of their businesses by doing just that: stimulating the development of ecosystems that parallel the ones they first created. For instance, Amazon has expanded from a books ecosystem to an e-commerce ecosystem, a cloud-based computing ecosystem, and to an autonomous delivery solutions ecosystem. Each has leveraged assets and knowhow from an earlier ecosystem. Books paved the way for e-commerce, Amazon's massive IT infrastructure for e-commerce spawned the idea of offering cloud-computing, and autonomous delivery services are an extension of its e-commerce operations. Although related, each required a new ecosystem to be developed. Therefore, the partners and relationships that underpin the AWS ecosystem are different from those with which Amazon engaged in building its e-commerce ecosystem. Likewise, Amazon's quest to turn autonomous delivery into reality has forced it to engage with a completely new set of partners.

The pattern is similar at ARM. While its ecosystem supplying mobile phones is still growing, with an over 95 percent market share for RISC chip architectures in the market, the growth potential is limited. ARM perceives a huge opportunity for its products in the nascent market for the IoT. Targeting that will require the company to engage with partners it hasn't worked with in the past, such as manufacturers of products ranging from thermostats and sensors to heavy machinery, as well as a range of service providers, from property managers to telecommunications companies and city governments.

When an existing ecosystem leader spawns a new ecosystem, it must recognize that it isn't starting from ground zero. It can leverage much from its existing assets and relationships to data and experience. The process must start with applying the ecosystem leadership mind-set we discussed in chapter 9 to the new opportunity. That means focusing on the potential to create new value for customers, the conviction that no single company can unlock the value opportunity acting alone, learning how to attract, engage, and motivate people who are not employees, and concentrating on increasing the size of the value pie rather than focusing on how the benefits should be divided.

Then, companies must redeploy executives with experience in partner engagement and building the capabilities required to lead an ecosystem. Alibaba's Jack Ma has an eye for spotting new opportunities, which is backed up by the company's ability to count on managers with years of experience in catalyzing and scaling an ecosystem. Daniel Zhang, Alibaba's CEO, and many of his team, have accumulated a deep understanding about leading ecosystems over nearly two decades.

As Alibaba's CEO, Daniel Zhang, explained: "It would be wrong . . . to describe Alibaba as an e-commerce platform. The company's core strength is becoming clear as it sucks up data through its mobile super-apps, which cover shopping, entertainment, finance, and social networking. We are positioning ourselves as a data company." He adds, "We have half a billion customers with shopping intentions and a method to pay. We know who they are, what they want, what they hate. This data revolution has enabled Alibaba to create personal credit profiles, known as Sesame Scores, for most of its users. Such scores are based on indicators, for example, the intensity with which users shop online, pay their utility bills on time, have a stable residential status, and have been using the same mobile phone number for a long time. In turn, that has facilitated the development of unrelated new businesses, such as Mobike bicycle hire, which assumes that those with high Sesame Scores are trustworthy enough not to pay a deposit."[9]

In fact, Alibaba has used its Sesame Scores to make it easier for partners to extend credit for everything from car loans to mobile-phone service contracts and a host of other types of consumer credit. That has enabled the company's partners to open up the credit market to those who have little or no credit history at traditional credit agencies. When Alibaba wanted to create an ecosystem to provide credit to small businesses outside China, it partnered with the US peer-to-peer lender Lending Club and small business lending specialists Iwoca and Orange Money in the UK. It promoted their financial services on the e-credit section on Alibaba.com and the 1688.com B2B platform, supplied them with data on the trading activities of loan applicants, and helped them refine their risk models.

When the company entered China's cloud computing market with Ali-Cloud, it targeted Taobao sellers that needed cloud capacity and trusted Alibaba, rather than trying to sell to users outside its network. When Alibaba was building a new ecosystem for financial services outside China, it ran into the entry barrier of Visa's and Mastercard's high customer penetration rates in the United States and Europe. It decided to focus on its existing customer base in China by enabling the use of Alipay for purchases, currency exchange, and tax refunds by the rapidly increasing numbers of Chinese traveling abroad (in 2016 more than 122 million Chinese ventured abroad).[10] It initially entered into partnerships with duty free shops, airport operators, and even small stores in Asia's night markets, who were keen to engage with relatively wealthy Chinese tourists. By opening doors to these new partners, Alibaba's employees developed an understanding of what different parties wanted, and tested their models. It gradually recruited a wider range of partners to expand the ecosystem.

Likewise, the team that ARM charged with developing its new IoT ecosystem includes a host of veterans from its mobile phone ecosystem, who bring a diversity of experience to the new challenge.

Leveraging the company's reputation as a dynamic, and yet fair, ecosystem leader can give it a head start when creating an adjacent ecosystem. How the ecosystem leader managed the first ecosystem will determine its credibility in future ecosystems. A commitment to maintaining the health of an ecosystem and the care ecosystem leaders take not to tread on partners' toes, for example, will help them develop other ecosystems quickly. By contrast, a reputation for encroaching on partners' territories or changing direction in ways that render obsolete partners' investments will impede the ability to build new ecosystems. Intel, for example, has participated in open source communities since 1999, but it is sometimes criticized for a lack of commitment to nurturing its ecosystems. The company faced a barrage of complaints after the release of its Intel Pro/Wireless products in 2005 because it refused to grant free redistribution rights for the firmware that must be included in the operating system for wireless devices to function.[11] Some commentators labeled Intel "an Open Source fraud," accusing it of favoring its biggest customer, Microsoft, over the ecosystem.[12] Whatever the truth is, the perceptions about Intel have not helped it create an ecosystem for mobile device chips, an area where it has struggled.

Companies that follow this growth path will be able to create a portfolio of ecosystems around each of their businesses. Each will be at a different stage of development: some will be trying to address a new opportunity, some will be trying to scale, and others will have reached a level of maturity. There will be no single operating model that will apply to all of them. The ecosystem leader's task is to nurture the portfolio, ensuring that each ecosystem in its universe is managed by executives with the mind-sets, processes, tools, and styles that match the opportunity and the stage of its development. A key part of its role will also be to facilitate the transfer of assets, experience, and knowledge between the different ecosystems on which the company's businesses depend.

A New Way of Doing Business

James Moore, who coined the term *business ecosystem*, spent a considerable amount of time in Central America, studying forests and ecology after a long and successful career at AT&T.[13] That led him to write a book in 1996 entitled, *The Death of Competition: Leadership and Strategy in the Age of Business Ecosystems*.[14] Competition hasn't died. But Moore's fundamental argument that companies fail because they focus on perfecting their capabilities, internal processes, and products and services, but fail to evolve with the changing external environment appears even more prescient today than it did two decades ago. The central theme of his book was that in order to have a successful business, the leaders of the organization must learn about, and lead, the external environment—the ecosystem of the organization—as well as get the fundamentals of the internal operations right. Most business failures result from the organization's inability to "co-evolve" intelligently with its surrounding business and societal environment. He believed that too many executives focused their time primarily on day-to-day struggles with direct competitors. They worked "in" the business, rather than "on" the business. Instead, they needed to begin by redefining the nature of the value their company could offer to the customer, and then focus on orchestrating the contributions of a network of players under their leadership.

Moore saw a future where competitive formations went beyond multidivisional organizations and the workings of the invisible hand of the market. He believed that successful business leaders would need to lead not only their organizations, but also myriad partners. They would have to serve as catalysts, bringing together different capabilities from which new businesses, new not-for-profit organizations, new rules of competition and cooperation, and new industries would emerge.

Our aim has been to help you, the reader, succeed in that future, which is almost upon us. It is a world in which no company can succeed without harnessing the potential of different partners to help it access a broader range of capabilities, speed up its rate of learning and innovation, and achieve a level of flexibility impossible for even the most agile corporation. It is a world where leaders must go beyond setting their own strategies, beyond developing their own organizations, beyond responding to their current competitors, and embrace the challenge of reshaping their external environment.

Rather than taking the business environment as a given that CEOs only need to understand and respond to, competing will mean catalyzing the growth and development of a new environment in the future. To accept the ecosystem in which a company is embedded as the set of customers, suppliers, competitors, and regulators that interact with it is to surrender the potential of the world of diverse capabilities and knowledge beyond the boundaries of your company and your industry. Having read this book to its very end, we hope you will now be both equipped and motivated to grasp that challenge, and the future, with both hands.

Notes

Chapter 1

1. Mohanbir Sawhney, "Why Investors Should Think Twice before Buying into Tesla," *Fortune*, April 11 2017, http://fortune.com/2017/04/11/tesla-market-cap-general-motors-ford/.

2. Bill Ford, "A Future beyond Traffic Gridlock," online video, March 2011, TED Talks, https://www.ted.com/talks/bill_ford_a_future_beyond_traffic_gridlock.

3. Ernest Gundling, "Disruption in Detroit: Ford, Silicon Valley, and Beyond," Berkeley Haas Case Series, University of California, July 1, 2016, http://cases.haas.berkeley.edu/documents/best_case_award/2016_2_ford_5875.pdf.

4. Gundling, "Disruption in Detroit."

5. "AlixPartners Study Indicates Greater Negative Effect of Car Sharing on Vehicle Purchases," AlixPartners, press release, February 5, 2014, http://legacy.alixpartners.com/en/MediaCenter/PressReleases/tabid/821/articleType/ArticleView/articleId/950/AlixPartners-Study-Indicates-Greater-Negative-Effect-of-Car-Sharing-on-Vehicle-Purchases.aspx#sthash.5aEKm3np.m8yxsDxo.dpbs.

6. Gundling, "Disruption in Detroit."

7. Mike Timmermann, "These Major Retailers Have Closed More than 5,000 Stores in 2017," Clark, December 13, 2017, http://clark.com/shopping-retail/major-retailers-closing-2017/.

8. "Five Industries under Threat from Technology," *Financial Times*, December 26, 2016, https://www.ft.com/content/b25e0e62-c6ca-11e6-9043-7e34c07b46ef.

9. Aircraft power by the hour is a term trademarked by Rolls Royce, but widely used in the aircraft engine industry to describe a programme to provide the aircraft operator with a fixed engine maintenance cost over an extended period of time.

10. “Speed to Scale,” Future Agenda, https://www.futureagenda.org/insight/speed-to-scale.

11. Kevin Kelleher, “How Facebook Learned from MySpace’s Mistakes, *Fortune*, November 19, 2010, http://fortune.com/2010/11/19/how-facebook-learned-from-myspaces-mistakes/.

12. All currency is in US dollars unless stated otherwise.

13. “Culture and Values,” Alibaba Group, https://www.alibabagroup.com/en/about/culture.

14. Peter Williamson and Michelle Wang, “Alibaba Group’s Taobao: From Intermediary to Ecosystem Enabler,” University of Cambridge, 2014, Judge Business School, case 10 (Case Centre case number 314-139-1, https://www.thecasecentre.org).

15. Ibid.

16. Ibid.

17. Ibid.

18. Ibid.

19. Ron Adner, “Ecosystem as Structure: An Actionable Construct for Strategy,” *Journal of Management* 43, no. 1 (2017): 39–58

20. Marco Iansiti and Roy Levien, *The Keystone Advantage: What the New Dynamics of Business Ecosystems Mean for Strategy, Innovation and Sustainability*, Boston, MA: Harvard Business School Press; Charles Dhanarg and Arvind Pharke, “Orchestrating Innovation Networks,” *Academy of Management Review* 31, no. 3 (2006): 659–69.

21. David B. Yoffie and Mary Kwak, “With Friends Like These: The Art of Managing Complementors,” *Harvard Business Review* 84, no. 9 (September 2006): 88–98, 157, https://hbr.org/2006/09/with-friends-like-these-the-art-of-managing-complementors; Ron Adner, “Match Your Innovation Strategy to Your Innovation Ecosystem,” *Harvard Business Review*, April 2006, 107.

22. James F. Moore, “Predators and Prey: A New Ecology of Competition,” *Harvard Business Review* 71, no. 3 (May–June 1993): 75–86.

23. Adner, “Ecosystem as Structure.”

Chapter 2

1. James F. Moore, “Predators and Prey: A New Ecology of Competition,” *Harvard Business Review*, May/June 1993, https://hbr.org/1993/05/predators-and-prey-a-new-ecology-of-competition.

2. Michael G. Jacobides, Carmel Cennamo, and Annabelle Gawer, “Towards a Theory of Ecosystems,” *Strategic Management Journal* 39, no. 8 (March 2018): 2255–76

3. James M. Acheson, *The Lobster Gangs of Maine* (Hanover, NH: University Press of New England, 1998); James M. Acheson, *Capturing the Commons: Devising Institutions to Manage the Maine Lobster Industry* (Lebanon, NH: University Press of New England, 2004).

4. “All about Lobsters,” Gulf of Maine Research Institute, accessed August 8, 2018, http://www.gma.org/lobsters/allaboutlobsters/lobsterhistory.html#sthash.suicOB1J.dpuf.

5. David Sneath, "State Policy and Pasture Degradation in Inner Asia," *Science*, August 21, 1998, 1147–48.

6. Elinor Ostrom et al., "Revisiting the Commons: Local Lessons, Global Challenges," *Science*, April 9, 1999, 278–82.

7. Kazuo Kadokawa, "Applicability of Marshall's Agglomeration Theory to Industrial Clustering in the Japanese Manufacturing Sector: An Exploratory Factor Analysis Approach," *Journal of Regional Analysis and Policy* 41, no. 2 (2011): 83–100.

8. Paul Krugman, "Increasing Returns and Economic Geography," *Journal of Political Economy* 99, no. 3, (June 1991): 483–99.

9. Michael Porter, *The Competitive Advantage of Nations* (New York: Free Press, 1990).

10. Mancur Olson, *The Logic of Collective Action: Public Goods and the Theory of Groups* (Cambridge, MA: Harvard University Press, 1965).

11. Robert Michels, *Political Parties: A Sociological Study of the Oligarchical Tendencies of Modern Democracy*, trans. Eden and Cedar Paul (New York: Hearst's International Library Co., 1915); Max Weber, *From Max Weber: Essays in Sociology*, edited by Hans Gerth and C. Wright Mills (New York: Oxford University Press, 1958).

12. Garrett Hardin, "The Tragedy of the Commons," *Science*, December 13, 1968, 1243–48.

13. Elinor Ostrom et al., "Revisiting the Commons: Local Lessons, Global Challenges," *Science*, April 9, 1999, 278–82.

14. Robert Axelrod, *The Evolution of Cooperation* (New York: Basic Books, 1984).

15. Paul S. Adler, "Market, Hierarchy, and Trust: The Knowledge Economy and the Future of Capitalism," *Organization Science* 12, no. 2(2001): 215–34.

16. Jacobides et al., "Towards a Theory of Ecosystems."

17. Charles Dhanarg and Arvind Pharke, "Orchestrating Innovation Networks," *Academy of Management Review* 31, no. 3 (2006): 659–69.

18. These opportunities may be more restricted by data privacy laws in some jurisdictions, such as Europe where companies are required to conform to the General Data Protection Regulation (GDPR).

19. Zheng He, Lez Rayman-Bacchus, and Yiming Wu, "Self-Organization of Industrial Clustering in a Transition Economy: A Proposed Framework and Case Study Evidence from China," *Research Policy* 40, no. 9 (November 2011): 1280–94;

Lee Fleming and Olav Sorenson, "Technology as a Complex Adaptive System: Evidence from Patent Data," *Research Policy* 30, no. 7 (August 2001): 1019–39; Elizabeth Garnsey, "The Genesis of the High Technology Milieu: A Study in Complexity," *International Journal of Urban and Regional Research* 22, no. 3 (September 1998): 361–77; Martin Kenney, *Understanding Silicon Valley: The Anatomy of an Entrepreneurial Region* (Palo Alto, CA: Stanford University Press, 2000).

20. Alfred Marshall, "Industrial Organization, Continued: The Concentration of Specialized Industries in Particular Localities," chap. 79 in *Principles of Economics*, 8th edition (London: Macmillan, 1920).

21. Ron Adner, "Ecosystem as Structure: An Actionable Construct for Strategy," *Journal of Management* 43, no. 1 (2017): 39–58.

22. Niklas Zennstroem, “Silicon Valley Is No Longer the Only Game in Town,” *Financial Times*, January 7, 2014, https://www.ft.com/content/156569c4-6c06-11e3-85b1-00144feabdco.

23. Julian Birkinshaw and Simon Best, “Responding to a Potentially Disruptive Technology: How Big Pharma Embraced Biotechnology,” *California Management Review* 60, no. 4 (2018): 74–100

24. David B. Yoffie and Mary Kwak, “With Friends Like These: The Art of Managing Complementors,” *Harvard Business Review*, September 2006, 89–98.

25. Jack Fuller, Michael G. Jacobides, and Martin Reeves, “The Myths and Realities of Business Ecosystems,” *MIT-Sloan Management Review*, February 25, 2019. https://sloanreview.mit.edu/article/the-myths-and-realities-of-business-ecosystems/

Chapter 3

1. Data about Dassault Systèmes is based on published materials, interviews, and their own website: www.3DS.com.

2. “Dassault Systèmes and National Research Foundation Collaborate to Develop the Virtual Singapore Platform,” Dassault Systèmes press release, June 16, 2015, https://www.3ds.com/press-releases/single/dassault-systemes-and-national-research-foundation-collaborate-to-develop-the-virtual-singapore-pla/.

3. “Bernard Charlès,” *Compass*, https://compassmag.3ds.com/4/all/bernard-charles-bernard-charles

4. “China’s Didi Bets $1Billion on Auto-Services Sector,” *Wall Street Journal*, August 6, 2018.

5. Ranjay Gulati and David Kletter, “Shrinking Core, Expanding Periphery,” *California Management Review* 47, no. 3 (April 1, 2005): 77–104.

6. Ibid.

7. Chihmao Hsieh et al., “Does Ownership Affect the Variability of the Production Process? Evidence from International Courier Services,” *Organization Science* 21, no. 4 (July–August 2010): 892–912; Ranjay Gulati, Paul R. Lawrence, and Phanish Puranam, “Adaptation in Vertical Relationships: Beyond Incentive Conflict.” *Strategic Management Journal* 26, no. 12 (December 2005): 415–40.

8. M. Peltoniemi, “Preliminary Theoretical Framework for the Study of Business Ecosystems,” *Emergence: Complexity & Organization* 8, no. 1 (2006): 10–19.

9. See the Dassault Systèmes website, www.3DS.com.

10. “Dassault Systèmes Introduces a New Release of 3DSwYm, Its Social Innovation Application,” Dassault Systèmes press release, April 12, 2012. https://www.3ds.com/press-releases/single/dassault-systemes-introduces-a-new-release-of-3dswym-its-social-innovation-application/.

11. C. H. Loch, A. De Meyer, and M. T. Pich, *Managing the Unknown: A New Approach to Managing High Uncertainty and Risk in Projects*. London: John Wiley and Sons, 2006.

12. W. B. Arthur, “Increasing Returns and the New World of Business,” *Harvard Business Review* 74, no. 4 (July–August 1996): 100–109.

13. "Renault Chooses Dassault Systèmes Full V6 PLM to Improve the Company's Productivity and Product Quality," Dassault Systèmes press release, June 29, 2009, https://www.3ds.com/press-releases/single/renault-chooses-dassault-systemes-full-v6-plm-to-improve-the-companys-productivity-and-product-q/

14. Robert F. Higgins and Erin Trimble, "athenahealth's More Disruption Please Program," Harvard Business School Case 816-060 (Boston: Harvard Business Publishing, November 18, 2015), 6.

15. "Creating a Disrupter Ecosystem: How Athenahealth Did It," Innovation Leader, https://www.innovationleader.com/how-athenahealth-created-a-community-around-disruptive-innovation/.

16. "More Disruption Please Datasheet," athenahealth, accessed August 8, 2018, http://www.athenahealth.com/~/media/athenaweb/files/data-sheets/mdp_datasheet

17. Higgins and Trimble, "athenahealth's More Disruption Please Program."

18. A. Agrawal, A. De Meyer, and L. Van Wassenhove, "Managing Value in Supply Chains: Case Studies on the Sourcing Hub Concept," *California Management Review* 56, no. 2 (2014): 23–54.

19. The information about Amazon in this and following chapters is based on a combination of interviews and published materials.

20. Julia Kirby and Thomas A. Stewart, "The Institutional Yes: An Interview with Jeff Bezos," *Harvard Business Review*, October 2007.

21. See Chris Seper, "Is the athenahealth Accelerator Term Sheet Disruptive or Just Awful?" *MedCityNews*, May 14, 2015, http://medcitynews.com/2015/05/more-disruption-please-term-sheet/; Stephani Baum, "athenahealth's More Disruption Please Accelerator Gives Startups Another Way to Shake Up Healthcare," *MedCityNews*, March 11, 2016, http://medcitynews.com/2016/03/athenahealths-more-disruption-please-accelerator/?rf=1; Athenahealth, http://www.athenahealth.com/more-disruption-please/accelerator.

22. "Karl Florida on the Legal Tech Innovation Challenge," Legal Current, accessed October 30, 2016, http://www.legalcurrent.com/karl-florida-on-the-legal-tech-open-innovation-challenge/.

23. "Thomson Reuters and CodeX Announce 2015 Legal Tech Open Innovation Challenge Winners," Thomson Reuters press release, December 15, 2015, accessed October 30, 2016, http://thomsonreuters.com/en/press-releases/2015/december/2015-legal-tech-open-innovation-challenge-winners.html.

Chapter 4

1. Andrew J. Hawkins, "Ford Expands Its Mobility Empire with a Couple of Acquisitions," *The Verge*, January 25, 2018, https://www.theverge.com/2018/1/25/16932868/ford-autonomic-transloc-acquistion-mobility.

2. Darrell Etherington, "Ford and Autonomic Are Building a Smart City Cloud Platform," TechCrunch, January 10, 2018, https://techcrunch.com/2018/01/09/ford-and-autonomic-are-building-a-smart-city-cloud-platform/?ncid=mobilerecirc_featured.

3. "Annual Reports," Thomson Reuters, https://ir.thomsonreuters.com/financial-information/annual-reports.

4. "Thomson Reuters Announces Definitive Agreement to Sell its Intellectual Property & Science Business to Onex and Baring Asia for $3.55 billion," Thomson Reuters press release, July 11, 2016, http://thomsonreuters.com/en/press-releases/2016/july/thomson-reuters-announces-definitive-agreement-to-sell-its-intellectual-property-science-business.html.

5. William Launder, "Thomson Reuters to Expand Eikon Instant Messaging," *Wall Street Journal*, August 3, 2013, http://www.wsj.com/articles/SB10001424127887323420604578647983409888730.

6. David Dawkins, "Clear Daylight Emerges between Bloomberg and the Competition," WatersTechnology, February 3, 2016, https://www.waterstechnology.com/industry-issues-initiatives/2444608/clear-daylight-emerges-between-bloomberg-and-the-competition.

7. Scott Carey, "Thomson Reuters Opens Up Eikon APIs in Bid to Take On Rival Trading Data Platforms," *ComputerworldUK*, January 18, 2016, http://www.computerworlduk.com/applications/thomson-reuters-opens-up-eikon-apis-in-bid-take-on-rival-trading-data-platforms-3633596/.

8. "Thomson Reuters Adds Futures and Options Execution Application for Commodities Traders in Eikon," Thomson Reuters press release, July 19, 2016, https://www.thomsonreuters.com/en/press-releases/2016/july/thomson-reuters-adds-futures-and-options-execution-application.html.

9. Thomson Reuters Labs, "Shareable by Default: Creating Resilient Data Ecosystems," accessed October 31, 2016, https://innovation.thomsonreuters.com/en/labs/shareable-data.html.

10. Andrew Fletcher, "Extracting Value from New Sources of Data," Thomson Reuters *Answers On* (blog), September 9, 2016, https://blogs.thomsonreuters.com/answerson/extracting-value-new-sources-data/.

11. Karl Florida, "The Legal Tech Innovation Challenge," online video, June 18, 2015, http://www.legalcurrent.com/karl-florida-on-the-legal-tech-open-innovation-challenge/.

12. Eleanor O'Keeffe and Peter Williamson, "ARM Holdings Plc—From Beleaguered Computer Company to Industry Standard," INSEAD Euro-Asia Centre, April 1, 2002 (Case Centre case number 302-170-1, www.thecasecentre.org).

13. Ibid.

14. Arnoud De Meyer et al., "Rolls-Royce in Singapore: Harnessing the Power of the Ecosystem to Drive Growth," Singapore Management University, 2014, case no. SMU-13-0031.

15. Ibid.

16. Ibid.

17. Ibid.

18. Matthias Hendrichs, "Why Alipay Is More Than Just the Chinese Equivalent of PayPal," *Tech in Asia*, August 3, 2015, https://www.techinasia.com/talk/online-payment-provider-alipay-chinese-equivalent-paypal.

19. Oscar Williams-Grut, "This £20 billion Data Giant Wants to Build the App Store for Finance: 'We're Leading the Charge,'" *Business Insider*, January 22, 2016, http://www.businessinsider.com/thomson-reuters-albert-lojko-on-fintech-and-app-studio-2016-1.

20. De Meyer et al., "Rolls-Royce in Singapore."

21. Thomson Reuters Labs Homepage, accessed October 25, 2016, https://innovation.thomsonreuters.com/en/labs.html.

22. "IDSS and Thomson Reuters Collaborate to Advance Innovation in Data Science, Finance, and Risk Analytics," MIT Institute for Data, Systems, and Society, accessed October 22, 2016, https://idss.mit.edu/idss-and-thomson-reuters-collaborate-to-advance-innovation-in-data-science-finance-and-risk-analytics/.

Chapter 5

1. See Amazon's AWS page: https://aws.amazon.com/.

2. Ron Miller, "How AWS Came to Be," *TechCrunch*, July 2, 2016, https://techcrunch.com/2016/07/02/andy-jassys-brief-history-of-the-genesis-of-aws/.

3. Steven Levy, "Jeff Bezos Owns the Web in More Ways Than You Think," *Wired*, November 13, 2011, https://www.wired.com/2011/11/ff_bezos/.

4. Robert S. Huckman, Gary P. Pisano, Liz Kind, "Amazon Web Services," Harvard Business Publishing, February 3, 2012, HBS No. 609-048, 14, 24.

5. "Amazon Partnership Model," Amazon Web Services, accessed August 10, 2017, https://www.slideshare.net/AmazonWebServices/awsome-day-warsaw-aws-partnership-model/31.

6. Ron Miller, "AWS Won't Be Ceding Its Massive Market Share Lead Anytime Soon," *TechCrunch*, July 28, 2017, https://techcrunch.com/2017/07/28/aws-wont-be-ceding-its-massive-market-share-lead-anytime-soon/.

7. Jessica Lyons Hardcastle, "Amazon Dominates the Cloud as AWS Revenue Soars in Q1," SDxCentral, April 28, 2017, https://www.sdxcentral.com/articles/news/aws-revenue-soars-q1/2017/04/.

8. "Amazon Partnership Model," Amazon Web Services, accessed August 10, 2017, https://www.slideshare.net/AmazonWebServices/awsome-day-warsaw-aws-partnership-model/31.

9. James Bourne, "AWS Lays Down Its Vision for the Success of Cloud Computing," *CloudTech*, March 27, 2014, https://www.cloudcomputing-news.net/news/2014/mar/27/aws-lays-down-its-vision-success-cloud-computing/.

10. "So You Want to Be an AWS Partner?," Amazon Web Services, accessed September 6, 2016, http://www.slideshare.net/AmazonWebServices/so-you-want-to-be-an-aws-partner.

11. "Global Partner Summit," AWS Events, accessed August 10, 2017, https://reinvent.awsevents.com/partners-sponsors/global-partner-summit/.

12. "AWS Partner Network (APN) Blog," Amazon, accessed August 10, 2017, https://aws.amazon.com/blogs/apn/thank-you-to-all-of-our-aws-partner-network-apn-partners/.

13. Asha McLean, Stephanie Condon, "Andy Jassy Warns AWS Has No Time for Uncommitted Partners," *ZDNet*, November 29, 2016, http://www.zdnet.com/article/andy-jassy-warns-aws-has-no-time-for-uncommitted-partners/.

14. "ARM Approved Program," ARM, accessed August 11, 2017, https://www.arm.com/support/arm-approved-program.

15. "2017 Letter to Shareholders," Amazon, accessed August 11, 2017, http://phx.corporate-ir.net/phoenix.zhtml?c=97664&p=irol-reportsannual.

16. Carliss Y. Baldwin and Kim B. Clark, "Managing in an Age of Modularity," *Harvard Business Review* 75, no. 5 (1997): 84-93.

17. "AWS Marketplace," Help and FAQ, Amazon, accessed August 11, 2017, https://aws.amazon.com/marketplace/help.

18. N. Lang, K. von Szczepanski, and C. Wurzer, "The Emerging Art of Ecosystem Management," BCG Henderson Institute, January 16, 2019, https://www.bcg.com/publications/2019/emerging-art-ecosystem-management.aspx.

19. Lyra J. Colfer and Carliss Young Baldwin, "The Mirror Hypothesis: Theory, Evidence and Exceptions," *Industrial and Corporate Change* 25, no. 5 (2016): 709-38.

20. Michael G. Jacobides, Carmel Cennamo, and Annabelle Gawer, "Towards a Theory of Ecosystems," *Strategic Management Journal* 39, no. 8 (2018): 2255-76.

21. A. Gawer, and R. Henderson, "Platform Owner Entry and Innovation in Complementary Markets: Evidence from Intel," *Journal of Economics & Management Strategy* 16, no 1 (Spring 2007): 1–34.

22. Barney Jopson, "From Warehouse to Powerhouse," *Financial Times*, July 8, 2012.

23. Peter Williamson and Michelle Wang, "Alibaba Group's Taobao: From Intermediary to Ecosystem Enabler," University of Cambridge, Judge Business School, 2014, case study, 10 (Case Centre case number 314-139-1, https://www.thecasecentre.org).

24. Ibid.

25. Ibid.

26. Adriana Neagu, "Figuring the Costs of Custom Mobile Business App Development," *Formotus*, last modified June 23, 2017, https://blog.formotus.com/enterprise-mobility/figuring-the-costs-of-custom-mobile-business-app-development.

27. Anita Balakrishnan, "Apple's Services Revenue Topped $9 Billion in the March Quarter," CNBC, TECH, May 1, 2018, https://www.cnbc.com/2018/05/01/apple-earnings-software-and-services-revenue.html.

28. W. J. Abernathy and J. M. Utterback, "Patterns of Industrial Innovation," *Technology Review* 80, no. 7 (1978): 40–47.

29. Paul Mooney, "The Story behind China's Tainted Milk Scandal," *U.S. News*, October 9, 2008, https://www.usnews.com/news/world/articles/2008/10/09/the-story-behind-chinas-tainted-milk-scandal.

Chapter 6

1. A. Agrawal, A. De Meyer, L. Van Wassenhove, "Managing Value in Supply Chains: Case Studies on the Sourcing Hub Concept," *California Management Review* 56, no. 2 (2014): 23–54.

2. A similar argument has been made in N. Lang, K. von Sczepanski, and C. Wurzer, "The Emerging Art of Ecosystem Management," BCG Henderson Institute, 2019, https://www.bcg.com/publications/2019/emerging-art-ecosystem-management.aspx.

3. C. H. Loch, A. De Meyer, M. T. Pich, *Managing the Unknown, A New Approach to Managing High Uncertainty and Risk in Projects* (Hoboken, NJ: John Wiley and Sons, 2006).

4. H. A. Simon, "A Formal Theory of the Employment Relationship," *Econometrica* 19, no. 3 (1951): 293–305.

5. W. C. Kim, R. Mauborgne, "Fair Process: Managing in the Global Economy," *Harvard Business Review*, 75, no. 4 (July–August 1997): 65–75.

6. Loch et al., *Managing the Unknown*.

7. Ibid.

8. Jessica Lyons, "Arm Partners with Vodafone, China Unicom on IoT," SDxCentral, March 1, 2019, https://www.sdxcentral.com/articles/news/arm-partners-with-vodafone-china-unicom-on-iot-launches-security-certification/2019/03/.

9. "Guardian Open Platform," Terms and Conditions, accessed October 4, 2016, https://www.theguardian.com/open-platform/terms-and-conditions.

10. E. Von Hippel, *Cooperation between Rivals: Informal Know How Trading Research Policy*, no. 16 (1987): 291–302.

11. "ARM Approved Program," ARM, accessed August 11, 2017, https://www.arm.com/support/arm-approved-program.

12. Susan Martin, "Karl Florida on the Legal Tech Open Innovation Challenge," *Legal Current*, June 18, 2015, http://www.legalcurrent.com/karl-florida-on-the-legal-tech-open-innovation-challenge/.

13. Eagan Minn, "Thomson Reuters and CodeX Announce 2015 Legal Tech Open Innovation Challenge Winners," *Thomson Reuters*, press release, December 15, 2015, https://www.thomsonreuters.com/en/press-releases/2015/december/2015-legal-tech-open-innovation-challenge-winners.html.

14. Paul S. Adler, "Market, Hierarchy, and Trust: The Knowledge Economy and the Future of Capitalism," *Organization Science* 12, no. 2 (2001): 215–34.

15. Ranjay Gulati, Paul R. Lawrence, and Phanish Puranam, "Adaptation in Vertical Relationships: Beyond Incentive Conflict." *Strategic Management Journal* 26, no. 12 (December 2005): 415–40.

16. "So You Want to Be an AWS Partner?," Amazon Web Services, accessed September 6, 2016, http://www.slideshare.net/AmazonWebServices/so-you-want-to-be-an-aws-partner.

17. Peter Williamson and Michelle Wang, "Alibaba Group's Taobao: From Intermediary to Ecosystem Enabler," University of Cambridge, Judge Business School, 2014, case study, 10 (Case Centre case number 314-139-1, https://www.thecasecentre.org).

18. A. Tencate and L. Zsolnai, "The Collaborative Enterprise," *Journal of Business Ethics* 85 (2009): 367–76.

19. "App Store Review Guidelines," App Store, Apple, accessed September 6, 2016, https://developer.apple.com/app-store/review/guidelines/#developer-information.

20. Williamson and Wang, "Alibaba Group's Taobao.

21. Y. L. Doz, and G. Hamel, *Alliance Advantage* (Boston: Harvard Business School Press, 1998), 201.

Chapter 7

1. SimilarWeb, "The Guardian.com," accessed March 19, 2019, https://www.similarweb.com/website/theguardian.com.

2. Judith Townsend, "Alan Rusbridger on His Vision for a 'Mutualised Newspaper,'" Journalism.co.uk (blog post), April 30, 2010, https://blogs.journalism.co.uk/2010/04/30/alan-rusbridger-on-his-vision-for-a-mutualised-newspaper-video/.

3. Matthew Ingram, "Guardian Says Open Journalism Is the Only Way Forward," *GigaOm*, March 1, 2012, https://gigaom.com/2012/03/01/guardian-says-open-journalism-is-the-only-way-forward/.

4. Mike Butcher, "The Guardian Launches Open API for All Content—but They Still Control the Ads," *TechCrunch*, March 11, 2009, https://techcrunch.com/2009/03/10/the-guardian-launches-open-api-for-all-content-but-they-still-control-the-ads/.

5. Matt McAlister, "An Open Community News Platform: n0tice.com," *Matt McAlister* (blog), May 16, 2011, http://www.mattmcalister.com/blog/2011/05/16/1785/an-open-community-news-platform-notice-com/.

6. Justin Ellis, "The Guardian Creates an API for n0tice, Its Open News Platform," NiemanLab, May 22, 2012, http://www.niemanlab.org/2012/05/the-guardian-creates-an-api-for-notice-its-open-news-platform/.

7. Ibid.

8. Contribly, accessed August 10, 2018, http://www.contribly.com/.

9. GNM Press Office, "GuardianWitness to Open Up Guardian Journalism as Never Before," *The Guardian*, April 16, 2013, https://www.theguardian.com/gnm-press-office/guardianwitness-to-open-up-guardian-journalism-as-never-before.

10. "About athenaInsight," athenahealth website, accessed August 10, 2018, https://insight.athenahealth.com/about/.

11. "PayerView 2016: Industry Trends," athenahealth website, accessed August 10, 2018, http://www.athenahealth.com/network-data-insights/payerview?intcmp=10033987.

12. AWS Partner recruitment slide pack.

13. John Ellis, "The Guardian, CNN, Reuters, and More Enter into a Global Ad Alliance," *NiemanLab*, March 18, 2015, http://www.niemanlab.org/2015/03/the-guardian-cnn-reuters-and-more-enter-into-a-global-ad-alliance/.

14. Jack Marshall, "News Publishers Form Programmatic Advertising Alliance," *Wall Street Journal, CMO Today* (blog), March 18, 2015, https://blogs.wsj.com/cmo/2015/03/18/news-publishers-form-programmatic-advertising-alliance/.

15. Lara O'Reilly, "*The Guardian*, *Financial Times*, Reuters, CNN, and *The Economist* have formed an Ad Alliance to Take On Google and Facebook," *Business Insider*, March 8, 2015, https://www.businessinsider.com.au/publishers-form-pangaea-advertising-alliance-2015-3.

16. Dassault Systèmes Website, "Why Become a Technology Partner?," accessed August 24, 2017, https://www.3ds.com/partners/partnership-programs/technology-partners/why-become-a-technology-partner/.

17. Steven Levy, "Jeff Bezos Owns the Web in More Ways Than You Think," *Wired*, November 13, 2011, https://www.wired.com/2011/11/ff_bezos/.

18. "2nd Watch", AWS Partner Network, accessed August 24, 2017, http://www.aws-partner-directory.com/PartnerDirectory/PartnerDetail?Name=2nd+Watch; "Coca-Cola North America" case study, 2nd Watch website, accessed August 24, 2017, http://2ndwatch.com/resources/customers/coca-cola-migration/.

19. "Breakfast Seminar: Simulation Driven Design," Dassault Systèmes Events, accessed August 24, 2017, https://www.3ds.com/events/single/breakfast-seminar-simulation-driven-design/.

20. "Innovation Unbridled," ARM, accessed August 24, 2017, http://www.arm.com/innovation.

Chapter 8

1. "Looking Ahead," *Byte Magazine* 8, no. 1 (1983), accessed February 6, 2017, https://archive.org/stream/byte-magazine-1983-01-rescan/1983_01_BYTE_08-01_Looking_Ahead#page/n189/mode/2up.

2. "Aboard the Columbia," *PC Magazine*, June 1983, https://books.google.co.uk/books?id=14Kfbrc6cbAC&pg=PA451&lpg=PA451&dq=&redir_esc=y#v=onepage&q&f=false.

3. Paul Freiberger, "Bill Gates, Microsoft and the IBM Personal Computer," *InfoWorld*, August 23, 1982, https://books.google.com.sg/books?id=VDAEAAAAMBAJ&lpg=PA19&pg=PA22&redir_esc=y%20-%20v=onepage&q&f=true#v=onepage&q&f=false.

4. Andrew Ross Sorkin, Floyd Norris, "Hewlett-Packard in Deal to Buy Compaq for $25 Billion in Stock," *The New York Times*, September 4, 2001, https://www.nytimes.com/2001/09/04/business/hewlett-packard-in-deal-to-buy-compaq-for-25-billion-in-stock.html.

5. Stewart Brand, *Whole Earth Software Catalog* (Garden City, NY: Quantum Press, 1984), https://archive.org/stream/Whole_Earth_Software_Catalog_1984_Point/Whole_Earth_Software_Catalog_1984_Point_djvu.txt.

6. Corey Sandler, "IBM: Colossus of Armonk," *Creative Computing* 10, no. 11 (1984): 298.

7. Charles Bermant, "Endangered PCs," *PC Magazine*, May 14, 1985, 33.

8. Tom R. Halfhill, "The MS-DOS Invasion / IBM Compatibles Are Coming Home," *Compute!*, December 1986, 32.

9. Paul Thurrott, "IBM's PC Division: No Profit in More Than 3 Years," *IT Pro Today*, January 2, 2005, https://www.itprotoday.com/windows-8/ibms-pc-division-no-profit-more-3-years.

10. M. Iansiti and R. Levin, *The Keystone Advantage: What the New Dynamics of Business Ecosystems Mean for Strategy, Innovation, and Sustainability* (Boston: Harvard Business School Press, 2004).

11. Jay Barney, "Firm Resources and Sustained Competitive Advantage," *Journal of Business* 17, no. 1 (1991): 99–120.

12. Tony Smith, "Nokia Grabs 40% of Phone Market for First Time," *The Register*, January 24, 2008, accessed March 28, 2017, http://www.theregister.co.uk/2008/01/24/sa_q4_phone_figures/.

13. Charles Arthur, "Nokia's Chief Executive to Staff: 'We Are Standing on a Burning Platform,'" *The Guardian*, February 9, 2011, accessed March 28, 2017, https://www.theguardian.com/technology/blog/2011/feb/09/nokia-burning-platform-memo-elop.

14. Gregory Gromov, *Roads and Crossroads of the Internet History* (published online 1995–2012), accessed March 29, 2017, http://history-of-internet.com.

15. "Browser Market Share," Net Marketshare, accessed March 27, 2017, https://www.netmarketshare.com/browser-market-share.aspx?qprid=0&qpcustomd=0.

16. Tim Mackenzie, "App Store Fees, Percentages, and Payouts: What Developers Need to Know," *TechRepublic*, May 7, 2012, http://www.techrepublic.com/blog/software-engineer/app-store-fees-percentages-and-payouts-what-developers-need-to-know/.

17. "Architecting a Secure and Connected World," ARM, accessed March 30, 2017, http://www.arm.com/company.

18. "Amazon S3 Pricing," Amazon Web Services, accessed March 30, 2017, https://aws.amazon.com/s3/pricing/.

Chapter 9

1. We use the expression *ecosystem head* for the individual who leads the ecosystem leader. In previous chapters we used the concept of ecosystem leader to describe the team and the organization that provides leadership to the ecosystem.

2. Peter Williamson and Michelle Wang, "Alibaba Group's Taobao: From Intermediary to Ecosystem Enabler," University of Cambridge, Judge Business School, 2014, case study 10. (Case Centre case number 314-139-1, https://www.thecasecentre.org).

3. L. D. Parker, "Control in Organizational Life: The Contribution of Mary Parker Follett." *Academy of Management Review* 9, no. 4 (1984): 736–45.

4. Arnoud De Meyer, "Collaborative Leadership: A New Perspective for Leadership Development," in *The Future of Leadership Development*, ed. Jordi Canals (Basingstoke, UK: Palgrave Macmillan, 2011).

5. Susan Schneider and Arnoud De Meyer, "Interpreting and Responding to Strategic Issues: The Impact of National Culture," *Strategic Management Journal* 12, no. 1 (1991): 307–20.

6. The reader who wants to know more about the role of dualities in management is referred to Fons Trompenaars and Charles Hampden Turner, *Riding the Waves of Culture: Understanding Cultural Diversity in Global Business* (New York: McGraw-Hill, 1998).

7. Michael L. Tushman, Wendy K. Smith, and Andy Binns, "The Ambidextrous CEO," *Harvard Business Review*, 89, no. 6 (June 2011): 74–80.

8. A. De Meyer, "The Flow of Technical Information in an R&D Department," *Research Policy* 14, no. 6 (1985): 315–28.

9. Tim Ocock, "Symbian OS—One of the Most Successful Failures in Tech History," *TechCrunch*, November 9, 2010, https://techcrunch.com/2010/11/08/guest-post-symbian-os-one-of-the-most-successful-failures-in-tech-history-2/.

10. Jo Best, "'Android before Android: The Long, Strange History of Symbian and Why It Matters for Nokia's Future," *ZD Net*, April 4, 2013, https://www.zdnet.com/article/android-before-android-the-long-strange-history-of-symbian-and-why-it-matters-for-nokias-future/.

Chapter 10

1. Of course, we don't argue that all business activities will be organized in ecosystems. As we mentioned in chapter 2, there will always be room for supply chains, vertical integration, and so on. See also: J. Fuller M. G., Jacobides, and M. Reeves, "The Myths and Realities of Business Ecosystems," *Sloan Management Review*, February 2019.

2. "Baidu Unleashes Accelerated Innovation for Autonomous Driving at 'China Speed' at CES 2018 in Las Vegas," GlobeNewswire, January 8, 2018, https://globenewswire.com/news-release/2018/01/08/1285414/0/en/Baidu-Unleashes-Accelerated-Innovation-for-Autonomous-Driving-at-China-Speed-at-CES-2018-in-Las-Vegas.html.

3. Michael E. Porter, *Competitive Strategy* (New York: Free Press, 1980); Michael E. Porter, *Competitive Advantage* (New York: Free Press, 1985).

4. Liz Flora, "Alibaba's Luxury Ambitions," Gartner L2, *Daily Insights*, April 2, 2018, https://www.l2inc.com/daily-insights/alibabas-luxury-ambitions.

5. Porter, *Competitive Advantage*, 15.

6. Cristina B. Gibson and Julian Birkinshaw, "The Antecedents, Consequences and Mediating Role of Organizational Ambidexterity, *Academy of Management Journal* 47, no. 2 (April 2004): 209–26.

7. "CST—Computer Simulation Technology," Dassault Systèmes, accessed August 26, 2017: https://www.cst.com/company/3ds.

8. Simon Erickson, "This 'Secret' Amazon Technology Could Be Worth $15 Billion to Shareholders," *The Motley Fool*, September 19, 2017, https://www.fool.com/investing/2017/09/19/this-secret-amazon-technology-could-be-worth-15-bi.aspx.

9. John Thornhill, "Daniel Zhang of Alibaba on Leading a Supercharged Empire," *Financial Times*, September 3, 2017, https://www.ft.com/content/5a14153c-6d53-11e7-b9c7-15af748b60d0.

10. "Chinese Outbound Tourism Statistics in 2016: 122 Million Chinese Tourists Make Outbound Trips, Spend $109.8 Billion," Travel168, http://news.travel168.net/20170203/43145.html.

11. Sam Varghese, "OpenBSD to Support More Wireless Chipsets," *The Age*, March 1, 2005, https://www.theage.com.au/national/openbsd-to-support-more-wireless-chipsets-20050301-gdku1p.html.

12. Theo de Raadt, "Intel: Only 'Open' for Business," *OpenBSD Journal*, September 30, 2006, http://www.undeadly.org/cgi?action=article&sid=20060930232710&mode=expanded.

13. Herb Rubenstein, "Book Review of *The Death of Competition: Leadership and Strategy in the Age of Business Ecosystems*, by James F. Moore," Herb Rubenstein Consulting, http://www.herbrubenstein.com/articles/THE-DEATH-OF-COMPETITION.pdf.

14. James F. Moore, *The Death of Competition: Leadership and Strategy in the Age of Business Ecosystems* (New York: Harper Business, 1996).

Index

www.ingramcontent.com/pod-product-compliance
Ingram Content Group UK Ltd.
Pitfield, Milton Keynes, MK11 3LW, UK
UKHW042143151224
452205UK00002B/5/J